English Teaching & New Literacies Pedagogy

Colin Lankshear and Michele Knobel
General Editors

Vol. 61

The New Literacies and Digital Epistemologies series
is part of the Peter Lang Education list.
Every volume is peer reviewed and meets
the highest quality standards for content and production.

PETER LANG
New York • Washington, D.C./Baltimore • Bern
Frankfurt • Berlin • Brussels • Vienna • Oxford

English Teaching & New Literacies Pedagogy

Interpreting and Authoring Digital Multimedia Narratives

EDITED BY
Len Unsworth & Angela Thomas

PETER LANG
New York • Washington, D.C./Baltimore • Bern
Frankfurt • Berlin • Brussels • Vienna • Oxford

Library of Congress Cataloging-in-Publication Data

English teaching and new literacies pedagogy:
interpreting and authoring digital multimedia narratives /
edited by Len Unsworth, Angela Thomas.
pages cm. — (New literacies and digital epistemologies; vol. 61)
Includes bibliographical references and index.
1. Language arts (Elementary)—Australia—Computer-assisted instruction.
2. Interactive multimedia—Australia. 3. Computers and literacy—Australia.
I. Unsworth, Len. II. Thomas, Angela.
LB1576.7.E55 2014   372.6—dc23   2014002013
ISBN 978-1-4331-1907-1 (hardcover)
ISBN 978-1-4331-1906-4 (paperback)
ISBN 978-1-4539-1311-6 (e-book)
ISSN 1523-9543

Bibliographic information published by **Die Deutsche Nationalbibliothek**.
Die Deutsche Nationalbibliothek lists this publication in the "Deutsche
Nationalbibliografie"; detailed bibliographic data are available
on the Internet at http://dnb.d-nb.de/.

The paper in this book meets the guidelines for permanence and durability
of the Committee on Production Guidelines for Book Longevity
of the Council of Library Resources.

© 2014 Peter Lang Publishing, Inc., New York
29 Broadway, 18th floor, New York, NY 10006
www.peterlang.com

All rights reserved.
Reprint or reproduction, even partially, in all forms such as microfilm,
xerography, microfiche, microcard, and offset strictly prohibited.

Printed in the United States of America

Table of Contents

Acknowledgments vii

Preface ix
    Len Unsworth & Angela Thomas

Chapter 1: Toward a Metalanguage for Multimedia Narrative
    Interpretation and Authoring Pedagogy: A National Curriculum
    Perspective from Australia 1
    Len Unsworth

Chapter 2: Using Contemporary Picture Books to Explore
    the Concept of Intermodal Complementarity............................. 23
    Angela Thomas

Chapter 3: Digital Fiction... 39
    Angela Thomas

Chapter 4: A Model for Critical Games Literacy 63
    Thomas Apperley & Catherine Beavis

Chapter 5: Enabling Students to Be Effective Multimodal Authors 79
    Paul D. Chandler

Chapter 6: The Image/Language Interface in Picture Books as Animated Films: A Focus for New Narrative Interpretation and Composition Pedagogies 105
Len Unsworth

Chapter 7: Using Focalisation Choices to Manipulate Audience Viewpoint in 3-D Animation Narratives: What Do Student Authors Need to Know? 123
Annemaree O'Brien

Chapter 8: Social Media, Education, and Contentious Literacies................. 151
Martin Waller

Chapter 9: Teaching *Inanimate Alice* 173
Angela Thomas, Jenny White, & Ros Lippis

Chapter 10: Empowering Older Adolescents as Authors: Multiliteracies, Metalanguage, and Multimodal Versions of Literary Narratives 191
Julie Bain & Len Unsworth

Chapter 11: Augmented Reality in the English Classroom 213
Winyu Chinthammit & Angela Thomas

Chapter 12: Virtual Macbeth: Using Virtual Worlds to Explore Literary Texts 233
Angela Thomas, Kerreen Ely-Harper, & Kate Richards

Contributors... 259

Index... 263

Acknowledgments

The editors would like to acknowledge the Australia National Council of Deans of Education whose Commonwealth Government innovation funding supported a local Teaching Teachers for the Future (TFF) project at the University of Tasmania. The TTF project was designed to explore how new forms of digital multimedia technology can be infused into the teaching of English. This edited book derives from the extensive and intensive work with high-profile international teacher educators and researchers as well as with local and international teachers as a result of the funding granted for this project.

To publishers Allen and Unwin, thank you for granting permission for use of artwork from Margaret Wild and Ron Brooks's picture book *Fox*.

We thank Passion Pictures Australia Pty. Ltd. for permission to include still images from the animated movie *The Lost Thing*.

We would also like to thank the journal editors of e-Learning and Digital Media for allowing us to use a version of the article "A Model for Critical Games Literacy" (*E–Learning and Digital Media*, Volume 10, Number 1, 2013) in our book.

Finally, we thank Damon Thomas for the time spent formatting and checking references across all chapters.

Preface

LEN UNSWORTH & ANGELA THOMAS

As the use of sophisticated digital multimedia communication software is becoming increasingly routine in the lives of many children and young people, school systems, teacher education, and curriculum authorities need to adjust to meet the needs of all students in the context of rapidly changing forms of literacy. This has recently been brought into sharp focus in Australia with the release of the new national curriculum in English. In both primary and secondary schools, students will now be expected to demonstrate competence in digital multimodal literacy. For example, the new national curriculum in English (ACARA, 2010) will require Year 4 students to

> Explore the effect of choices when framing an image, placement of elements in the image, and salience on composition of *still and moving images* in a range of types of texts.

In Year 6 students will be required to

> Plan, draft and publish imaginative, informative and persuasive texts, choosing and experimenting with text structures, language features, images and digital resources appropriate to purpose and audience.

And in Year 8 they will be expected to

> Explore and explain the ways authors combine different modes and media in creating texts, and the impact of these choices on the viewer/listener.

Such requirements reflect international longstanding and ongoing calls in the UK (Jewitt, 2002, 2006; Kress, 1995; Marsh, 2011) and the United States (Calvo, O'Rourke, Jones, Yacef, & Reimann, 2011; Gee, 2003; Lemke, 2006) for changes in English and literacy education to address the changing educational needs of a rapidly evolving and essentially digital multimedia communication world. However, it is also clear that internationally a significant proportion of teachers and teacher educators will need a great deal of professional development to enable them to address the implementation of these curriculum requirements.

The distinctive emphasis of the book is on new forms of digital multimedia narrative and the development of students as effective multimedia authors from the relatively early years of primary school through secondary school. This addresses a gaping chasm between the growing participation of children and adolescents in a variety of forms of multimedia authoring outside of school and the hegemonic mono-modal writing pedagogy of the past that dominates most students' experience of textual composition at school. This book will help prospective and practicing teachers to see how they can contribute to changing pedagogic practice and that the incorporation of multimedia authoring has both a theoretical and strong practical basis in the experience of those who are already involved in enacting this change in primary and secondary schools.

The first four chapters set the scene and explore the necessary awareness and fundamental knowledge bases for innovative practice. These chapters indicate the explicit, systematic knowledge about the meaning-making resources of image and language, separately and interactively, that teachers and students can draw on to enhance their effectiveness as multimodal authors. The subsequent chapters deal with the possibilities of new forms of storytelling for young children and the practical pedagogies of multimodal authoring in the primary school. The four chapters following these deal with new forms of narrative experience in middle school and secondary school classrooms, including emerging forms of new narrative experience based on Augmented Reality Technology, which enables mobile technology to overlay virtual content onto real-world contexts, blending the actual and the virtual in new forms of textual experience. What is important to recognize is that, although there are four chapters that focus on the classroom experience of this work in the primary school and the secondary school, in each case the broad potential of what is discussed can be transferred across levels of schooling.

English teachers will recognize the valuing of literature and appreciate the practical pedagogy and fostering of creativity as students are encouraged to explore new forms of narrative in the context of developing expertise in knowing and deploying the meaning-making resources of language as well as other digital multimedia. We expect this book to be valued not only as a course text but also as a professional resource for primary school and secondary school teachers.

REFERENCES

ACARA. (2010). *The Australian curriculum: English*. Retrieved from http://www.australiancurriculum.edu.au/English/Curriculum/F-10

Calvo, R., O'Rourke, S., Jones, J., Yacef, K., & Reimann, P. (2011). Collaborative writing support tools on the cloud. *IEEE Transactions on Learning Technologies, 4*(1), 88–97.

Gee, J. (2003). *What computer games have to teach us about learning and literacy*. New York: Palgrave Macmillan.

Jewitt, C. (2002). The move from page to screen: The multimodal reshaping of school English. *Visual Communication, 1*(2), 171–196.

Jewitt, C. (2006). *Technology, literacy and learning: A multimodal approach*. London: Routledge.

Kress, G. (1995). *Writing the future: English and the making of a culture of innovation*. Sheffield: National Association of Teachers of English.

Lemke, J. (2006). Towards critical multimedia literacy: Technology, research and politics. In M. McKenna, L. Labbo, R. Kieffer, & D. Reinking (Eds.), *International handbook of literacy and technology* (Vol. 2, pp. 3–14). Mahwah, NJ: Lawrence Erlbaum.

Marsh, J. (2011). Young children's literacy practices in a virtual world: Establishing an online interaction order. *Reading Research Quarterly, 46*(2), 101–118.

CHAPTER ONE

Toward a Metalanguage for Multimedia Narrative Interpretation and Authoring Pedagogy

A National Curriculum Perspective from Australia

LEN UNSWORTH

INTRODUCTION

In the current and evolving digital multimedia communication age a fundamental challenge for the English curriculum, and for teachers, is to embrace, as a pedagogic priority, the development of students' understanding of new forms of multimodal grammar. Developing students' explicit understanding of how meanings are made within distinct semiotic systems such as language, image, movement, music and sound, as well as their understanding of how these resources are articulated in making complex meanings in multimodal texts, is a crucial aspect of a socially responsible English curriculum and pedagogy concerned with equity and effectiveness in preparing students for the constantly changing communication contexts they are living in. This metasemiotic understanding of multiple, integrated, meaning-making resources is fundamental to effective new literacies pedagogies. What we are concerned with here goes beyond simply using or comprehending language (and/or images and other semiotic resources) effectively. It concerns building students' conscious awareness of why particular linguistic or visual semiotic choices are effective in different contexts through developing their knowledge of the systems of meaning-making options within language or images or other semiotics. This metasemiotic understanding requires a metalanguage that describes how linguistic forms and visual features of images and aspects of other semiotic systems relate to meaning, both within and across the different semiotics in multimodal texts (New London Group, 1996, 2000). The chapter seeks to further promote the development of an intermodal metalanguage, such as that proposed by the New London Group based on systemic functional linguistic (SFL) accounts of grammar (Halliday & Matthiessen, 2004) and genre (Martin, 1992; Martin & Rose, 2008) and extrapolations from this work to related social semiotic descriptions of images (Kress & van Leeuwen, 2006), three-dimensional art (O'Toole, 1994, 2004), music (van Leeuwen, 1999), gesture (Martinec, 2000, 2004), and film (van Leeuwen, 1991, 1996). The systemic functional linguistic work on grammar and genre as well as the work on images have become significantly incorporated into literacy research and pedagogic practice in Australia and internationally (Achugar, Schleppegrell, & Oteíza, 2007; Christie, 1989, 2005; Lemke, 1989, 1990, 1998, 2002, 2006; Love, 1996, 2000; Love, Pigdon, Baker, & Hamston, 2002; Macken-Horarik, 1996, 2008; Macken-Horarik & Adoniou, 2008; Macken-Horarik & Morgan, 2011; Schleppegrell, 2004; Schleppegrell, Achugar, & Oteíza, 2004). It is now strongly reflected in the new National Curriculum in English for Australian schools from the beginning of schooling to Year 10 (ACARA, 2012).

This chapter shows how the new Australian Curriculum: English (ACE) (ACARA, 2012) represents an innovative, albeit partial, introduction of metalanguage for verbal and visual grammar, clearly largely derived from SFL and related work (although not acknowledged as such). First, some basic concepts in SFL descriptions of grammar are briefly outlined. Then attention is drawn to the strong reflection of these SFL grammatical descriptions in the explicit requirements for the use of metalanguage as set out in the "Content Descriptions" of the Australian Curriculum: English (ACARA, 2012), which specify "the knowledge, understanding, skills and processes that teachers are expected to teach and students are expected to learn" (p. 5). Examples of the metalanguage required at different grade levels that distinctively reflect SFL descriptions will be identified and brief illustrations of their practical application in teaching narrative interpretation and text creation will be provided. The next section of the chapter shows the significant ACE emphasis on developing students' interpretation and creation of multimodal texts in paper and digital media through a sampling of content descriptions at different grade levels. The focus is then on the nature, extent, and distribution of the metalanguage required in the ACE content descriptions describing the meaning-making resources of images, and the similarity of this metalanguage to the grammar of visual design extrapolated from systemic functional linguistics (Kress & van Leeuwen, 2006). The ways in which images and language interact to construct meaning is also emphasized in the ACE as an important focus for student learning, and recent research further developing systemic functional initiatives in this area of intermodality are also briefly discussed in this chapter.

In concluding, the chapter suggests that while there are clear curricula and pedagogic advantages to the incorporation of systemic functional semiotic perspectives, determining the nature and extent of the metalanguage(s) apposite for supporting new literacies pedagogies at the various stages of schooling requires a much clearer, consistent, and comprehensive theoretical basis underpinning the curriculum (Unsworth, 2006, 2008) as well as substantial classroom-based research (Macken-Horarik, Love, & Unsworth, 2011). In progressing the discussion of metalanguage we will seek to address the following three key questions:

1. How can descriptions of the knowledge about language (KAL) required in school curricula be articulated with corresponding knowledge about the meaning-making resources of images to provide the metalanguage necessary to support digital multimodal literacy pedagogy?
2. How can such a metalanguage facilitate multimedia narrative interpretation and authoring pedagogy?
3. How can official curricula enhance new literacies development through more explicit and comprehensive inclusion of metalanguage adopted from multimodal semiotic theory?

BASIC CONCEPTS IN SYSTEMIC FUNCTIONAL GRAMMAR

Only a sketch of some basic concepts of systemic functional grammar (SFG) is possible here (for an accessible, chapter-length summary framework for SFG see Ravelli, 2000; Unsworth, 2001; and Williams, 1993. For book-length introductions to SFG for teachers see Butt, Fahey, Feez, Spinks, & Yallop, 2000; Droga & Humphrey, 2003; Humphrey, Love, & Droga, 2011). SFG proposes that all clauses in all texts simultaneously construct three types of meanings:

- Experiential meanings involve the representation of objects, events, and the circumstances of their relations
- Interpersonal meanings involve the nature of the relationships among the interactive participants
- Textual meanings deal with the ways in which language coheres to form texts

Experiential meanings are realized grammatically by Participants, Processes, and Circumstances of various kinds. Circumstances correspond to what is traditionally known as adverbs and adverbial phrases. Processes correspond to the verbal group, but Processes are semantically differentiated. Material Processes (action verbs), for example, express actions or events (such as *walk*, *sit*, or *travel*), while Mental Processes (sensing verbs) deal with thinking, feeling, and perceiving (*understand*, *detest*, *see*) and Verbal Processes deal with saying of various kinds (*demand*, *shout*, *plead*). Relational Processes link a Participant with an Attribute (She is tall; He appears tired) or identify or equate two Participants (She is the School Captain; Cu symbolizes copper.) These different kinds of Processes have their own specific categories of participants. Material Processes, for example, entail Actors (those carrying out the process) and Goals (those to whom the action is directed), while Mental Processes entail a Sensor and a Phenomenon. Relational processes that are attributive link a Carrier to its Attribute and if they are identifying they equate a Token and a Value.

Interpersonal meanings are realized by the mood and modality systems. Much of this aspect of SFG is familiar to those with experience of more traditional grammars. Statements are realized by declarative mood where the ordering within the clause is Subject followed by the Finite Verb (Grandad does enjoy his soup). Questions are realized by the interrogative mood where the ordering of Subject and Finite Verb is reversed (Does Grandad enjoy his soup?). The modal verbs (*can*, *should*, *must*, etc.) indicate degrees of obligation or inclination and modal adverbs such as *frequently*, *probably*, and *certainly* enable personal stance to be communicated through negotiating the semantic space between *yes* and *no*.

The personal stance aspect of interpersonal meaning was developed further in the *Appraisal* framework for conceptualizing and analyzing attitude (Martin & White, 2005). The framework has also been made available in a form easily accessible to teachers and students (Droga & Humphrey, 2003). In this framework, shown in Figure 1.1, attitude is subdivided into the categories of affect, appreciation, and judgment. Affect refers to the expression of feelings, which can be positive or negative, and may be descriptions of emotional states (e.g., *happy*) or behaviors that indicate an emotional state (e.g., *crying*). Subcategories of affect are *happiness*, *security*, and *satisfaction*. Appreciation relates to evaluations of objects, events, or states of affairs and is further subdivided into *reaction*, *composition*, and *valuation*. Reaction involves the emotional impact of the phenomenon (e.g., *thrilling, boring, enchanting, depressing*). Composition refers to the form of an object (e.g., *coherent, balanced, haphazard*), and valuation refers to the significance of the phenomenon (e.g., *groundbreaking, inconsequential*). Judgment can refer to assessments of someone's capacities (*brilliant, slow*), their dependability (*tireless, courageous, rash*), or their relative normality (*regular, weird*). Judgment can also refer to someone's truthfulness (*frank, manipulative*) and ethics (*just, cruel, corrupt*).

TOWARD A METALANGUAGE | 5

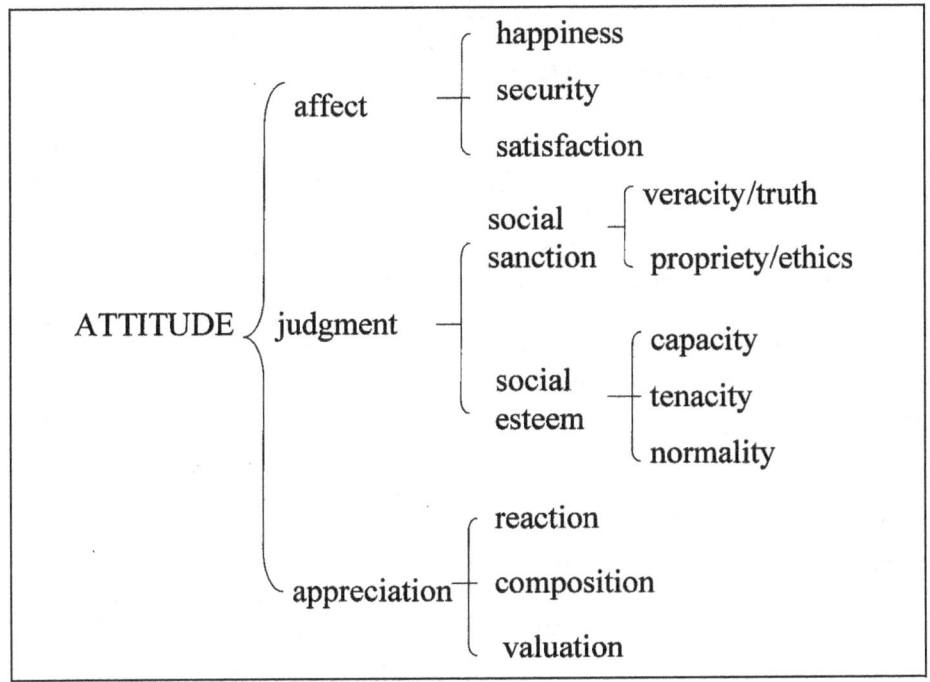

Fig 1.1. The Appraisal Framework, derived from Martin and Rose (2007).

Textual meanings are realized in part by the Theme/Rheme system. The Theme is the point of departure (Halliday & Matthiessen, 2004, p.64), orienting the clause in its context, and is the element that is in first position. This is usually the Subject ("The weather is mild in Australia"), but another element, such as a Circumstance (adverbial element) could be placed in Theme position ("In Australia the weather is mild"). This is not as common and is likely to occur more frequently in more formal written language than in informal spoken language. When some experiential element other than the Subject is placed in first position in a clause, it is referred to as a Marked Theme, in that it draws more attention due to its relatively less frequent use.

The three different grammatical systems realize the three main types of meaning simultaneously. For example, in the sentence, "The leader usually carries the flag on parade," the first element in the clause, *The leader*, is the Theme from the textual perspective. From the experiential perspective *The leader* is also the Actor (the doer of the action) and from the interpersonal perspective, in the mood system, *The leader* is the Subject. We could change the Theme—"On parade the leader usually carries the flag"—so the orientation of the clause in its context is different. Now *The leader* is not the Theme, but remains the Actor in experiential terms, and the Subject in interpersonal terms.

SFG-INFLUENCED METALANGUAGE: CURRICULUM REQUIREMENTS AND PEDAGOGIC APPLICATION

After the Foundation year, which is a preparatory or kindergarten year, the requirement for explicit learning of knowledge about language occurs from Year 1 of the Australian Curriculum: English (ACE). For example, students in Year 1 are expected to know that "a basic clause represents: a happening or a state (verb), who or what is involved (noun group/phrase), and the surrounding circumstances (adverb group/phrase)." Year 1 students are also expected to "understand that the purposes texts serve shape their structure in predictable ways." In addition, the students need to become "familiar with the typical stages of types of text including recount and procedure" (ACARA, 2012, p. 28). Progressively advanced knowledge expectations of grammar and genre permeate the curriculum, and the terminological formulation of most of these will be recognizable to those familiar with traditional school grammar. The examples of "Content Descriptions" to be discussed here illustrate the distinctive SFL influence on the approach to grammar. The grammatical construction of experiential meaning is illustrated by the approach to verbs in Year 3. An example of the SFL approach to the grammatical construction of textual meaning is shown with the introduction of grammatical "Theme" in Year 5. The grammatical resources for constructing interpersonal meaning are illustrated in the Year 6 requirements regarding modal verbs and adverbs and in the Year 7 requirements regarding resources for expressing evaluative meanings. It is expected that students will develop explicit knowledge of such grammatical concepts and use them to discuss their interpretation and creation of multimodal texts. This expectation is made clear in the curriculum. In Year 4, for example, Content Description (ACARA, 2012, p. 52)[1] states that students will "use metalanguage to describe the effects of ideas, text structures and language features of literary texts" (ACARA, 2012, p. 52) and in Year 5 students are required to "present a point of view about particular literary texts using appropriate metalanguage" (ACELT1609) and "use metalanguage to describe the effects of ideas, text structures and language features of literary texts" (ACELT1604) (ACARA, 2012, p. 59).

DIFFERENTIATING VERB TYPES AND LITERARY INTERPRETATION IN CLASSROOM WORK

The content descriptions for Year 3 in the ACE include the requirement that students will "understand that verbs represent different processes (doing, thinking, saying, and relating)" (ACELA1482) (ACARA, 2012, p. 43). This differentiation of verbs according to types of experiential meaning is consistent with, and distinctive to, SFG. Case study research shows that children in Year 2 classes are able to learn to distinguish different types of verbs and apply this knowledge in understanding how the distribution of verb types in a literary narrative is co-patterned with the different stages of the narrative genre (French, 2010a). Year 2 students learned to distinguish "action" verbs and "saying" verbs in the context of procedural genres such as instructions for making a polystyrene cup telephone (French, 2010b). Subsequently, the class worked with a picture book, *Pumpkin Soup* (Cooper, 1999). Learning experiences included whole-class and small-group shared reading and discussion of the book and activity-based learning involving concrete resources such as green ("verb coloured") cards featuring a stylised mouth shape on those that represented a saying verb. The children learned to confidently identify a wide range of "saying" verbs in the text (*murmured, said, squeaked, snapped, wailed, stormed, scoffed, muttered, sniffed, wept, whispered, yelped, shrieked, didn't say*). They were familiar with the Orientation, Complication, Resolution stages of the narrative genre and eventually were able to see a co-patterning of the "saying" verbs with these narrative stages. They were able to discuss the patterning of "saying" verbs that selected those showing increasing upset and trouble in the first part of the complication, leading to unhappiness and regret, and then a change to shrieking with delight and a thoughtful, accommodating silence as the characters dealt with their differences in the resolution (French, 2009, 2010a).

Children in Year 6 were able to combine their knowledge of different verb types with their understanding of the associated participant roles in thematic interpretation of Anthony Browne's (1986/1996) picture book, *Piggybook* (French, 2010a; Williams, 2000). The children learned about the participant roles of Actor and Goal in relation to Material Processes and were able to see how the differing statuses of the characters were reflected in this aspect of the grammar. For example, Mrs. Piggott, as an Actor, participated in Material Processes where the Goals were predominantly domestic items. Mr. Piggott and the boys were Actors but the Material Processes they participated in had no Goals, reflecting that they did a lot but did not act on things around the house. When Mrs. Piggott leaves the household the males do become Actors in Material Processes with Goals at the end of the story while they do these things around the house. Mrs. Piggott mends the car, so her Goals now extend beyond the household domestic items. With some guidance the children were able to reflect on the shift in the patterning of the Participant roles in the Material Processes in the story, and particularly on how this related to the structure of the narrative.

THE LANGUAGE OF EVALUATION: COMMUNICATING PERSONAL STANCE

Knowledge of the grammatical systems of Mood and Modality is clearly specified as a requirement in several ACE content descriptions across grade levels.

For example, in Year 3 students explore how modal verbs "indicate degrees of certainty, command or obligation" (ACELA1477) (ACARA, 2012, p. 43) and in Year 6 students learn "how degrees of possibility are opened up through the use of modal verbs…as well as through other resources such as adverbs" (ACELT 1615) (ACARA, 2012, p. 66). The manner in which the curriculum draws closely on recent SFL work is abundantly clear in the Year 6 content description elaboration, which requires students to develop "a knowledge base about words of evaluation, including words to express emotional responses to texts, judgment of characters and their actions, and appreciation of the aesthetic qualities of text" (ACELA1782) (ACARA, 2012, p. 71). This aligns directly with the Appraisal framework for conceptualizing and analyzing attitude (Martin & White, 2005) as briefly described above and outlined in Figure 1.1.

A comparative study of different versions of the *Shrek* story can be used to achieve the recommended integration of the content descriptions of the language and literature stands of the ACE and to initiate explicit teaching of the Appraisal framework (Unsworth, 2007). The original *Shrek* picture book by William Steig was published in 1990 and the animated movie, based on the book, was released in 2001 (Elliott, 2001). Also published in 2001 was an e-book by Ruth Ashby based on the movie and including still images from the movie. While the plot of both stories concerns the ogre Shrek and his eventual marriage to the ugly princess, beyond this the stories are very different. In the book the theme is about Shrek being himself and accepting himself for what he really is without caring about other people's attitudes toward him. Hence, he is quite active and confident with high self-esteem and pride in himself ("How it tickled him to be so repulsive!"). By contrast, in the electronic versions the theme is about the inappropriateness of judging things by appearance and perpetuating stereotypical values of beauty and physical perfection. Shrek is "stunned" when he believes Princess Fiona rejects him for his ugliness. He is shy and passive, needing social acceptance and encouragement to act.

In the final episode the book celebrates the attraction of Shrek and the princess to each other's conventionally regarded ugliness and the explicit positive valuing of this ugliness. The electronic version reconstrues conventional ugliness (or at least lack of conventional beauty) as, in fact, beauty in the eyes of the beholder. Students can be taught how to adopt a "text analytic" role in their reading (Freebody & Luke, 1990) to appreciate how grammatical resources have been deployed to construct this difference between the two versions. The starting point for this analysis could be with the vocabulary differences. Children will quite readily identify the significant number of words associated with ugliness in the book compared with the relatively few in the e-narrative. Children can be shown how to systematically articulate their informal impressions of the effects of vocabulary differences between the two texts, by teaching them how to use part of the Appraisal framework for analysing attitude (Droga & Humphrey, 2003; Martin & Rose, 2003; Martin & White, 2005).

When the selected segments from the different versions of *Shrek* are analysed, the ways that the language choices construct different dimensions of attitude can be clearly seen. In the original book version there is a co-patterning of invoked negative appreciation as a reaction to the repulsive description of either Shrek or the ogress and an inscribed positive expression of Affect, as indicated in Figure 1.2.

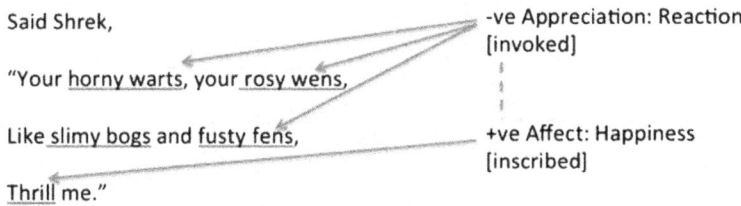

Fig 1.2. Co-patterning of APPRAISAL in *Shrek* (Steig, 1990).

This pattern is repeated several times in the dialogue between Shrek and the ogress. For example:

Said Shrek:
Oh <u>ghastly</u> you,
With <u>lips of blue</u>,
Your <u>ruddy eyes</u>
With <u>carmine sties</u>
<u>Enchant</u> me.
(Steig, 1990)

This contrasts starkly with the language of the exchange in the e-book:

"Fiona, I <u>love</u> you,"
Shrek admitted.
"I <u>love</u> you too,"
Fiona said.
(Ashby, 2001)

Throughout this section of the e-book positive Affect is dominant. The only examples of invoked negative Appreciation: Reaction are the three occurrences of the word *ogress*.

Fiona looked down at herself <u>in wonder</u>.
She was still an <u>ogress</u>!
"But I'm supposed to be <u>beautiful</u>,"
she said.
"You are <u>beautiful</u>,"
Shrek said.
(Ashby, 2001)

Once this kind of systematic patterning is established the students can be engaged in further analyses based on the Appraisal framework (Unsworth, 2007). By introducing students to analysis using this framework, they can be provided with a way of systematizing their observations about these texts and also develop a heuristic they can use to investigate the evaluative language of other texts.

GRAMMATICAL THEME: ORIENTING THE CLAUSE IN ITS CONTEXT

The concept of grammatical Theme is distinctive to SFG. In English, what comes first in the clause provides the "point of departure" or orientation to the message. If I say, "My daughter is coming home this weekend," the discussion is primarily about my daughter. On the other hand if I say, "This weekend my daughter is coming home," the orientation is more about the weekend. So the "point of departure" or orientation is one kind of prominence achieved through selection of first position in the clause. This concept (although not labeled grammatical Theme at this point) is introduced in the ACE in Year 5. Content description (ACELA1505) indicates that students will

> Understand that the starting point of a sentence gives prominence to the message in the text and allows for prediction of how the text will unfold (ACARA, 2012, p. 57).

The term *grammatical theme* does occur later in the ACE in Year 8 in content description (ACELA1809) (ACARA, 2012, p. 78), but there is no mention of Marked Theme and no further elaboration of grammatical theme. Here the interpretive utility of the concept of Marked Theme in understanding the "constructedness" of literary narrative will be briefly illustrated.

In some picture books such as *Drac and the Gremlin* (Baillie, 1991), Marked Themes signal the episodic development of the story. Of the 67 clauses in this story only five have marked Themes (for example, "At last Drac traps the Gremlin"; "At that moment, an emerald eaglon slips"). All five marked Themes are positioned at the boundaries of the four episodes in the story: Drac's subduing of the Gremlin; the encounter with General Min; the encounter with the Terrible Tongued Dragon; and finally Drac and the Gremlin receiving their reward. Similarly, marked Themes occur in only five clauses in *Zoo* (Browne, 1994) and they are all located at the boundaries of episodes in the story.

The patterning of Theme selection can draw attention to other aspects of story apart from episodic structure. This can be seen in *Five Times Dizzy* (Wheatley, 1982), which is a short novel about a Greek migrant family in Sydney, Australia. Yaya has recently arrived from Greece and is terribly lonely and homesick. Her nostalgia for the things she cannot find in her new environment (nature, animals, particularly her goat, the village community) and the fact that, with nothing to do, she spends her days alone in her room, drain her energy and make her seem older and melancholic. In Yaya's thoughts there is a constant comparison between her new environment and the old country, between the past and the present. Language choices draw attention to the significance of this difference. It is interesting to note how often time and place are marked Themes in this chapter as the following examples illustrate:

> <u>In Greece</u>, people look at their neighbours all the time. In Greece, you don't live behind walls and fences. (p. 18)

> <u>At home</u> she used to walk seven or eight kilometres a day, up and down the mountain-sides, leading Poppy to new grazing spots. <u>Here</u> she only dared walk at dawn, before the traffic. (p. 18)

> At home the child had had lots of friends but here she was always serving in the shop. (p. 21)

Mareka, her granddaughter, is not prepared to see her Yaya like this and is determined to find anything for Yaya to keep her busy, preferably something she used to do back home. Her solution is to obtain a goat for Yaya to tend in their inner-city terrace house. This causes much hilarity as well as some consternation in the neighbourhood and, happily, eventually draws Yaya into positive social prominence in the community. In the latter part of the book, marked Themes draw attention to the significance of this change in Yaya:

> Mareka pauses and shifts uncomfortably, remembering back to that day months ago when she'd come home and thought Yaya was dead. <u>These days</u>, it's hard to keep up with her. (p. 88)

Further accounts of the role of the pattern of Theme selection in highlighting readers' perception of the structure of narrative and drawing attention to experiential meanings integral to interpretive possibilities of text segments can be found in the discussions of *The Secret Garden* (Burnett, 1992) by Knowles and Malmkjaer (1996) and of *Bridge to Terabithia* (Paterson, 1977) by Unsworth (2001).

INTERPRETING AND CREATING MULTIMODAL TEXTS IN PAPER AND DIGITAL MEDIA

The ACE emphasizes the importance of students learning to interpret and create multimodal paper and digital media texts from the beginning of schooling. For example, in the first year of school children are expected to learn to

> Understand concepts about print and screen, including how books, film and simple digital texts work (ACELA1433). (ACARA, 2012, p. 20)

In the middle years of the primary school they are expected to

> Collaboratively plan, compose, sequence and prepare a literary text along a familiar storyline, using film, sound and images to convey setting, characters and points of drama in the plot (ACELT1794). (ACARA, 2012, p. 53)

And by Year 9 students will

> Investigate and experiment with the use and effect of extended metaphor, metonymy, allegory, icons, myths and symbolism in texts, for example poetry, short films, graphic novels, and plays on similar themes (ACELT1637). (ACARA, 2012, p. 87)

From Years 4 through 10 there are multiple content descriptions such as the above. For example, there are the following:

- Six content descriptions involving the interpretation of picture books
- Seven involving film creation and four involving the creation of animation
- Eight involving the creation of multimodal paper texts

In the interpretation and creation of such texts the ACE requires the use of metalanguage that describes the meaning-making resources of language as well as metalanguage that describes the meaning-making resources of images.

A METALANGUAGE DESCRIBING THE MEANING-MAKING RESOURCES OF IMAGES

Just as systemic functional grammar (SFG) describes language as a resource for simultaneously constructing three types of meanings (experiential, interpersonal, and textual), Kress and van Leeuwen (2006) proposed that images also always simultaneously construct these three types of meanings (which they named slightly differently as *representational*, *interactive*, and *compositional*). They described in detail the nature of representational, interactive, and compositional meanings and the features of images that construct those meanings in their account of the grammar of visual design (Kress & van Leeuwen, 2006). The metalanguage describing *interactive* (interpersonal) meanings constructed by images seems to be included in the ACE to a much greater extent than the metalanguage describing *representational* (experiential) or *compositional* (textual) meanings. This section of the chapter indicates the nature, extent, and distribution across the year levels of the ACE of the metalanguage dealing with the meaning-making resources of images. This mapping indicates how a closer articulation in the ACE of the metalanguage derived from systemic functional linguistics and that from the grammar of visual design could enhance the benefit of their common theoretical base and advance the conceptualization of a multimodal grammar as envisaged by the New London Group (1996, 2000). It also highlights practical issues for teachers striving to support their students to achieve cumulative metasemiotic understanding of language and image in the context of working with an emerging multimodal literacy curriculum.

A large proportion of the interactive meanings specified in the Kress and van Leeuwen (2006) grammar of visual design are entailed in content description ACELA1483 for Year 3 of the ACE:

> Identify the effect on audiences of techniques, for example shot size, vertical camera angle and layout in picture books, advertisements and film segments
> - noting how the relationship between characters can be depicted in illustrations through: the positioning of the characters (for example facing each other or facing away from each other); the distance between them; the relative size; one character looking up (or down) at the other (power relationships); facial expressions and body gesture.
> - observing how images construct a relationship with the viewer through such strategies as: direct gaze into the viewer's eyes, inviting involvement and how close ups are more engaging than distanced images, which can suggest alienation or loneliness. (ACARA, 2012, p. 44)

For Kress and van Leeuwen (2006), "direct gaze into the viewer's eyes" distinguishes a "Demand" image requiring interactive contact with the viewer as opposed to an "Offer" where no such interactive contact occurs and the viewer is a detached outside observer. Close up and distanced images are part of the continuum of Social Distance realized by the distance of the camera from the represented participants. The vertical angle can refer to the relationship between the represented participants and the viewer or the relationships among the represented participants (one character looking up [or down] at the other [power relationships]). A high angle view looks down on the represented participants affording power to the viewer, whereas a low angle view means that the viewer looks up at the more powerful represented participant. The diagrammatic summary of potential interactive meanings in images (Kress & van Leeuwen, 2006, p. 149) is indicated in Figure 1.3 along with annotations showing the coverage of this summary by the Year 3 ACE content description ACELA1483.

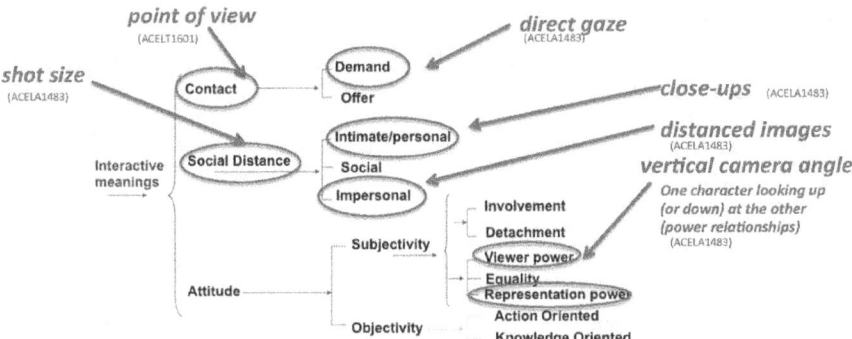

Fig 1.3. Addressing Interactive Meanings in Images in the Australian Curriculum: English Year 3.

What can be seen is that only two aspects of interactive meaning are not addressed in ACELA1483. The first of these is the viewer Involvement/Detachment option. This is realized by the horizontal angle of view. When the horizontal angle is such that the frontal plane of the represented participants is parallel to the frontal plane of the viewer, this indicates maximum involvement of the viewer in the world of the represented participants. An oblique horizontal angle, however, constructs the relationship between the viewer and the represented participants as "other." In fact, this aspect of interactive meanings is not addressed at any year level in the ACE, which is of concern as students are not learning about a significant means by which certain participants are marginalized in visual representations. The other aspect not addressed in ACELA1483 and also not in any other year level is that of Objectivity. This most frequently occurs in scientific and technical images such as diagrams and maps. The objectivity is achieved by either a directly frontal or perpendicular top-down angle. Such views represent special viewer positions that neutralize the distortions that usually come with perspective because they neutralize perspective itself (Kress & van Leeuwen, 2006). The question to be asked here is: If one content description at Year 3 can deal so comprehensively with interactive meanings in images, why are these two important aspects of such a well-established account of the semiotics of images not included at some point in the curriculum?

With respect to representational or experiential meanings, Kress and van Leeuwen distinguish between Narrative and Conceptual images. The three main categories of conceptual images are classificational (which represent taxonomic, superordinate/subordinate relations); analytic (which represent part/whole relations); and symbolic images. Symbolic images are addressed in Year 5 (ACELT1608) and Year 9 (ACELA1560) of the ACE. Classificational and analytic images are addressed in Year 6 (ACELA1520). Nowhere in the curriculum are narrative images addressed. The Kress and van Leeuwen account of narrative images distinguishes images involving actions and reactions, and whether these are transactional or not (involving a "doer" and a "receiver" or just a "doer"), verbal processes (speech bubbles), and mental processes (thought clouds). Included in the account are various kinds of circumstances related to narrative processes such as setting, means, and accompaniment. Narrative images are clearly significant in multimodal texts in the humanities disciplines and in various contemporary media texts, so one wonders why such images are not explicitly addressed in a multimodal English curriculum document.

Compositional meanings concerning various aspects of layout are addressed in Year 4 of the ACE:

> Explore the effect of choices when framing an image, placement of elements in the image, and salience on composition of still and moving images in a range of types of texts (ACELA1496). (ACARA, 2012, p. 51)

Apart from two occurrences of the word *layout* (AECLY1686; AECLT1805) this is the only content description that deals with compositional meanings. While "framing," "placement," and "salience" are mentioned, no further detail is provided, which is different from the elaborations of interactive meanings in Year 3 as discussed above. The elaboration of ACELA1496 does go on to indicate that this entails

> examining visual and multimodal texts, building a vocabulary to describe visual elements and techniques such as framing, composition and visual point of view and beginning to understand how these choices impact on viewer response (ACELA1496). (ACARA, 2012, p. 51)

However, there is no further reference to what such a metalanguage might include and no reference at all to any detail of what metalanguage might be involved in "visual point of view" (Painter, Martin, & Unsworth, 2013; Unsworth, 2013).

While attention to the metalanguage describing interactive meanings in images is reasonably comprehensive in the ACE, relatively little metalanguage is included for representational and compositional meanings. What has been excluded from ACE are not arcane visual meaning-making resources but those that could complement what is included in the metalanguage of verbal grammar. For example, distinguishing verb types in Anthony Browne's picture book *Zoo* (1994) reveals that only Mum is associated with *thinking* verbs (mental processes of cognition) and that while the *saying* processes for Mum and the boys are simply *said*, for Dad they are saying verbs such as *snorted, bellowed, howled*, and *jeered*. However, not only are the verb types indicative of the characterization in the story, but also the images depict Mum predominantly engaged in *reactional* processes (contemplative) while Dad and the boys are never depicted this way (Unsworth, 2001). Clearly the visual grammar of narrative images is a fundamental interpretive resource, and while it is well developed in the Kress and van Leeuwen (2006) grammar of visual design it does not appear in ACE at all. Since it has been decided that a metalanguage of meaning-making resources in images will be required knowledge in the ACE, the basis for determining the nature, extent, and distribution of the metalanguage needs further examination.

INTERMODALITY

The Australian Curriculum: English consistently emphasizes the need for students to negotiate the meanings constructed through the interaction of images and language, as indicated in Figure 1.4 by the examples of expectations of students at successive year levels.

- Explore the different contribution of words and images to meaning in stories and informative texts

  ACELA1786 | Content description | Foundation Year | English | Language | Expressing and developing ideas

- Identify visual representations of characters' actions, reactions, speech and thought processes in narratives, and consider how these images add to or contradict or multiply the meaning of accompanying words

  ACELA1469 | Content description | Year 2 | English | Language | Expressing and developing ideas

- making connections between information in print and images

  ELBE808 | Elaboration | Year 2 | English | Literacy | Interpreting, analysing, evaluating

- making connections between the information in print and images

  ELBE875 | Elaboration | Year 3 | English | Literacy | Interpreting, analysing, evaluating

- making connections between information in print and images

  ELBE934 | Elaboration | Year 4 | English | Literacy | Interpreting, analysing, evaluating

- making connections between information in print and images

  ELBE1051 | Elaboration | Year 6 | English | Literacy | Interpreting, analysing, evaluating

- using display advertising as a topic vehicle for close analysis of the ways images and words combine for deliberate effect including examples from the countries of Asia (for example comparing Hollywood film posters with Indian Bollywood film posters)

  ELBE1036 | Elaboration | Year 6 | English | Literacy | Texts in context

- recognising the similarities and differences between types of texts (for example a complex picture book and a feature film) in order to understand how different combinations of words and images lead readers to interpret visual texts in particular ways, according to audience, purpose and context

  ELBE1135 | Elaboration | Year 8 | English | Literature | Responding to literature

Fig 1.4. Requirements for Interpreting Image-Language Relations in the Australian Curriculum: English (ACARA, 2012).

But there is also the expectation that students will be able to draw on knowledge about the meaning-making resources of images and language to discuss how meanings are constructed intermodally as indicated, for example, in the following content description for Year 9 students:

> Explore and explain the combinations of language and visual choices that authors make to present information, opinions and perspectives in different texts (ACELY1745). (ACARA, 2012)

Recent research on picture books and illustrated literary narratives has related systemic functional linguistic and visual semiotic frameworks to develop an approach to the description of meaning-making through the combination of images and language (Painter & Martin, 2011; Painter et al., 2013). In this approach the contributions to meaning made by language and image are mapped out separately by tracking the choices made in particular texts in the visual and verbal systems of meaning-making options as described by SFG and in the grammar of visual design (Kress & van Leeuwen, 2006) and additional theoretical accounts of visual narratives (Painter & Martin, 2011; Painter et al., 2013). The interrelationship of these visual and verbal meaning-making systems has been described in detail by Painter and her colleagues (Painter et al., 2013). While the full account cannot be included here, Table 1.1 indicates in outline form just one example from each of the categories detailed by Painter and her colleagues to show how this approach relates the complementary visual and verbal meaning-making systems.

Table 1.1. Exemplifying Relationships Among Visual and Verbal Meaning-Making Resources

Metafunction		Visual Meaning	Visual Realization	Verbal Meaning	Verbal Realization
Interpersonal	Affiliation	Power	Vertical view: high, mid, low by viewer and by characters relative to each other	Power	Naming, forms of address, distribution of speech functions such as questions and commands
	Feeling	Affect	Emotion depicted in facial features and bodily stance	Affect	Language of emotion such as happiness, sadness, affection, antipathy
Ideational	Action	Action	Vectors (action lines, such as angle of limbs indicating movement)	Action	Material and behavioural (physical and physiological action) processes
	Character	Character attribution	Depiction of physical attributes	Participant description	Relating processes, noun groups, including describing and classifying adjectives
	Setting	Circumstance	Visual depiction of place and time (such as setting sun), lines indicating speed	Circumstance	Specification of time, place, manner, etc., usually by adverbs and adverbial phrases
Textual	Prominence	Focus	Compositional arrangement such as use of size of elements and colour to give emphasis	Information flow	Theme/rheme structure in clauses, intonation prominence
	Phasing	Genre stages and phases	Visual continuity and discontinuity across images	Genre stages and phases	Conjunction linking text segments, text reference

Painter and her colleagues (2013) emphasize that bimodal texts, like picture books, instantiate meaning choices from two meaning systems. From this perspective the question of how choices combine across modalities, and how they complement one another, needs to give priority to the distinctiveness of the two modes of meaning. This is dealt with by considering the different affordances for meaning of the visual and verbal semiotics, the degree to which each "commits" meaning in a particular instance, and the extent to which that commitment converges with or diverges from that of the other modality. Sometimes meaning committed in one mode is not committed in the other. For example, in the first two pages of David McKee's (1987) picture book, *Not Now Bernard*, the first image shows a young boy talking to his father, who has his back to the boy and is about to hammer a nail into the wall. The second image shows the father crying out in pain at the moment he has hit his finger with the hammer and the little boy now with his back to his father's back and walking away. There is no verbal commitment to what is depicted visually. The text under the first image says:

"Hello, Dad," said Bernard.
And the text under the second image says:
"Not now, Bernard," said his father.

But, subsequently, in the story there is frequent intermodal ideational coupling with concurrence between actions depicted and those narrated (e.g., picture of Bernard descending steps into garden + *Bernard went into the garden*, picture of monster throwing toy across room + *the monster broke Bernard's toy*, picture of Mum holding plate of dinner speaking and looking sideways out of frame + *"Your dinner's ready," said Bernard's mother*). In their discussion of *Not Now Bernard*, Painter and Martin point out that

> neither the visual nor the verbal sequence of actions on its own carries the full meaning nor provides the full enjoyment and fun of the text—this requires negotiating the gap between the two modalities and thus arriving at a new meaning that results from the co-patterning of semiotic resources. (Painter & Martin, 2011, p. 147)

CONCLUSION

The Australian Curriculum: English represents formal government recognition and practical action in relation to the multimodal reconceptualization of literacy and literacy pedagogy, requiring schools to address new literacies as mandated in the national curriculum (ACARA, 2012). A fundamental aspect of the new curriculum is the requirement that teachers will teach and students will learn metalanguage describing the meaning-making resources of language and images. The nature of this required metalanguage has been strongly influenced by systemic functional linguistics and related theoretical accounts of the semiotics of images.

As part of the language strand of the curriculum students are required to learn metalanguage relating to *Language for interaction*, *Text structure and organization*, and *Expressing and developing ideas* (ACARA, 2012), corresponding directly to the SFL theorization of language as simultaneously constructing experiential, interpersonal, and textual meaning (Halliday & Matthiessen, 2004). While there is substantial professional literature illustrating the pedagogic usefulness of systemic functional linguistic approaches to grammar, discourse, and genre, the ACE has not comprehensively adopted these accounts, nor has it comprehensively adopted the related grammar of visual design. While the fusion of more traditional grammatical description with that of SFL is no doubt in response to widely differing community and professional views on the relative advantages of various approaches to grammar, the basis for curriculum decisions about the extent and detail of the verbal and visual grammar to be included remains unclear. Notwithstanding the long history of research relating to grammar in schooling (Locke, 2010), there is no established research basis for determining how much detail of what aspects of grammar are appropriate to be taught at differing levels of schooling. Less surprisingly, there is likewise no research basis for determining how the grammar of visual design might be optimally infused into the curriculum for the successive levels of schooling. While some larger scale studies across primary and secondary schooling are beginning to investigate such issues (Macken-Horarik et al., 2011), much of the relevant informing evidential advice needs to be aggregated from more modest studies of single grade levels. For example, Chandler (Chapter 5, this volume), in the context of digital animated movie making with students in the upper primary school, explores the ways in which teacher knowledge of multimodal design elements helps to shape the pedagogy, curriculum, and assessment of multimodal authoring. In the same context, O'Brien (Chapter 7, this volume) explores the teaching of visual point of view, and in the senior secondary school Bain and Unsworth (Chapter 10, this volume) report on initiatives to develop older adolescents' understanding and use of a metalanguage of multimodality as a resource for text interpretation and composition. The ACE provides a locus for national and international discussion about the nature and role of a metalanguage of multimodality in relation to multimodal narrative interpretation and authoring and in relation to new literacies pedagogy more generally. It is hoped that this chapter may stimulate such discussion, critical response, collaborative research, and reflective classroom-based enquiry by teachers.

REFERENCES

ACARA. (2012). *Australian Curriclum English Version 3*. Retrieved from http://www.australiancurriculum.edu.au

Achugar, M., Schleppegrell, M., & Oteíza, T. (2007). Engaging teachers in language analysis: A functional linguistics approach to reflective literacy. *English Teaching: Practice and Critique, 6*(2), 8–24.

Ashby, R. (2001). *Shrek.* New York: ipicturebooks.com.
Baillie, A. (1991). *Drac and the Gremlin,* Ringwood, Victoria: Penguin/Puffin.
Browne, A. (1986/1996). *Piggybook.* London: Julia MacRae.
Browne, A. (1994). *Zoo.* London: Random House.
Burnett, F. H. (1992). *The Secret Garden,* London, Sainsbury: Walker.
Butt, D., Fahey, R., Feez, S., Spinks, S., & Yallop, C. (2000). *Using functional grammar: An explorer's guide.* Sydney: National Centre for English Language Teaching and Research.
Christie, F. (Ed.). (1989). *Writing in schools: Study guide.* Geelong: Deakin University Press.
Christie, F. (2005). *Language education in the primary years.* Sydney: University of New South Wales Press.
Cooper, H. (1999). *Pumpkin soup* (1st ed.). London: Picture Corgi.
Droga, L., & Humphrey, S. (2003). *Grammar and meaning: An introduction for primary teachers.* Berry, New South Wales: Target Texts.
Elliott, T. (Writer). (2001). *Shrek* [Movie]. Glendale, CA: Dreamworks.
Freebody, P., & Luke, A. (1990). "Literacies" programs: Debates and demands in cultural context. *Prospect, 5,* 7–16.
French, R. (2009). Pumpkin soup and grammatics: A critical literacy case study with Year 2. In T. Hays & R. Hussain (Eds.), *Bridging the gap between ideas and doing research—Proceedings of the 3rd Annual Postgraduate Research Conference, The Faculty of the Professions, University of New England, Armidale NSW* (pp. 69–84). Armidale, Australia: University of New England.
French, R. (2010a). Primary school children learning grammar: Rethinking the possibilities. In T. Locke (Ed.), *Beyond the grammar wars: A resource for teachers and students on developing language knowledge in the English/literacy classroom* (pp. 206–229). New York: Routledge.
French, R. (2010b). Starting points in teaching grammatics: Children learning about verbs. In T. Hays (Ed.), *Bridging the gap between ideas and doing research—Proceedings of the 4th Annual Postgraduate Research Conference, Faculty of the Professions, University of New England, Armidale NSW* (pp. 79–106). Armidale, Australia: University of New England.
Halliday, M. A. K., & Matthiessen, C. (2004). *An introduction to functional grammar* (3rd ed.). London: Arnold.
Humphrey, S., Love, K., & Droga, L. (2011). *Working grammar: An introduction for secondary English teachers.* Melbourne: Pearson.
Knowles, M., & Malmkjaer, K. (1996). *Language and control in children's literature.* London: Routledge.
Kress, G., & van Leeuwen, T. (2006). *Reading images: The grammar of visual design* (2nd ed.). London: Routledge.
Lemke, J. (1989). Making text talk. *Theory into Practice, 28,* 136–141.
Lemke, J. (1990). *Talking science: Language, learning and values.* Norwood, NJ: Ablex.
Lemke, J. (1998). Metamedia literacy: Transforming meanings and media. In D. Reinking, M. McKenna, L. Labbo, & R. Kieffer (Eds.), *Handbook of literacy and technology: Transformations in a post-typographic world* (pp. 283–302). Mahwah, NJ: Erlbaum.
Lemke, J. (2002). Travels in hypermodality. *Visual Communication, 1*(3), 299–325.
Lemke, J. (2006). Towards critical multimedia literacy: Technology, research and politics. In M. McKenna, L. Labbo, R. Kieffer, & D. Reinking (Eds.), *International handbook of literacy and technology* (Vol. 2, pp. 3–14). Mahwah, NJ: Erlbaum.
Locke, T. (Ed.). (2010). *Beyond the grammar wars: A resource for teachers and students on developing language knowledge in the English/literacy classroom.* London: Routledge.
Love, K. (1996). Talk around text: Acquiescence or empowerment in secondary English. *Australian Review of Applied Linguistics, 19*(2), 1–25.

Love, K. (2000). Personal response or critical response in secondary English discussions: A linguistic analysis. *Australian Review of Applied Linguistics, 23*(1), 31–52.
Love, K., Pigdon, K., Baker, G., & Hamston, J. (2002). *BUILT—Building Understanding in Literacy and Teaching*. CD ROM: The University of Melbourne.
Macken-Horarik, M. (1996). Literacy and learning across the curriculum: Towards a model of register for secondary school teachers. In R. Hasan & G. Williams (Eds.), *Literacy in society* (pp. 232–278). Harlow: Addison Wesley Longman.
Macken-Horarik, M. (2008). Multiliteracies and "basic skills" accountability. In L. Unsworth (Ed.), *New literacies and the English curriculum: Multimodal perspectives*. London: Continuum.
Macken-Horarik, M., & Adoniou, M. (2008). Genre and register in multiliteracies. In B. Spolsky & F. M. Hult (Eds.), *The handbook of educational linguistics* (pp. 367–382). Malden, MA: Blackwell Publishing.
Macken-Horarik, M., Love, K., & Unsworth, L. (2011). A grammatics "good enough" for school English in the 21st century: Four challenges in realizing the potential. *Australian Journal of Language and Literacy, 34*(1), 9–23.
Macken-Horarik, M., & Morgan, W. (2011). Towards a metalanguage adequate to linguistic achievement in post-structuralism and English: Reflections on voicing in the writing of secondary students. *Linguistics and Education, 22*(2), 133–149.
Martin, J. R. (1992). *English text: System and structure*. Amsterdam: Benjamins.
Martin, J. R., & Rose, D. (2003). *Working with discourse: Meaning beyond the clause* (1st ed., Vol. 1). London/New York: Continuum.
Martin, J. R., & Rose, D. (2007). *Working with discourse: Meaning beyond the clause* (2nd ed., Vol. 1). London/New York: Continuum.
Martin, J. R., & Rose, D. (2008). *Genre relations: Mapping culture*. London: Equinox.
Martin, J. R., & White, P. (2005). *The language of evaluation: Appraisal in English*. London/New York: Palgrave/Macmillan.
Martinec, R. (2000). Types of process in action. *Semiotica, 130*(3/4), 243–268.
Martinec, R. (2004). Gestures that co-occur with speech as a systematic resource: The realization of experiential meanings in indexes. *Social Semiotics*(14), 2.
McKee, D. (1987). *Not now, Bernard*. London: Arrow.
New London Group. (1996). A pedagogy of multiliteracies: Designing social futures. *Harvard Educational Review, 66*(1), 60–91.
New London Group. (2000). A pedagogy of multiliteracies: Designing social futures. In B. Cope & M. Kalantzis (Eds.), *Multiliteracies: Literacy learning and the design of social futures* (pp. 9–37). Melbourne: Macmillan.
O'Toole, M. (1994). *The language of displayed art*. London: Leicester University Press.
O'Toole, M. (2004). Opera Ludentes: The Sydney Opera House at work and play. In K. O'Halloran (Ed.), *Multimodal discourse analysis: Systemic functional perspectives* (pp. 11–27). London: Continuum.
Painter, C., & Martin, J. R. (2011). Intermodal complementarity: Modelling affordances across image and verbiage in children's picture books. In F. Yan (Ed.), *Studies in functional linguistics and discourse analysis* (pp. 132–158). Beijing: Education Press of China.
Painter, C., Martin, J. R., & Unsworth, L. (2013). *Reading visual narratives: Image analysis of children's picture books*. London: Equinox.
Paterson, K. (1977). *Bridge to Terabithia*. Harmondsworth: Puffin.
Ravelli, L. (2000). Beyond shopping: Constructing the Sydney Olympics in three-dimensional text. *Text, 20*(4), 489–515.
Schleppegrell, M. (2004). *The language of schooling: A functional linguistic perspective*. Mawah, NJ: Erlbaum.

Schleppegrell, M., Achugar, M., & Oteíza, T. (2004). The grammar of history: Enhancing content-based instruction through a functional focus on language. *TESOL Quarterly, 38*(1), 67–93.

Steig, W. (1990). *Shrek*. New York: Michael Di Capua Books.

Unsworth, L. (2001). *Teaching multiliteracies across the curriculum: Changing contexts of text and image in classroom practice*. Buckingham, UK: Open University Press.

Unsworth, L. (2006). Towards a metalanguage for multiliteracies education: Describing the meaning-making resources of language-image interaction. *English Teaching: Practice and Critique, (5)*1, 55–76. Retrieved from http://education.waikato.ac.nz/research/ files/etpc/2006v5n1art4.pdf

Unsworth, L. (2007). Multimodal text analysis in classroom work with children's literature. In T. Royce & W. Bowcher (Eds.), *New directions in multimodal text analysis* (pp. 331–360). Mahwah, NJ: Erlbaum.

Unsworth, L. (2008). *Multiliteracies and metalanguage: Describing image/text relations as a resource for negotiating multimodal texts*. In D. Leu, J. Corio, M. Knobel & C. Lankshear (Eds.), *Handbook of research on new literacies* (pp. 377–405). Mahwah, NJ: Erlbaum.

Unsworth, L. (2013). Point of view in picture books and animated movie adaptations. *Scan, 32*(1), 28–37.

van Leeuwen, T. (1991). Conjunctive structure in documentary film and television. *Continuum, 5*(1), 76–114.

van Leeuwen, T. (1996). Moving English. In S. Goodman & D. Graddol (Eds.), *Redesigning English: New texts, new identitities*. London: Open University Press.

van Leeuwen, T. (1999). *Speech, music, sound*. London: Macmillan.

Wheatley, N. (1982). *Five Times Dizzy*. Melbourne: Oxford University Press.

Williams, G. (1993). Using systemic grammar in teaching young leraners: An introduction. In L. Unsworth (Ed.), *Literacy learning and teaching: Language as social practice in the primary school* (pp. 197–254). Melbourne: Macmillan.

Williams, G. (2000). Children's literature, children and uses of language description. In L. Unsworth (Ed.), *Researching language in schools and communities: A functional linguistic perspective* (pp. 111–129). London: Cassell.

FURTHER READING

Butt, D., Fahey, R., Feez, S., Spinks, S., & Yallop, C. (2000). *Using functional grammar: An explorer's guide*. Sydney: National Centre for English Language Teaching and Research.

Droga, L., & Humphrey, S. (2003). *Grammar and meaning: An introduction for primary teachers*. Berry, New South Wales: Target Texts.

Halliday, M. A. K., & Matthiessen, C. (2004). *An introduction to functional grammar* (3rd ed.). London: Arnold.

Humphrey, S., Love, K., & Droga, L. (2011). *Working grammar: An introduction for secondary English teachers*. Melbourne: Pearson.

Martin, J. R., & White, P. (2005). *The language of evaluation: Appraisal in English*. London: Palgrave/Macmillan.

NOTES

1. "These describe the knowledge, understanding, skills and processes that teachers are expected to teach and students are expected to learn" (ACARA, 2012, p. 5). Each content description is coded with an alphabetical prefix: ACELT, ACELA, ACELY, referring to the ACE and either literature, language or literacy. For example: ACELY1745.

CHAPTER TWO

Using Contemporary Picture Books to Explore the Concept of Intermodal Complementarity

ANGELA THOMAS

Multimodal literary texts are recognized as a prominent textual form in the landscape of children's literature. Whether it is a picture book, film, animation, computer game, or digital fiction, children experience these multimodal forms as part of their everyday encounters with literature. Curricula such as the Australian Curriculum: English (ACARA, 2012) have foregrounded the role of multimodal texts within the field of study of literature in English, signifying their importance in contemporary classroom contexts.

A multimodal text is a text that consists of more than one mode or meaning-making system. Modes might include the following: linguistic (words), visual (images, including moving images), audio (sound), gestural (gesture), and spatial (space) (Cope & Kalantzis, 2009). A picture book consists of two modes: linguistic and visual. A film consists of three modes: linguistic, visual, and audio. A piece of digital fiction typically consists of four modes: linguistic, visual, audio, and spatial. A virtual world includes five modes: linguistic, visual, audio, spatial, and gestural.

As teachers explore multimodal texts with children, it is not only the meaning-making potential of each mode that is important, but it is also how those modes work together that is significant. The ways in which individual modes work together is termed *intermodality* or "intermodal complementarity" (Painter & Martin, 2011). An ideal way to explore the concepts of intermodality is to begin with picture books, where two modes only are at play together: the linguistic and the visual. This chapter will examine how the linguistic and visual work together in picture books and how intermodality might be introduced to children. As such, it will address the following three key questions:

1. How do the images and words in picture books work together to create meaning?
2. What understandings about intermodality are important in the study of multimodal texts?
3. How can teachers use picture books to explore concepts of multimodality?

Contemporary children's picture books have developed in sophistication and complexity, evolving from earlier forms in which an illustration was simply a depiction of meanings also conveyed by words on the page. Today, pictures in a picture book work to complement the meanings of the words on the page, such that understanding the narrative requires careful reading of both modes—words and images. Hunt (1991) argues:

> as Sonia Landes has said,… "What today's illustrators understand is that picture books really deal with <u>two story lines</u>, the visual and the verbal; and each can be separately phased so as to reinforce, counterpoint, anticipate or expand, one another." They have great semiotic/semantic potential; they are emphatically *not* simply collections of pictures. (p. 176)

Exploring the meanings of words in a picture book with students offers teachers opportunities to scaffold understandings about the beauty of language, and the choices made by authors about words they use to construct meanings about the characters and themes of a text. Exploring the meanings of illustrations in a picture book affords the same possibilities—teachers can scaffold student understandings about the ways images make these similar meanings. However, treating images and language as independent systems does not do justice to the ways contemporary picture books work, nor how they are designed to be read. Readers do not engage with the two modes independently; rather, they are always reading and interpreting a text using the combination of modes together. As Lewis (2001) argues,

> When we read picture books we look at the pictures and we read the words and our eyes go back and forth between the two as we piece together the meaning of the text. (p. 32)

Furthermore, each mode—visual and linguistic—is likely to influence the meaning of one another in some manner, and most picture books are only completely understood when viewing the text as a unified whole. That is, both modes must be considered concurrently to comprehend the narrative.

Lewis (2001) draws from work by Meek (1992) to describe the interdependent relationship between words and images as an *interanimation*, explaining:

> words are never just words, they are always words-as-influenced-by-pictures. Similarly, the pictures are never just pictures, they are pictures-as-influenced-by-words. Thus the words

on their own are always partial, incomplete, unfinished, awaiting the flesh of the pictures. Similarly the pictures are perpetually pregnant with potential narrative meanings, indeterminate, unfinished, awaiting the closure provided by the words. (p. 74)

Understanding Lewis's (2001) concept of *interanimation*—the interdependent relationship of words and images—requires considerable effort on the part of the reader. Lewis argues the importance of teaching understandings about picture books through analysing them aesthetically, semiotically, and grammatically. Furthermore, he argues that they should be understood within the broader social and cultural contexts in which they are produced and consumed.

THE NATURE OF INTERMODALITY

One concept to begin such explorations into interanimation is that of *intermodality* (Painter & Martin, 2011). To explore intermodality I draw on systemic functional descriptions of language (Halliday & Matthiessen, 2004) and social semiotic descriptions of the ways images and sounds construct meaning (Kress & van Leeuwen, 2006; van Leeuwen, 1999). Intermodality is the way in which a multimodal text can be described through the relationship between specific grammatical meanings of words, and the specific complementary semiotic meanings of images. Such an approach provides a detailed account of how the semiotic resources within a picture book (or, indeed, any multimodal text) work together to make meaning.

In systemic functional linguistics, language is modeled as a social resource for making meaning, or a social semiotic system, which is organized into three broad functions that language has evolved to serve, which are called "metafunctions": *ideational* (how language expresses ideas); *interpersonal* (how language is used to interact with others); and *textual* (how language is used to construct cohesive and coherent texts) (Halliday & Matthiessen, 2004). Ideational meanings are concerned primarily with the topic or field of the text—the who, what, where, why, when, and how of the text. Interpersonal meanings relate to the tenor or the nature of the relationship between the writer/speaker and the reader/viewer; for example, the way in which language works to construct relative power or emotional positionings between those involved in the communication. Textual meanings relate to the mode of communication and how a text is organized in that mode. These three metafunctions, while originally designed to describe language and verbal meaning-making, provide a useful starting point for describing the meaning-making potential and use of different semiotic modes, and are therefore a powerful resource for teachers and students working with multimodal texts.

Adapting key principles of systemic functional linguistics to the interaction between modes in picture books, Painter and Martin (2011) have outlined an approach to exploring the intermodality between image and text that they term *intermodal complementarity* and define as

> the degree to which each [modality] commits meaning in a particular instance and the extent to which—for each metafunction—that commitment converges with or diverges from that of the other modality. (p. 132)

Painter and Martin (2011) elaborate in detail how intermodal complementarity is realized across visual and verbal modalities and demonstrate how meanings in the image and text might commit to the same meaning, which they term *convergence*, or how they might be oppositional in meaning, which they term *divergence*. They explain that by examining the meaning potentials of each metafunction, we can understand, for example, that the meaning of sadness might be achieved through both an illustration drawn in blue tones and the selection of certain interpersonal word choices such as the word *sad*. When the same meanings in a metafunction (e.g., the interpersonal metafunction, which conveys feelings such as sadness) are present in both image and words, then Painter and Martin describe their interaction as convergent. If the visual and verbal meanings are different, then the intermodal complementarity is divergent.

I will explain this further by exploring elements of the interpersonal metafunction relating to emotions, which in systemic functional linguistics is described by the umbrella term *attitude*. Attitude can be created through the use of some specific tools in words and specific tools in images. In words, the specific attitudinal tool relating to emotion is termed *affect*. Affect refers to those words that express happiness, security, satisfaction, or the opposite of these and any emotional states on un/happiness, in/security, and dis/satisfaction continua. Additionally, affect can be created through more implicit means, such as the repetition of certain words or phrases or the use of figurative language such as metaphors and similes (Martin & White, 2005). In images, attitude can be created through a range of tools, two of which are *affiliation* and *ambience* (Painter, 2008). Affiliation relates to the way in which a character makes contact or not with the viewer. For example, an image in which a character gazes directly at the viewer with a happy expression constructs a warm and inviting relationship with the viewer, while an image where the character hangs his or her head and makes no eye contact may construct a sense of sadness or a removal. Ambience refers to the choices of colour in an image. For example, an image containing a predominance of cool blue tones can reflect sadness, while an image containing a predominance of vibrant red tones might reflect happiness and excitement. In music, attitude can be created through *tone* (van Leeuwen, 1999). For example, a melody that uses a major key might signify happiness, while a melody in a minor key might signify sadness. Table 2.1, devised by Unsworth (this volume), further demonstrates the ways in which grammatical meanings of words relate to the semiotic meanings of images across all metafunctions.

To provide a practical example of how this works, I will use the children's picture book *Michael Rosen's Sad Book* (Rosen & Blake, 2008). This is a poignant true story dealing with the death of the author's son, Eddie. Michael Rosen's sparsely written tale described his grief at the loss of his son, while Quentin Blake's haunting illustrations reflect both the sadness in the present as well as the joys of the past between father and child. In the opening page of the book, the text begins: *This is me being sad*. Yet the image is a drawing of Michael Rosen with a large smile on his face, dressed in bright colours, on a sunny yellow background.

In terms of the interpersonal meaning of affect (feelings and emotions), the visual facial expression of a smile is positive, yet contrary to this, the word expressing emotion, *sad*, is negative. So in this instance, the intermodal divergence constructs an incredibly powerful moment of poignancy, particularly when coupled with the following two sentences, which read: *Maybe you think I am being happy in this picture. Really I am being sad but pretending I'm being happy*.

This is then followed by the next page in which the image is a shadowy ink sketch of a small hunched man on a large grey and black wash backdrop of clouds, and the words *Sometimes sad is very big. It's everywhere. All over me*. In this page the visual and verbal modes converge. The same meanings of affect are reflected through both the bodily stance of the figure and the word *sad*. They are also reflected in choice of cold colour tone, and scaled up in the *tone* of the repeated circumstances in the words *very big*, *everywhere*, and *all over me*. Both of these pages reflect the grief experienced by the author but the first page in which there is an intermodal divergence sets up a significant affectual, or emotional, impact that serves to shock the reader on first reading.

Teachers are encouraged to conduct *deep studies* of texts in their classrooms (Freebody, 2010). Integral to deep studies of multimodal texts (such as picture books) would be the investigation of how images and texts make meaning, and how images and text work together. An impotrant part of this would be to examine the changing intermodal meanings at key moments in the narrative. This would assist students to understand how authors carefully plan for and achieve the shifts and turns of plot, character, perspective, point of view, and structure to create rich and powerful stories. One approach to exploring the shifting narrative dynamics of a story is demonstrated next, using the picture book *Fox* (Wild & Brooks, 2000).

UNDERSTANDING IMAGE-TEXT RELATIONSHIPS IN THE PICTURE BOOK *FOX*

Fox (Wild & Brooks, 2000) is an award-winning picture book. In *Fox*, the character of Fox lures Magpie away from her friend Dog, with the promise of adventure, and then betrays her by leaving her stranded in the desert. A description of the book reads:

An injured magpie and a one-eyed dog live happily together in the forest, until a jealous fox arrives to teach them what it means to be alone. (Kane/Miller Book Publishers, 2011, para. 1)

The first 10 pages of the story build a sense of friendship and understanding between Magpie (who has a burnt wing) and Dog (who has lost the sight of one eye). Together they learn to live happily despite their injuries. The character of Fox is introduced midway through the narrative, with the words:

> a Fox comes into the bush; Fox with his haunted eyes and rich red coat. He flickers through the trees like a tongue of fire, and Magpie trembles.

A set of teacher notes (Anderson, 2000) for using *Fox* in the classroom was published by Allen and Unwin. In these notes, the book editor of *Fox*, Sarah Brenan, describes the two-year process it took to decide on the adjective *haunted*:

> One item remained—how to describe Fox's eyes when he first appears in the story. We spent the next two years, on and off, looking for the perfect word—there's a pile of correspondence centimetres thick on this. In the MS she sent us first, Margaret had, "After the rains, when saplings are springing up everywhere, a fox comes into the bush; Fox with his dead eyes and rich red coat. He flickers through the trees like a tongue of fire, and Magpie quails." It's a very powerful juxtaposition, "dead/rich, red," one that really makes you look again—but we felt "dead eyes" was too closed, it gave Fox no possibility of redemption …. We began the search for a word that would suggest hurt and damage without taking away from Fox's charisma and power. We tried "cold," "hard," "bleak," "empty," "hungry," "piercing," "haunting," "haunted," "glittering," "restless," "wild," "searching," "yearning," "wretched," "desolate," "knowing" and dozens of others. (Brenan, in Anderson, 2000, p. 12)

The amount of time taken puzzling over a single adjective is staggering, and when sharing this story about the hunt for *haunted* with students it provides a lovely moment to consider the power, meaning, and beauty of a single word. Similarly, each word or phrase could be discussed in detail with students. The verb *flickers*, for example, is used to describe Fox's movement. Students could explore the meanings of this word, or identify its use in other texts to contemplate its meaning. *Flicker* may signify unsteadiness and symbolize more than just the movement, but also a foreshadowing about the nature of Fox's character. The simile *like a tongue of fire* is also figurative, relating the movement to the irregular movements of flames of a fire. The use of this expression is both symbolic of the actual bushfires that had played havoc with the environment in the story and another example of foreshadowing, of the emotional destruction to come in the narrative. This leads to Magpie's reaction of *trembles*. Readers have learned that Magpie's damaged wing was burnt in a fire, so the sight of Fox flickering like a tongue of fire juxtaposed with this reaction makes the narrative link, offering a deeper insight into the inner world of Magpie.

The two words *haunted* and *trembles* represent each character's emotional history. They both realize interpersonal meanings, but in a slightly different way. *Haunted* suggests that Fox lives with, and is preoccupied, by negative emotions, memories, or ideas. It is a state of existence, related to Fox's cognitive processes. This is in contrast to Magpie's reaction *trembles*, which is a physical surge of behavior caused by her reaction triggered at a visceral level by Fox. Grammatically, the words *haunted* and *trembles* both realize interpersonal meanings of attitude: affect: insecurity (-ve) (Martin & White, 2005) but one is a disposition, or state of being, while the other is an involuntary reaction to a phenomenon. This offers insight into the difference between the two characters. Magpie has managed to overcome the emotional impact of losing her wing, and has moved on with life thanks to her relationship with Dog. Yet the fear is still embodied within her psyche and this is manifested through the trembling. In contrast, Fox's past seems to embody him so that it is always present, on the surface, inscribed in his body for all to see.

The image in Figure 2.1 shows the illustration of Fox's entrance in the narrative. This image stands alone and is not part of a larger image that crosses over the double-page spread. This image depicts Fox, curved around the right hand side of the page, his body long and lean, stretched out around the words. Fox's first appearance depicts his complete body, while Magpie has not only *receded* (Painter, Martin, & Unsworth, 2013) but is invisible in the image, and does not reappear until the following page. This marks an element of experiential divergence given that both Fox and Magpie are depicted in the text. Compositionally, Fox is also the most *salient* (Kress & van Leeuwen, 2006) element of the image, as instanced through the shape of his curved body taking up a large portion of the page, his bright red and orange coat, and the deep red eye that draws the reader's eye to it. His body encircles the words, serving to frame part of the page. While Fox is *thematised* (Halliday & Matthiessen, 2004) in three of the five clauses in the text, Magpie is also thematised once, so her invisibility on the page also constructs a divergence of textual meanings.

Interpersonally, Fox does not direct his gaze to the viewer, in this image described as an *offer* (Kress & van Leeuwen, 2006) or *unmediated observe* (Painter, Martin, & Unsworth, 2013), which has the effect of constructing the viewer as an outside observer rather than being invited into the story. His body is side on, angled away from the viewer, serving to construct distance between character and viewer. This sense of distance is juxtaposed with the meanings created through *ambience* (Painter, 2008), that is, the colours are vivid, warm, bright, and familiar. This ambivalence of interpersonal meanings (both distancing and yet at the same time familiar) work intra-modally to create a sense of uncertainty about what Fox's character and role in the narrative might be. However, when considering intermodal complementarity, the contradictory meanings in the image converge with what could also be conceived of as contradictory meanings in the text—Fox is haunted (negative attitudinal meanings), but he flickers like a tongue of fire, which implicitly and figuratively also suggests attitudinal meanings of his on/off emotions—negative and positive affect: security (Martin & White, 2005).

Fig 2.1. Image from *Fox*.

Another way of thinking about interanimation of words and images is to look not only at intermodal complementarity of meanings within a single page but also to consider the patterns or changes of intermodal meanings sequenced across in the narrative. In discussing this previously (Thomas, 2011; 2014) I have demonstrated how intersemiotic shifts between convergence and divergence and the combination of both serves to create moments of humour, pathos, and irony. So, to explore this idea, I have selected two contrasting moments in the narrative which, when examined together, demonstrate the changing intersemiotic shifts that build the interpersonal dimensions that create the significant impact of the betrayal. These moments are depicted on two double-page spreads—the first toward the middle of the story, and the second toward the end. Each excerpt will be analysed grammatically and visually, and then the relationships between words and images and between excerpts will be discussed.

Table 2.1 is a more detailed analysis of the words and images from two contrasting excerpts of *Fox*, illustrated on the double-page spreads shown in Figures 2.2 and 2.3.

Table 2.1. Written and Visual Analysis of Two Double-Page Spreads from the Picture Book *Fox* (Wild & Brooks, 2000)

Visual Analysis of Excerpt 1	
 Fig 2.2. Double-Page Spread from the Picture Book *Fox*.	
Experiential Meanings	Transactional action (Fox: outstretched limbs, off the ground as if caught in mid-flight; Magpie: outstretched wing, legs upturned; action lines appear in paint suggesting wind and movement around participants) and also transactional reaction (implied vectors made between the eyes of participants as they gaze at one another). Depiction of circumstances: Supporting Fox and Magpie's new freedom, the landscape is defined and open and has a lightness of colour, the subtle tinge of orange from Fox's fur is shown in the rocks (the rocks pointing toward Fox) and the sky. Magpie's scratched claws mirrored in the tree trunks, the whiteness of the cloud on Magpie's head, and Fox's snout also imply that they are in harmony with the landscape.
Symbolism	None evident
Contact	Offer
Social distance	Medium shot
Involvement	Participants angled away from viewer
Power	Equal angle
Ambience	Infused with colour, vibrant (fully saturated), warm with red hues, familiar (high colour differentiation)
Modality	Realistic rather than naturalistic
Salience	Fox's head (size and colour), Magpie's eye (colour)
Framing	Loosely framed

Written grammar analysis of the two paragraphs of text across the double-page spreads	
Experiential analysis: *(adverbials coded with italics, noun groups are bolded, verb groups underlined, any word not coded is a conjunction or connective)*	
Paragraph 1	*While* **Dog** <u>sleeps</u>, **Magpie** and **Fox** <u>streak</u> *past coolibah trees*, <u>rip</u> *through long grass*, <u>pelt</u> *over rocks*. **Fox** <u>runs</u> *so fast* that **his feet** *scarcely* <u>touch</u> **the ground**, and **Magpie** <u>exults</u>, "*At last* **I** <u>am flying</u>. *Really* <u>flying</u>!"
Paragraph 2	**He** <u>stops</u>, *scarcely* <u>panting</u>. There <u>is</u> **silence** *between them*. **Neither** <u>moves</u>, **neither** <u>speaks</u>. *Then* **Fox** <u>shakes</u> **Magpie** <u>off</u> **his back**, *as he would a flea*, and <u>pads away</u>. **He** <u>turns</u> and <u>looks at</u> **Magpie**, and **he** <u>says</u>, "*Now* **you** and **Dog** <u>will know</u> what **it** <u>is like</u> <u>to be</u> *truly* **alone**." *Then* **he** <u>is gone</u>. *In the stillness*, **Magpie** <u>hears</u> **a faraway scream**. **She** <u>cannot tell</u> if **it** <u>is</u> **a scream of triumph or despair**.

Interpersonal analysis: *(tool selected for analysis is judgment, coded with highlights)*	
Paragraph 1	While Dog sleeps, Magpie and Fox ==streak== past coolibah trees, ==rip== through long grass, ==pelt== over rocks. Fox ==runs so fast== that ==his feet scarcely touch the ground==, and Magpie exults, "At last I am flying. Really flying!"
Paragraph 2	He stops, ==scarcely panting==. There is silence between them. Neither moves, neither speaks. Then Fox ==shakes Magpie off== his back, ==as he would a flea==, and pads away. He turns and looks at Magpie, and he says, "Now you and Dog will know what it is like to be ==truly alone==." Then he is ==gone==. In the stillness, Magpie hears a faraway scream. She cannot tell if it is ==a scream of triumph or despair==.

Visual Analysis of Excerpt 2
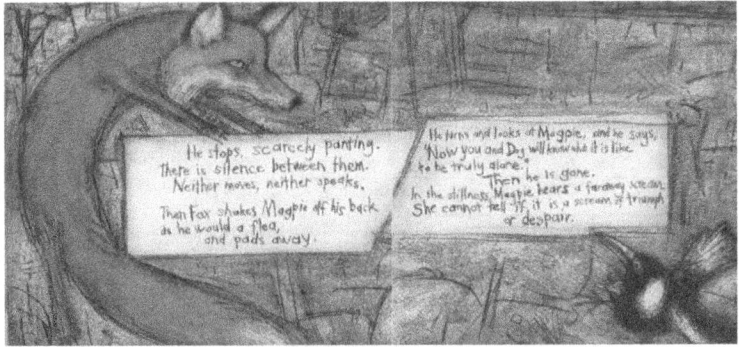
Fig 2.3. Double-Page Spread from the Picture Book *Fox*.

Experiential Meanings	Transactional reaction (eyes of participants linked together by implied vector of gaze at each other as well as respective snout/beak pointing toward each other). Depiction of circumstances: The landscape has now lost definition with rocks and trees represented by thin scratched lines.
Symbolism	"Torn" frame around the two pieces of text suggestive of the broken relationship and betrayal occurring. Terror is reflected in Magpie's eye through the small symbolic speck of orange, which is the same colour as Fox's fur.
Contact	Offer
Social distance	Long shot
Involvement	Participants angled away from viewer
Power	High angle (viewer power over magpie)
Ambience	Setting is muted, darker shades, cooler, and removed in its monochrome charcoals and blacks
Modality	Realistic rather than naturalistic
Salience	Fox's body (size, curved shape, and bright red colour), especially his head (top of page, eye contrast); Magpie's eye (red colour; red marks salience)
Framing	Elements of strong framing inside the image around the text. Fox's front legs break up the frame, frame torn in half. A sense of Fox closing in on Magpie is used by applying a dark shading effect, which frames the edge of the page.

DISCUSSION OF WRITTEN ANALYSIS

Differences in experiential meanings between the two selected paragraphs demonstrate the theme of betrayal in the story. Paragraph 1 uses a variety of high-octane action verbs (*streak; rip; pelt; runs; am flying*) to construct the movement and excitement shared between characters. Modal adverbs emphasise this thrill and energy (*so; scarcely; really*). In paragraph 2, Fox is depicted with quieter action verb groups (*pads; turns; is gone*) and Magpie is only represented with sensing verb groups (*hears; cannot tell*). The insight into Magpie's inner thoughts aligns readers with her point of view as she experiences confusion and struggles to make sense of what has happened.

The adverbials of place (*past coolibah trees; through long grass; over rocks*) in paragraph 1 indicate where action occurs and the adverbial of time (*at last*) indicates that Magpie's dream of flying is finally coming true, thanks to the actions of Fox. This is in contrast to the adverbial *in the stillness* in paragraph 2, which is more of an abstract space and sensation. Noun groups in paragraph 1 focused on the participants of the action: Fox and Magpie. In paragraph 2, more abstract and ephemeral nouns are used (*silence; a faraway scream; a scream of triumph or despair*). The noun *silence* is particularly striking because it contrasts with Magpie's joyous exultation and the imagined sounds of movement implied in paragraph 1. The jarring suddenness of the silence marks the change in the narrative arc.

The interpersonal tool of judgment has been selected for analysis as the theme of betrayal has been selected. Betrayal is a violation of trust resulting in moral conflict, and as it is the behavior of the one who betrays that results in social sanction, it is the judgment of Fox and how the author has used vocabulary to do this that is of significance for the analysis. There are no explicit statements of judgment; rather, they are all implicitly invoked as a result of references to social values in our culture. In paragraph 1, the reader is positioned to construct a positive judgment (social esteem) with respect to Fox's athletic prowess through use of vocabulary such as *streak, so fast*, and *his feet scarcely touch the ground*. This is also true at the beginning of paragraph 2, when we realize he was scarcely panting after such exertions. However, when Fox shakes Magpie off his back with the figurative expression *as he would a flea*, our judgment quickly becomes negative (social sanction). Fleas are pests and annoyances. When Fox shrugs off Magpie with such little regard it is interpreted as unkind, morally wrong treatment of Magpie. The words *truly alone* uttered by Fox suggest that he is well aware of the insecurity of loneliness. Because he is deliberately inflicting emotional pain on Magpie and Dog, the reader senses a cruelty in Fox, leading to a negative judgment (social sanction) about his behavior. This is then repeated with Fox's final action, *he is gone*, as he leaves the damaged-winged Magpie alone to fend for herself in the desert. At the end of paragraph 2, the reader is aware that Fox has uttered a scream from faraway, but Magpie's confusion about whether it is in triumph or despair leaves the reader undecided about their final judgment of Fox's morality.

DISCUSSION OF VISUAL ANALYSIS

A number of significant visual contrasts between the two images reflect the theme of betrayal. The difference in ambience in the circumstantiation of the text is marked: the first image has a setting of vibrant, warm, and familiar ambience—the colours are rich, deep, warm reds and oranges, while the second has a setting of muted, dark, cooler tones of blacks and charcoals. The warm ambience of image 1 constructs a sense of intimacy, representative of the close relationship portrayed. The coolness represented by the monotone background of image 2 constructs an interpersonal sense of distance, and the reader/viewer senses the deep chill of emotions that has replaced the previous warmth. Furthermore, some of Magpie's black-and-white body actually blends and disappears into the surrounding black background. This is distinctly opposed to the bright blue sky and *wind* (action lines in paint) surrounding her as she *flies* in image 1.

Experientially, there is a movement and joy of action depicted in image 1 with outstretched limbs/wings, which create vectors signifying both Fox's rapid movement across the ground and Magpie's thrilling bouncing ride/flying. The faint outline shadow of Magpie's beak above the actual depicted beak indicates the speed with which she is hurtling around. The fact that Magpie is drawn upside down with her feet up in the air, with only her one working wing touching and balancing her on Fox's back, suggests both a playfulness and a high degree of security and trust between the two. The scratched lines in the paint medium both around Magpie's feet and in between Fox's feet indicate the swooshing of wind and vectors (action lines) of movement, and there is a definite sense of the carefree—a joie de vivre being experienced together by the participants.

The closeness of the relationship is also reflected in the experiential meanings of the portrayal of the participants interacting with each other. This is matched by the close positioning of the participants, with Magpie's beak and Fox's snout close together, almost touching. Fox's head is turned to face and look at Magpie, with no regard for the direction he is running. This transactional reaction image of the participants looking into each other's eyes indicates a heightened intimacy.

This is a stark difference to the stillness of image 2. Magpie's cowering in a corner coupled with the high angle shot that gives the viewer power reflects the shift in Magpie's emotions, from being overjoyed to fear and trepidation. The framing of the text is also symbolically significant. In image 1, the text is layered over the image at the bottom of the page. In image 2, the text is tightly framed and positioned in the centre of the page, constructing a physical separation between Magpie and Fox. Furthermore, the way that the frame appears torn into two is symbolic of the broken trust and Fox's betrayal, suggestive of a ripped up contract that had existed between them. The way that Fox is leaning over the frame with front paws covering some of the frame and aimed in the direction of Magpie is somewhat menacing. Magpie's beak, while angled up at Fox, is pulled back away from the frame, just as she is pulling back away from Fox.

HOW IMAGES AND TEXT WORK TOGETHER

There is a high intermodal convergence (Painter & Martin, 2011) between the words and images on each double-page spread which serves to create maximum impact of the meanings in the contrasting phases of the narrative. Experiential meanings in the first double-page spread are focused on the actions of the characters (realized by action verb groups: *streak, runs, rip*) and the image reflects these actions through the use of vectors (Fox's outstretched limbs, action lines depicting wind, and motion scratched into paint). Fox and Magpie are depicted interacting with each other both through these actions and through their gaze at each other. Circumstances are concentrated on place in the words (*past coolibah trees, through long grass, over rocks*) and these places are represented in the image. Interpersonal meanings work together to create a sense of intimacy and playfulness between Fox and Magpie. The characters are depicted visually in an intimate proximity to each other, and the fact that Magpie is upside down conveys the thrill and playfulness of the interaction. This thrill is reflected in the words, with the saying verb *exults* capturing Magpie's joyful jubilance, and the adverbial *at last* reflecting Magpie's sense of recapturing her identity that was lost when her wing was damaged. The ambience is vibrant and warm, and this also works to create intimacy and familiarity (Painter, 2008). Fox is depicted as athletic and powerful visually, through the dominance of his form across the double-page spread, and by his legs outstretched in movement, feet caught mid-air. This depiction is evident in the words not only through action verbs but also with the expression *his feet scarcely touch the ground*. Both words and image serve to invoke an implicit positive judgment (Humphrey, Droga, & Feez, 2012) of Fox as highly capable.

Semiotic meanings of words and image in the second double-page spread converge intermodally (Thomas, 2013) to construct a breakdown in the relationship between Fox and Magpie and an invoked negative judgment (Humphrey, Droga, & Feez, 2012) of Fox's behavior. Most striking in the image is the framed text, torn in two, symbolizing the relationship breakdown, with the characters in distant proximity, divided by the words. The use of the figurative expression *as he would a flea* demonstrates Fox's total disregard of Magpie, invokes a negative judgment (social sanction), and the image reveals him posed menacingly over the words high above Magpie, who is depicted with a high angle shot (Kress & van Leeuwen, 2006), with a distinct loss of power, as she cowers in the corner, melting fearfully into the blackness of the background. Her confusion at what has happened and what she hears is evident in the sensing verb *cannot tell*. The ambience in the second image is distant and cold, and this is mirrored in word choices of noun groups such as *silence* and *stillness*. The shifts and contrasts between the words and images on each double-page spread evoke a strong emotional response in the reader, as the cruel betrayal of Magpie by Fox in the second double-page spread is made all the more poignant and heart-wrenching as a result of the high level of intense joyfulness depicted intermodally in the first.

CONCLUSION

This chapter has focused on the use of picture books to explore the concept of intermodal complementarity. This concept is one that is critical to fully understanding how multimodal literary texts work and is a concept that the Australian Curriculum: English (ACARA, 2010) suggests be introduced in simple terms to children in Year 1. As children progress through the years of schooling, deeper understandings about the concept will require a more systematic investigation of the grammar and semiotics of the modes within the text. Martin (2008), Painter and Martin (2011), and Painter, Martin, and Unsworth (2013) provide additional examples of intersemiotic analyses of picture books suitable for upper primary and secondary students, which illustrate intermodal complementarity. However, further research is still required to flesh out the variations and possibilities of meaning systems across modalities, particularly that of sound, space, and gesture. An ideal way to begin exploring the concept is to limit the number of modalities by looking only at image-text relationships. The picture book is a perfect literary text for such investigations and will lead well into further explorations with film, digital text, and beyond.

REFERENCES

ACARA. (2012). *Australian curriculum: English*. Retrieved from http://www.australiancurriculum.edu.au/English/Curriculum/F-10

Anderson. J. (2002). Teachers notes. Retrieved from http://www.allenandunwin.com/_uploads/BookPdf/TeachersNotes/9781864484656.pdf

Cope, B., & Kalantzis, M. (2009). A grammar of multimodality. *The International Journal of Learning. 16*(4), 361–426.

Freebody, P. (2010). *Introduction*. Retrieved from http://www.australiancurriculum.edu.au/English/Introduction

Halliday, M. A. K., & Matthiessen, C. M. I. M. (2004). *Introduction to functional grammar* (3rd ed.). London: Arnold.

Humphrey, S., Droga, S., & Feez, S. (2012). *Grammar and meaning*. Sydney: Primary English Teaching Association of Australia.

Hunt, P. (1991). *Literary criticism: Criticism, theory, and children's literature*. London: Blackwell.

Kane/Miller Book Publishers. (2001). *Fox by Margaret Wild*. Retrieved from http://www.goodreads.com/book/show/2651521-fox

Kress, G., & van Leeuwen, T. (2006). *Reading images: The grammar of visual design*. London: Routledge.

Lewis, D. (2001). *Reading contemporary picturebooks: Picturing text*. London: Routledge.

Martin, J. R. (2008). Intermodal reconciliation: Mates in arms. In L. Unsworth (Ed.), *New literacies and the English curriculum Multimodal perspectives* (pp. 112–148). London: Continuum.

Martin, J. R., & Rose, D. (2008). *Genre relations: Mapping culture*. London: Equinox.

Martin, J. R., & White, P. (2005). *The language of evaluation: Appraisal in English*. London: Palgrave Macmillan.

Meek, M. (1992). *How texts teach what readers learn*. Stroud: Thimble Press.

Painter, C. (2008). The role of colour in children's picture books: Choices in AMBIENCE. In L. Unsworth (Ed.), *New literacies and the English curriculum: Multimodal perspectives* (pp. 89–111). London: Continuum.

Painter, C., & Martin, J. R. (2011). Intermodal complementarity: Modelling affordances across image and verbiage in children's picture books. In F. Yan (Ed.), *Studies in functional linguistics and discourse analysis 3* (pp. 132–158). Beijing: Higher Education Press.

Painter, C., Martin, J. R., & Unsworth, L. (2013). *Reading visual narratives: Image analysis of children's picture books*. Sheffield: Equinox Publishing.

Rosen, M., & Blake, Q. (2008). *The sad book*. London: Walker.

Thomas, A. (2008). Machinima: Composing 3D multimedia narratives. In L. Unsworth (Ed.), *New literacies and the English curriculum: Multimodal perspectives* (pp. 167–185). London: Continuum.

Thomas, A. (2011). Children's writing goes 3D: A case study of one school's journey into multimodal authoring. *Learning, Media and Technology, 37*(1), 77–93.

Thomas, A. (2014). Intermodal complementarity and social critical literacy in children's multimodal texts. In E. Djonov & S. Zhao (Eds.), *Critical multimodal studies of popular culture*. London: Routledge.

Unsworth, L. (2001). *Teaching multiliteracies across the curriculum: Changing contexts of text and image in classroom practice*. Buckingham, UK: Open University Press.

Unsworth, L. (2006). *E-literature for children*. Oxon, UK: Routledge.

van Leeuwen, T. (1999). *Speech, music, sound*. London: Macmillan.

Wild, M., & Brooks, R. (Illustrator). (2000). *Fox*. St. Leonards, NSW: Allen & Unwin.

FURTHER READING

Nodelman, P., & Reimer, M. (2003). *The pleasures of children's literature* (3rd ed.). Boston, MA: Allyn & Bacon.

Sipe, L., & Pantaleo, S. (Eds.). (2008). *Postmodern picturebooks: Play, parody, and self-referentiality*. New York: Routledge.

van Leeuwen, T. (1999). *Speech, music, sound*. London: Macmillan.

WEB RESOURCES

Fox: http://www.allenandunwin.com/default.aspx?page=94&book=97 81864484656

CHAPTER THREE

Digital Fiction

ANGELA THOMAS

INTRODUCTION

Digital fiction is a contemporary narrative form, one that embodies the tradition of narrative yet uses the affordances of new technologies to create new kinds of narratives. It can combine art, music, film, and Web design with a multilayered complexity that, according to Campbell (2008), is both *compulsive* and *immersive*. The multimodal meaning-making resources are woven together to create narratives that can, Campbell (2008) argues,

> also change and mutate depending on a user/reader's interactions. It is as if the physical entity that is text itself has changed from static to liquid, has learnt to move around and react in response to other media—and is thus able to form new narratives-in-motion which require different methods of both writing *and* reading. (para. 4)

Digital narratives, digital fiction, or *e-literature* is a contested term. According to Strickland (2009), the purest definition of e-literature is as follows:

> What is meant by e-literature, by works called born-digital, is that computation is required at every stage of their life. If it could possibly be printed out, it isn't e-lit...[it] relies on code for its creation, preservation, and display: there is no way to experience a work of e-literature unless a computer is running it—reading it and perhaps also generating it. (para. 1–2)

The concept of e-literature being limited to *born-digital* works is constantly being challenged with the many new transformations and reversionings of *traditional* literature. Such transformations (for example, the iPad version of Lewis Carroll's *Alice in Wonderland*) offer reading experiences that incorporate computation and code such that it is not possible to print these versions out to replicate the experience. So it is useful to consider the body of digital fiction with reference to a typology whereby different types of digital fiction use the possibilities afforded by computers in degrees. These affordances redefine the reading experience and, indeed, may actually blur the boundaries of the reader and the writer, thus positioning the reader in new ways. The affordances include multimodality, hypertext, spatiality, and interactivity. Interactivity can range from clicking on a link to touching, moving, or shaking a screen (such an iPad), to moving and animating an avatar around a virtual space (such as Second Life). Fiction that is designed or *born* as digital will be designed to take advantage of many of these affordances, and so *born-digital* fiction is often a transformative experience for children. Furthermore, the affordances can be taught explicitly to children as meaning-making resources that can be incorporated into their own multimodal authoring compositions.

This chapter will address the following three key questions:

1. What kinds of digital fiction are available for teachers' use in the classroom?
2. What are the affordances of digital fiction and how is narrative affected through these affordances?
3. In which ways can teachers explore digital fiction in the classroom?

TYPES OF DIGITAL FICTION

Table 3.1 exemplifies the kind of typology that is useful for discussing works within the range of digital fiction and their respective possibilities for use in the English and literacy classroom. It is important to note that there will be slippage between and across categories, depending on the work or site.

Table 3.1. A Typology of Digital Fiction

A Digital Fiction Typology		
Type	Definition	Examples
Digital replications of known texts	This refers to the digitalisation of print-based fiction	• e-books • Project Gutenberg
Digital enhancements and embellishments to known stories	This refers to elements of the story world created by the original authors or publishers to enhance and promote their fiction	• *Pottermore* • *Donnie Darko*

Digital transformations of known texts	This refers to works that are faithful to an original print-based text, but are re-created in a new form to use the affordances of technology to enhance it	• *Alice in Wonderland* • *The Lost Thing*
Digital reversionings/ reconfigurations of known texts	This refers to works that use elements of an existing story or stories but are reconfigured to create new versions of those works	• *Virtual Macbeth* • Fan fiction • Remixes and mash-ups
"Born Digital" fictions	This refers to works that were designed for ("born in") the digital space—they do not exist in any print or traditional medium	• *The Fantastic Flying Books of Mr. Morris Lessmore* • *Dreaming Methods* • *Inanimate Alice* • *Machinima* • Blog/Twitter/mobile phone/ Facebook/wiki fiction • MMORPGs
Blended digital/print; real/virtual fictions	This refers to those works which overlay digital stories onto real spaces, and/ or incorporate a blend of digital and paper based fiction as part of the storyworld	• Alternate reality games • Cross media storytelling • Augmented Reality (e.g., *Street Museum*)

DIGITAL REPLICATIONS OF KNOWN TEXTS

Digital replications of existing texts, or e-books, have become increasingly widespread as an alternative to printed texts due to lower cost and convenience. As tablets such as the iPad and other mobile technologies continue to develop and improve, reading digital books (both fiction and nonfiction) will be a growing phenomenon. Fiction titles are often now released by publishers in hardback, paperback, and digital versions. Digital versions can include both written versions and audiobook versions. Furthermore, many online bookstores offer a range of free e-books, such as UK's book depository (http://www.bookdepository.co.uk/free).

Project Gutenberg (http://www.gutenberg.org/), which originated in 1971, was the first website to create a collection of free electronic books. Besides making books available in the public domain, its mission also included the preservation of fiction from the past that otherwise could become lost or have limited or no print runs in contemporary times.

DIGITAL ENHANCEMENTS AND EMBELLISHMENTS TO KNOWN TEXTS

Authors and publishers often create supplementary extras to their work, such as games, prequels, or a director's commentary. J. K. Rowling, for example, created an embellished universe with back-stories and facts about the Harry Potter story world, known as Pottermore (http://www.pottermore.com/). Pottermore offers fans of the Harry Potter universe a host of features, including the ability to interact with scenes from the movie (zooming in and out and across scenes to explore hidden extras), opportunities to unlock new content from author J. K. Rowling, and to purchase e-book versions of the Harry Potter series. Additionally, by becoming part of the community, users can collect their own wand, be sorted by the sorting hat into a school house (and gain house points for activity within the community), and collect digital items across the world explored to perform acts such as making potions and casting spells on other users. Pottermore provides fans with a way to continue exploring the story world by becoming part of it.

In terms of Pottermore, there is some blurring of its content between this category of the typology and the following two, and the distinction between these is that of interactivity. A digital enhancement or embellishment will typically have limited opportunities for the kind of interaction that would include user-created content. Pottermore certainly allows some level of interaction and user-created content, but it is primarily designed to offer users *extras*. While Pottermore is an official site for fans to come together, a multitude of unofficial fan sites, including role-playing sites and fan fiction sites, have existed since the Harry Potter phenomenon began. One such site, The Leaky Cauldron (http://www.the-leaky-cauldron.org/), was founded in 2000 and remains an active community today. User-created fan sites are discussed further below.

Another site popular with older users that offers enhancements and embellishments to a known text is a site that offers a prequel to the cult film *Donnie Darko* (http://archive.hi-res.net/donniedarko/). According to Hi_ReS! (2001), the creators of this interactive site:

> What attracted us to Donnie Darko, was its narrative structure and the possibilities it offered for an online expansion. While the film plays over a period of 28 days, the site becomes the narrative's prologue and epilogue and reflects the film's puzzle-like structure in the way it is constructed and left open-ended. (para. 1)

Another distinguishing factor for works in this category is that more often than not they are designed by authors (or producers or publishers) to create interest or buzz for the related fictional work.

DIGITAL TRANSFORMATIONS OF KNOWN TEXTS

A digital transformation of a known text is a work that is faithful to an original print-based text but re-created in a new form to use the affordances of technology to enhance it. Original images, text, and narrative are mostly retained, but the process of creating a digital version allows added enhancements that transform the text and add to it in new ways. The iPad version of *Alice in Wonderland*, for example, allows readers to touch or shake the screen and activate animations of the story, bringing it to life in new ways. The animated version of author Shaun Tan's picture book *The Lost Thing* (Tan, 2000) brings the still images to life and offers readers an expanded view of the story world. A comparison between meanings within picture book and animation is explained further by Unsworth in Chapter 6 of this book.

DIGITAL REVERSIONINGS OF KNOWN TEXTS

Digital reversionings use elements of an existing story or stories but are reconfigured to create new versions of those works. Prime examples of this include two specific online social practices—fan fiction and remixes. Both of these practices are typified by user-generated content. That is, users work together in like-minded communities to share, create, critique, and support each other in the construction of their own versions of favourite texts. This kind of digital fiction has great potential for the classroom, as it provides the space for students to have their own voice, and to reinterpret stories or rewrite them (or to remix and mash them) in ways that can subvert traditional stereotypes and inject elements of students' identity into the fictional world.

In fan fiction, fans will borrow settings, plots, characters, and ideas from a story (or a blend of several stories) to weave together new versions of those stories. Such stories sometimes feature the author or a representation of the author as a new character in that story. In other examples, fans have created their own prequels or sequels to a work. When the Harry Potter phenomenon was at its height and fans were waiting (not so patiently) for J. K. Rowling to complete the final books in the series, some fans wrote entire books imagining what could happen next.

The value of fan fiction as a rich scaffold for children's writing has been argued extensively (Black, 2005; Jenkins, 2004; Lewis, 2004; Thomas, 2005a, 2005b, 2006). As Lewis (2004) commented:

> What fan fiction offers to these young writers is a great, existing storyline; interesting, three-dimensional characters that have already been developed; and a wealth of back story to both pull from and write about. The inexperienced author doesn't have to spend all his or her time developing something original, but instead can focus on the actual skill of writing.

> It allows young authors to practice their craft without expending huge amounts of time and energy developing something "original". As they build their "writing muscles", their writing improves and they tend to stray farther and farther from the source material. (p. 3)

There are two characteristics of fan fiction sites that are of particular interest in terms of literacy and English development. The first of these is that users are encouraged to co-create works, that is, to write in pairs or groups. In previous research (Thomas, 2006) one of my research participants, a young girl named Tiana, explained the value of this approach for her own writing by stating:

> By working together in conjunction with someone who writes three times better than I do when it comes to dialogue—though I am probably better at viewpoints—we balance each other out, and contrast our individual skills. My spelling, for one thing, has improved, as has my grammar. A lot. I mean, a few months ago I would've spelt grammar as grammer and not known it was wrong... heh. But we contrast with our writing skills, and by that, make each other stronger. By focusing on strengthening another's weak points, you begin to allow yourself to write deeper in on your own weaknesses, and strengthen yourself in those points. But allowing yourself to see your weaknesses through another's eyes can strengthen your stronger points. I'll always prefer co-authoring fanfictions now.

The second characteristic is the support provided on/to some sites by more experienced users of the site whose role it is to be "beta writers." This role involves the beta writer providing detailed critical feedback to the user on their writing before it is permitted to be made public on the site. Jenkins (2006) argued that this provided an exceptional level of writing instruction—beyond what young writers might receive in classroom contexts.

In addition to such literacy benefits of fan fiction practices is that of the *critical* literacy potential of these practices and the empowerment this affords young people. As I have noted previously, "[o]ne of the features of most fan fiction is that fans of the text can take it and write in characters and plots that are relevant to their own identities and lives, giving them a voice in a text in which they might otherwise be marginalised" (Thomas, 2006, p. 234). Two girls in my research, for example, were able to create characters in their fan fiction that challenged the hierarchical world of their selected story world of *Star Wars*. In their own reversionings of *Star Wars*, these girls were able to create female Jedi Knights, something not possible in the original work of fiction. Through subverting the ways in which gender was constructed in the original story world, these girls were responding in critical ways to counter the hegemony of those texts.

Similarly, the social phenomenon of the "remix" has at its heart the sense of critically responding to texts. The term *remix* is defined as the appropriation of content from existing stories and reorganising that content to create new texts. The form of most remixes is short video clips, and young people create a remix by editing together excerpts from existing films using movie editing software. Often the purpose for remixing is for humour, parody, or to point out injustices or questionable values. As Jenkins (2006) noted:

> More and more literacy experts are recognizing that enacting, reciting, and appropriating elements from preexisting stories is a valuable and organic part of the process by which children develop cultural literacy. Parents should instead think about their kids' appropriations as a kind of apprenticeship. They learn by remixing. Indeed, they learn more about the form of expression they remix than if they simply made that expression directly. (p. 177)

This concept is not new, as writers of fan fiction have been doing this for decades. But what does seem to have evolved strongly with YouTube culture is the notion of subversion and using remix for political agendas.

One particular example serves well to demonstrate this new activism and political commentary through the textual form. It is a remix of scenes from the popular movie franchise *Twilight* with the TV series *Buffy*. In Buffy we had a strong female protagonist who exemplified the identity of the "girl power" movement in pop culture and literature that became mainstream in the last decades of the twentieth century. For many, the discourses surrounding gender in the newer *Twilight* saga have seemed a return to traditional notions of femininity and masculinity, with its heroes playing out stereotyped roles of desire and storylines of females being protected or rescued by males. Not content with this, young activist Jonathan McIntosh (2009) created a remix, which, in his own words, was a form of resistance to those discourses.

> In this re-imagined narrative, Edward Cullen from the Twilight Series meets Buffy the Vampire Slayer. It's an example of transformative storytelling serving as a pro-feminist visual critique of Edward's character and generally creepy behavior. Seen through Buffy's eyes, some of the more sexist gender roles and patriarchal Hollywood themes embedded in the Twilight saga are exposed. Ultimately this remix is about more than a decisive showdown between the slayer and the sparkly vampire. It also doubles as a metaphor for the ongoing battle between two opposing visions of gender roles in the 21st century. (para. 1)

This is one of many instances whereby youth are inserting themselves into the stories of pop culture, and where they are unable to find their place or voice, they re-create the stories in ways that allow them to become the heroes themselves. Such reinventions cause us to stop and reconsider identity, society, culture, and the tensions young people face on a daily basis as they are bombarded with images and expectations that serve to alienate them. As Lessig (2008) comments:

> There are two goods that remix creates, at least for us, or for our kids, at least now. One is the good of community. The other is education. (pp. 76–77)

Remixes are not just quirky, or fun, or a video that might go viral; rather, they have the power to change perspectives, thoughts, and behaviours. This is the kind of critical digital literacy teachers should be aiming for when they are working with students in classroom contexts.

BORN DIGITAL FICTION

A work defined as *born digital* has no traditional version and is one that is both created (or *born*) for the digital space and read/experienced within the digital space. That is, the work does not and cannot exist in a print form. Over the past three decades or so, born digital texts have been variously termed *electronic literature, interactive fiction, network fiction* (Hayles, 2000), *hypertext fiction, ergodic literature* (Aarseth, 1997), and more. The increasing growth and change resulting from emergent digital technology has affected the way that narrative theorists describe and define such works.

A number of excellent websites collect and archive examples of born digital fiction. One site is Dreaming Methods (One to One Development Trust, 2013), which hosts a range of highly creative *born digital* fiction, linking to works created by students, professional artists, writers, and producers. According to the site, it aims to create "powerful, compelling and visually stunning works that explore abstract, complex and contemporary themes" (para. 3). Other sites include the Electronic Literature Organization (http://eliterature.org/), which includes both a collection of digital fiction works and scholarly articles about the field. Similarly, Electronic Literature as a Model of Creativity and Innovation in Practice (ELMCIP; http://elmcip.net/) showcases both literary and scholarly works with a focus on European research and practice. The site if:book UK (http://www.ifbook.co.uk/) explores the future of the book by supporting projects that contribute to education with digital fiction. A companion site in Australia, if:book Australia (http://www.futureofthebook.org.au/), was established in 2010 and is exploring the intersection of technology and publishing. The New Media Writing Prize (http://www.newmediawriting prize.co.uk/) is a UK-based site, also established in 2010, and offers annual prizes for new media writing.

One of the student entrants in the 2011 New Media Writing prize was Simon Kerr, who created the work *5Haitis* (http://ispysi.org.uk/ 5Haitis/output/5Haitis.html). This work tells the stories of three people living during the 2010 earthquake in Haiti. It consists of a 2D interactive space and the three characters who interact with both the space and with each other. A reader explores the relationship between characters as well as the relationship of characters to the space by dragging the mouse across the scene. A few minutes into the exploration, an earthquake is simulated, and the contrast between before and after is both stark and haunting.

There are multitudes of forms that born digital fiction can take, and new forms continue to emerge as technology advances. Just a few examples include video stories told through YouTube, blog narratives told through regular blog posts, iPad stories (such as the award-winning *Fantastic Flying Books of Mr. Morris Lessmore*), machinima—animated stories created using gaming platforms—twitter fiction, sms poetry, and Facebook fiction where stories are woven together by characters interacting together on Facebook pages. Another award-winning digital novel popular with teachers is *Inanimate Alice*. This will be the focus of Chapter 9 of this volume.

BLENDED REALITY FICTIONS

Blended reality fictions are works that overlay digital stories onto real spaces and/or incorporate a blend of digital and paper-based fiction as part of the story world. Two examples of this type of digital fiction include alternate reality games and augmented reality storytelling. An alternate reality game is a fictional work that has its pieces distributed across both virtual and real spaces. It is called a game because users are required to hunt for clues to find each piece of the story and collaborate with others to share the pieces and make sense of the story. Augmented reality storytelling typically involves walking around a space with a mobile device and unlocking pieces of a story that are tagged to specific geographical locations. Streetmuseum (Museum of London, 2010), for example, is a mobile application that allows a user to walk around London and view images and stories from London's past overlaid onto the real space. Both of these forms of storytelling represent a new kind of digital fiction that is yet to be explored for its fullest literary and educational potential. Chapter 12 of this volume explains augmented reality in more detail and explores its potential use in literacy and English teaching contexts.

THE AFFORDANCES OF DIGITAL FICTION

Affordance 1: Multimodality

Lankshear and Knobel (2004) argue that literacy educators need to be taking into account the increasingly prominent contexts of multimodal texts. Kress (2003) argues that in these contexts, representation and meaning-making in textual forms are undergoing important changes compared to traditional printed texts. Kress (2003) notes a distinction between traditional writing, which is governed by linear space and time or sequencing, and images, which, as Lankshear and Knobel (2004) also argue, "are governed by a logic of space and function that attributes meaning to the placement of images, the spatial relations between an image and space or other images and text, to size, to colour and shape, and so on" (para. 37).

Kress (2003), Lankshear and Knobel (2003, 2004), Cope and Kalantzis (2000), Lankshear, Snyder, and Green (2000), and many others all argue for a new theoretical approach to reading that emphasises the multimodality of new forms of texts, particularly given the burgeoning nature of digital forms of texts with which young people are interacting on a daily basis. In fact, Kress (2003) calls for a move away from examining texts linguistically, arguing for a need for semiotic examinations and readings of such texts. Kress (2003) argues:

> The theoretical change is from linguistics to semiotics—from a theory that accounted for language alone to a theory that can account equally well for gesture, speech, image, writing, 3D objects, colour, music, and no doubt others. (pp. 35–36)

And as Lankshear and Knobel (2004) argue, such semiotic analysis and reading of texts no longer privileges the linguistic; instead, it "necessarily highlights the importance of the representational and *affordance* work carried out by these modes to meet a given social purpose" (para. 41). That is, Lankshear and Knobel's (2004) argument, following Kress (2003), is that within this new way of thinking,

> language becomes just one mode among many that people can draw on to communicate with others to represent meanings and that needs to be "dealt with" semiotically rather than linguistically. (para. 43)

According to Unsworth, Thomas, Simpson, and Asha (2005), the semiotic affordances of multimodal texts include any combination of written text, image, and sound. Digital forms of multimodal fiction have actually developed over the past decade to become art forms in their own right. As Walker (2003) remarks,

> The original form of publishing and distributing hypertext fiction was clearly within a literary model.... The web has a radically different delivery form... [but] in the last decade's web works, network-specific genres have been increasingly incorporated in web narratives and poems.... Webcams, web diaries and serial narratives have become more common both as artistic endeavours in their own right and as elements of and inspirations to hypertext and interactive narrative. (p. 14)

Understanding how each mode (text, image, sound, space, etc.) works grammatically to make meaning is significant in classroom contexts. English curricula such as the Australian Curriculum: English (ACARA, 2010) require students not only to grasp the ways in which words make meaning but also places an emphasis on the ways in which images and sounds make meaning. Also important is the way that the various modes of a text (words, images, sounds) interact together to make meaning.

Affordance 2: Hypertext/Hypermedia

In relation to digital fiction, a number of theorists (W. Morgan, 1999; H. Morgan, 2004; Moulthrop, 1997) have commented on the significance of hypertext to reading. H. Morgan (2004) claims that hypertext "forces a reconsideration of the role of the reader" (para. 4). Based on W. Morgan's (1999) argument, I have previously noted (Thomas, 2005a) that the cognitive work associated with reading hypertext fiction was related to readers' abilities to anticipate what might be uncovered by the link, by filling in the gaps, using background knowledge of expectations and linking together the individual pieces of hypertext information to form a coherent whole.

Following this notion of the gap or space in digital fiction, Moulthrop (1997) explains his idea that there are three types of spaces in digital texts: the imaginary space of the fictional world, the presentation space or interface used for the fiction, and the semantic space, the domain of writing. These spaces are all interconnected and he argues the reader needs to assemble meaning from each space to understand the world of the fiction.

Ever since the now classic and earliest known fictional hypertexts such as Joyce's (1989) *Afternoon, a Story*, the relationship between hypertext and the role of the reader has been widely discussed (Walker, 2003). Though strongly linear in narrative if the reader chooses, *Afternoon* has many possible reading paths due to its fragmentation and spatial scattering. The reader is asked yes/no questions, to which a "yes" response will bring up one lexia and "no" will bring up a different lexia. To press return would take the reader on a preset journey through the narrative, the default chronology of events, which is told in a *descriptive, poetic, dreaming*, and *reluctant* manner (Walker, 2003), which leaves the reader to imagine and assemble both the sequence and meaning of the narrative.

Affordance 3: Spatiality

The spatiality of hypertext fiction is discussed in detail by Hayles (2000). Discussing Jackson's (1995) notable digital fiction *Patchwork Girl*, Hayles (2000) argues:

> like many hypertexts, chronology is inherently tenuous because linking structures leap across time as well as space. As if recapitulating the processes of fragmentation and recombination made possible by digital technologies, *Patchwork Girl* locates its performance of subjectivity in the individual lexia.... Sequence is constructed by accumulating a string of present moments when the reader clicks on links.... This situation reverses our usual sense that time is passing as we watch. Instead, time becomes a river that always already exists in its entirety, and we create sequence and chronology by choosing which portions of the river to sample. (pp. 162–163)

Allen (2003) argues that hypertext as a concept is not necessarily new or innovative but it is the reader's role that is extended in dramatically different ways to traditional print-based texts. He terms this new agent the *wreader*—both the producer and consumer of textual, hypertextual practices. Allen states:

> In this new reader, both production and consumption of texts is combined into one process that is self-contained. The new reader navigates through lexias to find threads of connected meaning where no author placed them.... This new reader is reminiscent of the old reader who has always decoded texts and made new meanings with them, prowling them for paths that go toward new textual centers and make new experiences. These readers are... "radial" readers, which means that they read texts in an open-ended search for meaning. (para. 15)

Some exemplary types of digital fiction that require the reader to piece together a narrative across some form of space are those of distributed narratives—digital narratives that are divided into a number of components are distributed both spatially and temporally, such as the e-mail narrative *Daughters of Freya* and the Web narrative *Online Caroline*. In *Daughters of Freya*, a sequence of approximately 100 emails is delivered to your e-mail box over the period of several weeks. The e-mails are actual e-mail conversations between the characters in the narrative, and the reader is required to piece together the narrative from these letters.

In *Online Caroline*, the narrative is pieced together through a range of texts: e-mail, webcam video episodes, Caroline's diary and photo album, her phone messages, and more. What is particularly fascinating about *Online Caroline* is that the reader is required to fill out a personal facts form, and this information is then explicitly used throughout the e-mails and Web text to develop intimacy with the fictional character. Caroline calls the reader her friend. This results in the reader becoming a part of the diegesis of the fictional world. The reader is given agency to traverse the spaces of the text or to "perform" (Bolter, 2001) and "explore" (Saltz, 1997) the text.

The affordance of spatiality was also used to great effect in *5Haitis* as explained above, whereby users cross the visual terrain of the story and interact with it. This is explored further in Chapter 12 of this volume, relating to the virtual world of Second Life, and the creation of a virtual island called *Macbeth* that users needed to walk through and interact with to make meaning of this new interpretation of Shakespeare's play.

Affordance 4: Interactivity

The notion of reader interactivity and control is one that I have previously emphasised as a critical affordance of digital texts (Thomas 2005a, 2005b). In thinking about the nature of interactivity, I propose that interaction requires the reader to act upon the text in some way to access it. As Douglas (1996) comments, "the text draws us into it because it cannot exist without our participation" (p. 209). It seems to me that the element of interactivity and reader control is at the heart of the *radical change* (Dresang, 2003) in the reading of digital fiction. Walker (2003) argues that the relationship between the reader and the text is "central to the meaning of the work" (p. 11). In cases where digital fiction includes hypertext and distribution across online spaces (though not all examples of digital fiction do this), we are finding, as H. Morgan (2004) argues, "the distance between writing and reading is once again seriously reduced, only this time…the process of writing and reading nearly overlap" (para. 6).

The reader/writer overlap is a pronounced feature of blog fiction. In a previous study (Thomas, 2005a), I have argued that blog fiction is where author or authors have used a blog as a writing device, using all of the affordances of the blogging or journaling software, such as hyperlinks, graphics, and the commenting system. These authors are experimenting and manipulating the software to exploit it for their writing purposes, and in this way are creating a genre that has both continuities and disparities with other narrative genres. Their innovative play with the medium is creating a narrative, which at its best is multimodal, hypertextual, episodic, serialised, and interactive.

DIGITAL FICTION "DONE WELL"

In considering the range of digital fiction above, it is no longer conceivable to think of reading through a linguistic lens; instead, we need to see reading more about engagement through a piecing together of the multimodal, hypertextual, and spatial components of text to make meaning: the words, image, sound, and "bits" of information (lexia) that are positioned across several spaces that may or may not be directly linked through hypertext. In some instances, such as the blog fiction and, more so, the role-playing fiction, it is even more than piecing together and puzzling through the component parts of a text; instead, reading is intimately connected to characterisation, identity, and the performance of a text. The affordances of multimodality, hypertext, spatiality, and interaction are not necessarily unique to digital fiction, but in many cases the fact that they coexist in a concentrated form means that successful reading requires the reader to draw upon a multitude of resources simultaneously to make meaning from the text.

Technological affordances such as multimodality, hypertext, spatiality, and interactivity can affect the nature of narrative. Specifically, there are two significant ways in which narrative is affected, and these include the notions of active reading and multivocality. Barthes (1971) argued that "the goal of literary work is to make the reader no longer a consumer but a producer of text" (p. 4), and drawing from theories about hypertext (Deleuze & Guattari, 1987; Landow, 2006; Moulthrop, 1997) as discussed above, it is clear that hypertext, hypermedia, and the digital space challenge readers to assemble *bits* of semantic meanings or *lexia* to create their own journey through a text and use a range of semiotic meaning-making resources to construct a narrative. This in turn offers opportunities for readers to become authors as they navigate through a text, and insert themselves within it, as the boundaries between reader and author blur. Digital fiction has the potential to become what Bakhtin (1981) calls the *dialogic polyphonic multivocal novel*, leaving new gaps for readers to reimagine the text in new ways, with voices other than the textual voice given space to have a presence.

DEEP STUDIES OF DIGITAL FICTION: *5HAITIS*

A strong emphasis in the Australian English curriculum (ACARA, 2010) is that of deep studies of literature of all forms. As Freebody (2010) comments, "there will be more of an intense focus on the use of literature…I hope it will encourage teachers to deal with fewer texts, more deeply." A deep study of text involves studying its literary form, analyzing the techniques used by the author, illustrator, filmmaker, artist (those who have constructed the text), to create different kinds of effects through the different modes of the text (written words, images, sounds, space), and finally it also involves asking critical questions about how the text reflects values, issues, or ideas about the world.

5Haitis (mentioned above) is a remarkable piece of digital fiction that combines words, images, sounds, space, and interactivity to tell the story of the 2010 earthquake in Haiti. The narrative is divided into two parts. It opens with a snapshot of life in Haiti and is told from three characters' points of view. Text flickers next to each individual character revealing internal thoughts on the morning before the earthquake hits. Readers are able to click on a single character to see the world from his or her point of view only, and they are able to drag characters onto each other, which prompts dialogue between characters. The reader can also drag a character onto a location to reveal a relationship with that space. Themes that underscore the opening part of the narrative include the poverty in the slums of Port-au-Prince in Haiti, the nature of childhood in the slums as children are set to work and punished harshly for not doing chores, hunger, the role of aid workers, and faith. A typical snapshot from the opening is included in Figure 3.1.

DIGITAL FICTION | 53

Fig 3.1. Screenshot from *5Haitis*.

The three characters we are introduced to at the beginning include Bronte (the mother of four children living in the Port-au-Prince slums), Guerda (Bronte's eldest daughter), and Omar (an aid worker from the United States). We are given an insight into the life and concerns of each character. Following Bronte's point of view, readers learn that her husband is out of work and Bronte is struggling to make ends meet. She sets her two oldest children many chores each day while she cooks and tends to the two younger children. One evening each week she attends the free college. She is a good cook and thinks of setting up a stall to sell her sweetbread and make some money. She is proud of Guerda but disciplines her harshly if she fails to complete her chores. We learn that discipline takes the form of being whipped. Following Guerda's point of view, readers learn that the whole family lives in one room of a shack, and that the only toilet is a sewer drain outside, which is also where people throw all of their rubbish. The water pump outside the shack (shared by all of the neighbours) is a highly valued commodity. Guerda spends some time at school but the remaining time is spent working and completing her chores. Guerda is keen to see Haiti cleaned up of the slums and thinks it could be beautiful. Following Omar's point of view, readers learn that he is a deeply concerned aid worker, driven by faith to help the people of Haiti. Omar is from Pennsylvania and was *spared* from something two years previously, though what this was is unclear. Omar is concerned about the garbage in the slums, as well as the *prepackaged, hi-carb snacks* that he was issued to give them instead of real food, saying that this added to the rubbish problem in the area. He admires Bronte and also admits he is attracted to her. He shares a memory of one time when Bronte generously feeds him one day—food that would have fed the entire family—and he felt so guilty that he threw up.

After some time (three or four minutes) of reading and interacting with the story, the view changes—the screen appears to shake, blur over, and crack, as the *story page* simulates an earthquake, as illustrated in Figure 3.2.

Fig 3.2. Crisis Point in the Story *5Haitis*—the earthquake hits.

The section part of the narrative is told one year from the day of the earthquake, and the first visual is illustrated in Figure 3.3.

Fig 3.3. After the Earthquake in the Story *5Haitis*.

Readers quickly realize that Guerda has been killed in the earthquake, from the empty space where her character used to be. Omar is first shown as speechless, and the use of the ellipses in Bronte's first appearance after the earthquake is symbolically poignant. As the story proceeds (now told only from Bronte's and Omar's points of view) we learn that all but one child have perished, as has Bronte's husband. Bronte's first words are *Life ended a year ago*, and her grief is visible as her head is bowed and her gaze kept to the ground. Omar's first words are *There's been no time at all since the quake to stop and think about anything*, and readers learn that he has been busy rebuilding the town. Themes underscoring the second half of the narrative include the opportunities for regrowth and regeneration, resilience, grief, faith, and recovery.

Understanding the narrative only occurs after multiple readings, as each new reading can involve the reader interacting with the text in different ways to trigger different text. Also, as the three character viewpoints (or two in part two of the narrative) are shown simultaneously, it may take three viewings before each character is understood. Each character reveals a history, a relationship to place, and relationships with each other, so there is much to discover with each new reading.

A number of techniques used by Kerr (2011) could be examined in more detail for a deep study of *5Haitis*. Three particularly interesting techniques that could be the focus of a close study in the classroom include how words are used to create a picture of the poverty in the slums of Port-au-Prince; the contrasting attitudinal meanings of words, images, and sounds between the two phases of the narrative to reveal loss and grief; and the use of space and interactivity to unlock the significance of place to humankind. Each of these techniques is discussed on the following pages.

Table 3.2. Text Excerpts in *5Haitis* that Construct the Meaning of Poverty in Port-u-Prince, Haiti

Text excerpts that construct a sense of poverty in Port-au-prince	
Bronte's point of view	• 4am. Time to get up. I'm so tired. • Only a few people around as I relieve myself into the sewer drain outside. • The only thing of nature is the sky above me. • Life here is difficult. People don't get old in the slums. • We are all poor. • Everyone is sick of mudcakes, literally. • I wash my teeth with yesterday's water and search round for some wood. • They're both strong and need to learn how life is, in this place. • I look at the mirror on the wall. Tired, grey eyes gaze back at me.
Omar's point of view	• Looking out the hostel window I could see the garbage. It was everywhere. Flowing into the river, piled up against the shacks. Kids were playing on it. Pigs were eating off it. Bronte's dumb goat stood there peeing straight into an empty can of beans.

Omar's point of view	• And all we're giving these poor people is pre-packaged, hi-carb snacks. We're barely feeding them and at the same time burying them in crap. • I gave the kid my old shades and she was over the moon... funny. • They're all so generous despite the fact they have nothing. • The first thing to go was the shack.... No surprise there. It barely kept standing on its own anyway. Everything just collapsed like wet paper. It was a dump anyway. They all froze at night and in the day were overrun by vermin. Some of the rats I saw were gigantic! But you can't really expect hygiene in a place like this.
Guerda's point of view	• Mudcakes again for breakfast. • There was no delivery at Josias' shop. • Coming back I found some sugarcane in the trash... just needed rinsing and it was fine. • Our whole family lives in this one room. • The only toilet is the sewer drain. • That's where everyone throws their rubbish. • I love Haiti. I want to help get rid of this rubbish. It could be so beautiful here without the rubbish and the slums.

Text excerpts that construct a sense of poverty in *5Haitis* are included in Table 3.2. Poverty is built up through descriptions of the garbage, food, shack, and hygiene. Garbage is described with verbs such as *flowing into*, *piled up against*, and *burying* and adverbials such as *everywhere*. The shack is described with the noun group *a dump* and at the time of the earthquake, the verb used to describe it falling is *collapsed*, and the manner in which it falls is through the simile (an adverbial of manner) *like a wet piece of paper*.

Attributes to describe life include *difficult*, and to describe people include *poor* and as having *nothing*. The food people eat include either the mudcakes (which makes everybody literally sick) or the food supplied by aid workers, which is described in the nominal group *pre-packaged, hi-carb snacks*. The packaging is described as contributing to the garbage problem by creating *crap*. Another reference to food is the fact that Omar suggests that it *barely* feeds them—the modal adverb *barely* indicating the hunger experienced by people. Guerda's insights also indicate that food is scarce (no delivery of bread at the shop), so scarce that she eats sugarcane she finds from the rubbish.

Hygiene is referred to in a number of ways—water used for cleaning is described as *yesterday's water*, and *the only toilet* is *the sewer drain outside*. The fact that Bronte reveals that she has to *relieve herself* in the drain so matter-of-factly builds a sense of normalcy that is horrifying and vivid. The description of the shack being *overrun by vermin* and of the rats as *gigantic* further builds the sense of a lack of hygiene and the potential for rampant disease. This is suggested in Bronte's words: *people don't get old in the slums.*

Table 3.3 illustrates the second technique used by Kerr (2011) that could be the subject of closer study with students. This is the way that contrasting words, images, and sounds in the two phases of the narrative work to reveal the attitudinal meanings of grief and loss. There is a strong sense of intermodal convergence (Painter & Martin, 2011) between words, images, and sounds in the first phase of the narrative. The general mood constructed across all modes in the first phase is that of community, hope, and faith as the family struggles through difficult times. There is also a strong intermodal convergence in the second phase of the narrative. The general mood is that of emptiness, bleakness, despair, lack of faith (for Bronte), and a sense of nothingness. The shift of interpersonal meanings from the richly textured sense of hope, faith, and positivity to the richly textured layering of meanings of grief, sorrow, and emptiness is designed to create a dramatic impact—one of deep pathos—for the reader as he or she experiences the story.

Table 3.3. Contrasting Meanings Between the Two Phases of the Narrative that Reveal Attitudinal Meanings of Grief and Loss

Words	Images	Sounds
In phase 1 of the narrative, Bronte's words reflect a number of aspects about her character: her faith in God ("I see God every day in the strength he gives us to cope"), her own strength ("I'm determined to succeed"), and her love of family ("I feel proud"). In phase 2, her words relate to these themes: "Life ended a year ago" "Our family was split" "My life's buried only 10 feet away" "I feel nothing…about anything" "I'm stuck in a loop repeating the same things over	The two images of Figures 3.1 and 3.3 illustrate contrasts of the two phases of the narrative. The most striking characteristic of Figure 3.3, in contrast with Figure 3.1, is that of the empty space where daughter Guerda used to be. The emptiness symbolizes her death during the earthquake and instantly evokes sadness in the reader, who fills in the gaps without needing any words explaining what has happened. In the first image, Bronte is depicted with a direct gaze to the reader, which serves to invite the reader into her world. In the second image, Bronte is looking down, her gaze directed	The music that plays in phase 1 of the narrative is "Wongolo," which is a Haitian folk song. It is sung by a choir in four-part harmony, a capella. Wongolo is the name of a Haitian spirit, and the words of the song translate to: "Wongolo, you're leaving, when will you come and see me again. When will you come and see me again? The country is changing,

and over but never getting anywhere" "I can't see God anymore" "There's nowhere for me to go…and no-one to go to…there is noth-" Also, Bronte's language is interspersed with many uses of ellipses ("…") The use of strong modal verbs, the repetition of the concept of nothingness, and the expression "stuck in a loop…but never getting anywhere" create an image of Bronte's deep despair and sense of futility, as well as her loss of faith.	away from the viewer, serving to distance the reader, and constructing a sense of her grief. While the background of neither image could be described as vibrant, the colour tones in image 1 have a warmth to them with the use of earthy brown tones, whereas the background of image 2 is completely washed out with a monotone colour palette of greys. Using Painter's (2008) description of how colour constructs interpersonal meanings, the grey palette constructs meanings of unfamiliarity, coolness, and distance.	When will you come back and see me again, Wongolo?" The music is beautiful and is richly textured with four soft flowing legato harmonies in a minor key that suggests soulful lament—a prayer for the good of the country. The fact that it is a folk song suggests a sense of community, place, and tradition. The overall attitudinal meaning is that of a respectful, harmonious community, positive and brought together by faith. In contrast, the music in the second phase of the narrative is a short modern piano etude. It is thinly textured with a single, slow melody of notes played with many silences and pauses in between, and the notes are accented with occasional chords. The register is generally very low, with higher notes at regular intervals, and the key is minor. The mood created is somber, melancholic, and sad.

A third technique used by Kerr (2011) is that of the use of space as a means to unfold the narrative. The reader must traverse the space and interact with both the characters and the space to read the story. Dragging a character across particular elements of the space causes them to light up to signal the meaning potential of extra information. Dropping the character onto a highlighted object or building in the space then reveals additional story information about the relevance of that space to the lives of the people in Port-au-Prince and, in particular, the family at the centre of the story. Moving one character closer in proximity to another triggers an interaction between the two. As the narrative tells the story of an earthquake, which ravaged place and space, the technique of allowing a reader to interact with place and space in a variety of ways in the story is particularly innovative and apposite.

CONCLUSION

Digital fiction continues to grow and adapt as new technologies and social practices around technologies emerge. Reading and creating digital fiction will require an understanding of how modalities (such as words, images, sounds, space) work to construct meanings. It also requires new ways of thinking about how readers interact with a text. At the heart of any fiction worthy of deep study in a classroom is that the narrative explores themes of contemporary significance, in ways that challenge and extend students' understandings of the world. This is also true of digital fiction.

REFERENCES

Aarseth, E. (1997). *Cybertext: Perspectives in ergodic literature.* Baltimore: Johns Hopkins University Press.
ACARA. (2010). *The Australian Curriculum: English.* Retrieved from http://www.australiancurriculum.edu.au/English/Curriculum/F-10
Allen, M. (2003). *This is not a hypertext, but…:A set of lexias on textuality.* Retrieved from http://ctheory.net/text_file.asp?pick=389
Bakhtin, M. M. (1981). *The dialogic imagination: Four essasys by Michael Holquist.* Austin: University of Texas Press.
Barthes, R. (1971). *S/Z* (R. Howard, Trans.). New York: Hill and Wang.
Black, R. W. (2004). Access and affiliation: The new literacy practices of English language learners in an online animé-based fanfiction community. In *Proceedings of the 2004 National Conference of Teachers of English Assembly for Research.* Berkeley, CA.
Black, R.W. (2005). Access and affiliation: The literacy and composition practices of English language learners in an online fanfiction community. Journal of Adolescent & Adult Literacy, 49 (2), 118–128.
Bolter, J. D. (2001). *Writing space: Computers, hypertext and the remediation of print* (2nd ed.). London: Erlbaum.
Campbell, A. (2008). *Undreamt fiction.* Retrieved from http://www.dreamingmethods.com/uploads/resources/Undreamt_Fiction.pdf
Cope, B., & Kalantzis, M. (2000). Designs for social futures. In B. Cope & M. Kalantzis (Eds.), *Multiliteracies: Literacy learning and the design of social futures* (pp. 203–234). South Yarra, Melbourne: Macmillan.
Deleuze, G., & Guattari, F. (1987). *A thousand plateaus.* Minneapolis: University of Minnesota Press.
Douglas, J. Y. (1996). Virtual intimacy and the male gaze cubed: Interacting with narratives on CD-ROM. *Leonardo, 29*(3), 207–213.
Dresang, E. (2003). Radical change: A theory for reading and writing in the digital age. In *Proceedings of the Wisconsin Symposium on Reading Research.* Tallahassee, FL: Florida State University Press.
Freebody, P. (2010). *Introduction.* Retrieved from http://www.australiancurriculum.edu.au/English/Introduction)

Hayles, N. K. (2000). *Flickering connectivities in Shelley Jackson's* Patchwork Girl: *The importance of media-specific analysis.* Retrieved from http://www.iath.virginia.edu/pmc/text-only/issue.100/10.2ha yles.txt

Hi_ReS! (2001). *Donnie Darko.* Retrieved from http://archive.hi-res.net/donniedarko/

Jackson, S. (1995). *Patchwork Girl.* Eastgate Systems, CD-ROM.

Jenkins, H. (2006). *Convergence culture: Where old and new media collide.* New York: New York University Press.

Joyce, M. (1989). *Afternoon, a story.* (Eastgate Systems, CD-ROM, 1989 release).

Kerr, S. (2011). *5Haitis.* Retrieved from http://ispysi.org.uk/5Haitis /output/5Haitis.html

Kress, G. (2003). *Literacy in the new media age.* London: Routledge/Falmer.

Kress, G., Jewitt, J., Ogborn, J., & Tsatsarelis, C. (2001). *Multimodal teaching and learning: The rhetorics of the science classroom.* London: Continuum.

Landow, G. (2006). *Hypertext 3.0: New media and critical theory in an era of globalization.* Baltimore: Johns Hopkins University Press.

Lankshear, C., & Knobel, M. (2003). *New literacies: Changing knowledge and classroom learning.* Buckingham: Open University Press.

Lankshear, C., & Knobel, M. (2004). Text related roles of the digitally "at home." Retrieved from http://www.geocities.com/c.lankshear/roles.html

Lankshear, C., Snyder, I., & Green, B. (2000). *Teachers and techno-literacy: Managing literacy, technology and learning in schools.* St. Leonards: Allen & Unwin.

Lessig, L. (2008). *Remix: Making art and commerce thrive in the hybrid economy.* New York: Penguin.

Lewis, D. (2004). Understanding the power of fan fiction for young authors. Retrieved from http://www.thefreelibrary.com/Understanding+the+power+of+fan+fiction+for+young+authors.-a0114326743

McIntosh, J. (2009). *Buffy vs Edward (Twilight Remixed).* Retrieved from http://www.rebelliouspixels.com/2009/buffy-vs-edward-twilight-remixed

Morgan, H. (2004). *Exploring hypertext's new reader: Some theoretical approaches.* Retrieved from http://www.athabascau.ca/courses/engl/475/archive/morgan_exploring.pdf

Morgan, W. (1999). Heterotopics: Towards a grammar of hyperlinks. In *Proceedings of the Messenger Morphs the Media Conference.* Retrieved from http://www.wordcircuits.com/htww/morgan1.htm

Moulthrop, S. (1997). Practical criticism for hypertext. In *Proceedings of the Ohio State Univeristy Colloqium.* Retrieved from http://iat.ubalt.edu/moulthrop/talks/osu/

Museum of London. (2010). *Streetmuseum.* Retrieved from https://itunes.apple.com/app/id369684330

One to One Development Trust. (2013). Dreaming methods. Retrieved from http://www.dreamingmethods.com/

Painter, C. (2008). The role of colour in children's picture books: Choices in AMBIENCE. In L. Unsworth (Ed.), *New literacies and the English curriculum: Multimodal perspectives* (pp. 89–111). London: Continuum.

Painter, C., & Martin, J. R. (2011). Intermodal complementarity: Modelling affordances across image and verbiage in children's picture books. In H. G. Wen (Ed.), *Studies in functional linguistics and discourse analysis* (pp. 132–158). Beijing: Higher Education Press.

Saltz, D. (1997). The art of interaction: Interactivity, performativity and computers. *The Journal of Aesthetics and Art Criticism, 55*(2), 117–127.

Strickland, S. (2009). *Born digital.* Retrieved from http://www.poetryfoundation.org/article/182942

Tan, S. (2000). *The lost thing.* Sydney: Hachette.

Thomas, A. (2005a). Fictional blogs and the narrative identities of adolescent girls. In *Proceedings of the Blogtalk Downunder Conference*. Sydney, Australia.
Thomas, A. (2005b). Blurring and breaking through the boundaries of narrative, literacy and identity in adolescent fan fiction. In *Proceedings of the NRC Conference*. Miami, FL.
Thomas, A. (2006). Fan fiction online: Engagement, critical response and affective play through writing. *Australian Journal of Language and Literacy, 29*(3), 226–239.
Unsworth, L., Thomas, A., Simpson, A., & Asha, J. (2005), *Children's literature and computer-based teaching*. UK: Open University Press.
Walker, J. (2003). *Fiction and interaction: How clicking a mouse can make you part of a fictional world.* (Unpublished doctoral thesis). University of Bergen, Norway.

WEB RESOURCES

5Haitis: http://ispysi.org.uk/ 5Haitis/output/5Haitis.html
Donnie Darko: http://archive.hi-res.net/donniedarko/
Dreaming Methods: http://www.dreamingmethods.com/
Electronic Literature Organization: http://eliterature.org/
ELMCIP: http://elmcip.net/
if:book Australia: http://www.futureofthebook.org.au/
if:book UK: http://www.ifbook.co.uk/
Inanimate Alice: http://inanimatealice.com/
New Media Writing Prize: http://www.newmediawritingprize.co.uk/
Online Caroline: http://www.onlinecaroline.com
Pottermore: http://www.pottermore.com/
Project Gutenberg: http://www.gutenberg.org/
The Daughters of Freya: http://emailmystery.com/dof/index.php
The Leaky Cauldron: http://www.the-leaky-cauldron.org/
UK's book depository: http://www.bookdepository.co.uk/free
Virtual Macbeth: http://virtualmacbeth.wikispaces.com/

CHAPTER FOUR

A Model for Critical Games Literacy

THOMAS APPERLEY & CATHERINE BEAVIS

The centrality of new media and digitally mediated communication in young people's lives is an increasingly important concern for teaching practitioners in English and literacy education. Previous research into young people's out-of-school digital engagements and literacy practices highlights the role of digital texts as multimodal forms of meaning making, and the role of digital culture in formations of values, identity, and community (e.g., Jewett, 2008). The scholarly research that has endorsed the importance of digital texts has been accompanied by a more general recognition of the centrality of digital technological competence to economic and social well-being at both individual and national levels (OECD/CERI, 2009; Westbrook, 2011). Consequently, media literacy education has been embraced in many jurisdictions, including the United States, where media literacy was highlighted as one of three "21st-century competencies" in the U.S. National Education Technology Plan (Office of Educational Technology, 2010, p. 13). This recognition underlines the need for English and literacy curricula and pedagogies to actively incorporate the use and analysis of digital texts, knowledge, and practices in the classroom. This chapter will address the following three questions:

1. Why are digital games useful for the English and literacy curriculum?
2. In what ways does *how* digital games are played align with or challenge the strict conception of "text"?
3. How can English and literacy curriculum usefully draw on digital games in a manner that strengthens traditional classroom literacies while also connecting students to new literacy practices?

WHY DIGITAL GAMES AND LITERACY?

The premise of this focus of media—particularly digital—literacies is the need to prepare students to be active, literate participants in the rapidly changing world beyond school. Understanding the literacy practices involved in playing digital games, and reconceptualizing curriculum to support the learning affordances offered by digital games, has great potential to build strong bridges between students' out-of-school life-worlds and 21st-century curriculum. This chapter presents a model for use in developing English and literacy curriculum with digital games that will allow teachers and practitioners to capitalize on this connection. The chapter focuses on *gaming literacy*—the literacies required to analyze, design, and play digital games. Previous research has solidly established this connection between digital games and digital literacy (Buckingham & Burn, 2007; Gee & Hayes, 2010; Hayes & Gee, 2010; Hsu & Wang, 2010; Salen, 2007, 2008b; Zimmerman, 2009), particularly how they "recruit important literacy practices," both through play and participation in online gaming communities (Steinkuelher, 2010, p. 63).

While in many respects the literacy practices developed through digital games are similar to those required for any other digital media, we argue that digital games are different because they are *enacted* by the player. Thus, we define gaming literacy to include the following:

1. "Textual" literacy—the "new literacies" associated with digital iterations of "reading" (or playing) and "writing" (or producing) in combination and in multimodal forms (e.g., New London Group, 1996)
2. "Literacies" specifically linked to the *action*-based processes of digital game play (e.g., Atkins, 2006; Galloway, 2006)

The model of game literacy we present in this chapter draws on the insight of games scholars *and* literacy theorists to both emphasize the distinctiveness of digital games as cultural phenomena and situate this uniqueness against contemporary understandings of literacy and multimodal literacy practices.

This definition of gaming literacy underscores how digital games—including games played on computers, consoles, and mobile and handheld devices—present a complex challenge for researchers and practitioners of education. Digital games deserve a central place in an expanded repertoire of texts brought into the curriculum for study, but *they cannot be understood simply on textual terms*—successfully capitalizing on digital games in the classroom requires an understanding of students' out-of-school gaming practices on their own terms. While the "meanings" of digital games are negotiated and produced in the interaction between "text" and reader (as is the case with any text), we believe it is important that the model also demonstrates how digital games are enacted and instantiated through *action* (Apperley & Beavis, 2011).

A MODEL FOR CRITICAL GAMES LITERACY | 65

This is why the model is presented as two interlocking layers: games-as-action (Figure 4.1) and games-as-text (Figure 4.2). The games-as-action layer is presented first. It addresses the experience of gameplay by examining the virtual worlds of digital games and the dynamic interplay between game and player. This layer looks inward to the virtual world of the game to focus on and understand gameplay on its own terms and uncover the constellation of literacy practices involved in digital gameplay. Second, the games-as-text layer is outlined. This layer examines the connection between the digital game and the lifeworld of the player, where the game play is embedded, enacted, and given meaning. By looking outward to the experience of the player, this layer provides scope for connecting gameplay to literacy outcomes and events in the world more generally. Finally, we discuss how these two layers can be fruitfully combined (Figure 4.3). The boundary between the layers is permeable and overlapping, and this section endeavors to mark useful segues between games-as-action and games-as-text layers to demonstrate how the model operates holistically.

GAMES-AS-ACTION

The notion of "ergodic" (Aarseth, 1997, p. 1) is the crucial concept from game studies that marks the importance of understanding digital games as action. The term emphasizes the physical actions ("labour") of the player in the configuration of the final game "text." The notion conceptualizes the relationship between the final text—or output—of a digital game and the process of textual production—the interactions between the digital game software, hardware, and player that produce the text (see Bogost, 2007; Walsh, 2010; Wardrup-Fruin, 2009). Three crucial factors inform the ergodic process: *action, design,* and *situation*; alone and in combination, these factors constitute the games-as-action layer of the model (Figure 4.1).

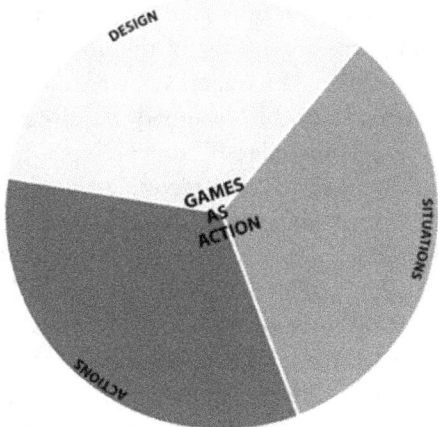

Fig 4.1. Games-As-Action.

ACTIONS

Digital games are enacted on two levels: by the players and by the console or computer that enacts the games' software. Actions refer to *interactions*—the reciprocal configuration and reconfiguration of the game software—performed both by the player and by the hardware (Galloway, 2006). This distinction allows practitioners to understand distinctive actions within what might otherwise be perceived—based on purely visual observations—as an amorphous, homogenous, and unspecific session of game play.

Action underscores the complex contradictory relationship between the player and the digital game. Players often—even within the same game—will alternate between playing *against* and playing *with* the digital game. The game software takes on an ambiguous position as an opponent, referee, and arbiter, who sometimes provides the conflict but always determines and enforces its outcome. In many cases the game software is responsible for the actions of all opponents and hazards, which will act only according to their designed remit. In such cases the players' actions are often informed by how well they observe and understand the actions that the software undertakes as their opponent. In multiplayer games this challenge is provided by other players, making the strategies involved considerably more complex. In these cases the software arbitrates the interactions between the parties and the physics of the virtual world. Software and players also play cooperatively in single-player digital games centered on building and management. For example, in the SimCity series (Maxis, 1989), the player and software cooperate to build/design a virtual city, the player makes the decisions and the software runs the simulation according to set rules, while notifying the player of areas needing particular attention (deforestation, pollution, etc.).

Digital games are defined by action. Actions determine *how* players will use their avatars, the virtual game space(s), and the objects in it. As Gee (2008b) points out: "in a game, the virtual character's powers and limitations mesh with the way in which the virtual world is designed in quite specific ways" (p. 259). Players must deploy their knowledge—from previous gaming experience, or from some other intertextual signal—to recognize actions available to an avatar. *Assassin's Creed II* (Ubisoft Montreal, 2009) illustrates this point; the fact that Ezio can climb makes Florence a different kind of city to explore. This is revealed right away in the game's tutorial along with other basic actions, but *Assassin's Creed II* constantly introduces new techniques as the player proceeds through the game. These are explained when Ezio comes to a new area or must perform a new challenge to proceed in the game. It is the introduction of the action by the game and its mastery by the player that allows the game to proceed.

DESIGNS

The concept distinguishes between two crucial forms of action: those that follow the rules of the game and those that shape the rules of the game. It is necessary to understand design in these two closely related—and sometimes virtually indistinct—ways. First, design includes the element of production within digital games that players encounter and with which they interact during the course of play. For example, in the Nintendo DS game *Lock's Quest* (5th Cell, 2008), to successfully play the game the player must design and upkeep protective fortifications. Second, previous research suggests that literacies are also developed through participation in online communities (Steinkuehler, 2010) by re-presenting and recontextualizing information from digital games in the creation of paratexts (Gutierrez & Beavis, 2010; Walsh & Apperley, 2008, 2009) and the process of designing and redesigning games (Buckingham & Burn, 2007; Hayes & Games, 2008; Peppler & Kafai, 2007; Salen, 2007; Zimmerman, 2009). The first form of design literacy is connected to action, while the second emphasizes multimodal meaning-making and design.

Many recent and contemporary digital games allow players a degree of control over elements of design. Control takes place on two levels: the appearance of the game and the game system. Aesthetic design choices—for example, the lengthy and detailed avatar design found in recent digital games such as *Fallout: New Vegas* (Obsidian Entertainment, 2010) and *Mass Effect 2* (BioWare, 2010)—have no impact on the rules of the game or how the game is played. Even in games such as *Grand Theft Auto IV* (Rockstar North, 2008) in which players have no choice over their avatars, forms of player customization of the avatar are possible because of the availability of clothing and accessory stores. *Grand Theft Auto: San Andreas* (Rockstar North, 2004), with barbershops, gyms, and junk food, is exemplary of this form of player customization.

Other design decisions act on the game system, and thus may have an impact on the processes and outcomes of digital game play. This is apparent in games—for example, *Grand Theft Auto IV* (Rockstar North, 2008), *Heavy Rain* (Quantic Dream, 2010), and *Star Wars: Knights of the Old Republic* (BioWare, 2003)—that are designed to have different narrative outcomes that are based on the actions of the player. For example, in *Dragon Age: Origins* (BioWare, 2009) particular choices made during the avatar design phase—specifically the selection of the avatar's race and class, rather than the size of the avatar's chin and nose, which does not change the game system—unlock different subplots within the overarching narrative.

Many digital games allow players to customize areas of the game world. While activity is central to some popular digital games, such as *Minecraft* (Mojang, 2009), *The Sims* (Maxis, 2000) series, and *WarioWare D.I.Y.* (Intelligent Systems/Nintendo, 2010), it is more commonly included as an optional feature. Often, design parameters are limited on consoles (and handheld devices) in comparison to computers because digital rights are more strictly controlled. Usually, this results in the console game exerting strong and inflexible control over the games' design features (see Sotamaa, 2010b). For example, the Wii game *Boom Blox* (Amblin Entertainment, 2008) allows players to design and distribute maps, but only through the Wii, to other players who also own *Boom Blox*. Computers offer more opportunities for thorough engagement with game design, using software such as *Game Star Mechanic* and *Game Maker* (Games & Squire, 2008; Richards & O'Mara, in press), although similar software like *Microsoft XNA* is also available on the Xbox live service. Game design is informally learned/taught through these platforms by a combination of trial and error, the use of paratexts, and the unofficial *mentorship* of online interest groups.

SITUATIONS

The situation of play refers primarily to its context. While emphasis is often given to the virtual elements of play, it is also important to conceptualize the spaces in which digital games are embedded and enacted (Flynn, 2003; Stevens, Satwicz, & McCarthy, 2008; Taylor, 2006). Examining the situation of game play foregrounds the learning and sociality that take place, and how digital gaming is connected with—and a part of—other mundane daily activities (Apperley, 2010; Gosling & Crawford, 2011; Pargman & Jakobsson, 2008; Pelletier, 2008). The concept provides scope for practitioners to focus on how pupils' out-of-school literacies are developed through digital gaming without excluding other environmental factors.

When digital games are played, people and technologies are aggregated in many different ways (Apperley, 2010; Steinkuehler, 2006; Taylor, 2009). Accounting for people in this aggregation is not as simple as it seems; while some people are clearly playing, other people are often also—directly or indirectly—involved. Other players may be playing from different locations over a network, as is common with massive multiplayer online games such as *World of Warcraft* (Blizzard Software, 2004); or in the same room, as is more common with console-based multiplayer games such as *Mario Kart Wii* (Nintendo, 2008). In other cases a group of people will play, with players taking turns to play and watch the others play while they wait—the *Mario Party* (Hudson Soft, 1999) series, for example, encourages this type of play (see Newman, 2004).

While many multiplayer games have a strong competitive focus, there is also considerable cooperation between players that can be understood only in the context of the situation. For example, in multiplayer games knowledge and information are shared between players in the process of play through observation—and experience—of new tactics. Similar information can be "researched" using digital game paratexts and online communities. This knowledge exchange may be facilitated by cooperation—one player looking up instructions on an online FAQ while giving instructions to another who manipulates the controller—or may involve a more direct mentorship, as a more experienced player leads another through a difficult part of the game. The process by which players learn from one another is described as the exchange of "gaming capital" (Consalvo, 2007; Sotamaa, 2010a; Walsh & Apperley, 2008, 2009).

It is from the situated perspective that the ergodic (games-as-action) and textual (games-as-text) modes of engagement intertwine and feed back into each other. The three dimensions—action, design, and situation—that organize the games-as-action layer of the model intersect with, overlap, and mutually constitute each other.

GAMES-AS-TEXT

Bringing a textual approach to bear provides a mode of connecting digital games, and the actions players take within them, to the wider world. Hayes and Gee (2010) observe, "Game literacy is itself multiple, embedded in different practices and fully *socioculturally situated*. Game literacy does not have one effect, but gives rise to different skills, values, and attitudes in different contexts" (p. 67; emphasis added). The role of the games-as-text layer of the model is to situate digital games in wider contexts: the classroom, students' out-of-school experiences, even world events. The games-as-text layer also fleshes out a spectrum of literacy and learning outcomes that are intimately related to context. Steinkuehler (2006, 2007, 2010), for example, demonstrates how in-game play in massively multiplayer online games develops and relies on a "constellation" of literacy practices. However, a quite different constellation is required in playing first-person shooter games such as *Counterstrike* in an Internet café (Beavis & Charles, 2007) or fantasy sports games such as *AFL Supercoach* (Gutierrez & Beavis, 2010) or fantasy baseball (Halverson & Halverson, 2008). Furthermore, following the New Literacies Studies tradition (e.g., Corio, Knobel, Lankshear, & Leu, 2008), this layer of the model explores the role of the multimodal meaning-making taking place in the digital game text in the formation of values, identity, and community.

To connect new literacies frameworks for understanding digital and out-of-school literacies with conventional iterations of literacy as presented in state and national curriculum documents, the games-as-text layer maps four foci for study in relation to the model of gameplay outlined in the games-as-action layer. The games-as-text layer also calls on and presupposes a "3D" view of literacy (Green, 1999; Durrant & Green, 2000) that "thinks together" literacy and technology (Green, 1999, pp. 42–43) and requires attention to "cultural," "critical," and "operational" dimensions of language use (pp. 43–44) in relation to digital games and game play. The four foci addressed in this layer are

- Knowledge about games
- The world around the game
- "Me" as a game player
- Learning through games

Each focus traces a trajectory from the immediacy of game play to the world outside the game, providing teachers and practitioners different segues between the unofficial knowledges of out-of-school literacy practices and the demands of the literacy curriculum. The four foci act as lenses or vectors that reciprocally illuminate—and are illuminated by—the model of game play presented in the games-as-action layer. The active experience of play, described in the games-as-action layer, is in the model's center.

KNOWLEDGE ABOUT GAMES

While attending to and historicizing narrative and aesthetic aspects of digital game play the key role of the "knowledge about games" focus is to bring critical literacy perspectives to bear on digital games and game play, to consider digital games as cultural artifacts and the aesthetic and technological forms that have emerged. This requires a balanced approach that recognizes that digital games are not simply "remediated" versions of related forms—film, literature, or television—while still acknowledging the "family resemblances" between digital games and previous media forms. Crucially, digital games draw on intertextual knowledge to build narratives across forms and platforms; not simply a matter of branding, digital games also pioneered transmedia storytelling, using more than one medium to deliver a narrative (for example, *The Matrix* film series and *Enter the Matrix* digital game) (see Jenkins, 2006).

For example, a curriculum that focuses on a digital game's narrative structures and features might trace the relation between the game and narratives from other "texts" (e.g., the narrative of the novel *Lord of the Rings* could be compared with the narrative presented in the film trilogy, or in the series of games that accompanied the films *The Fellowship of the Ring*, *The Two Towers*, and *Return of the King*). Using digital games in curriculum in this manner calls on and develops students' multimodal understanding of the characteristics and features of the relevant genre—in this case, fantasy—by examining how those generic features are used, and to what effect, across different mediums. Burn (2005), for example, describes how the "same" scene from the Harry Potter book, film, and digital game—Harry's encounter with the giant spider Aragog—changes across genres and discusses children's commentary on the differences they found. He explores such questions as how a particular image or narrative moment "translates" across different media, what "character" means in the context of a game, and how the "verb" differs in the interactive medium of the digital game.

"ME" AS GAME PLAYER

This focus encourages reflexivity about oneself as a games player and includes attention to issues of value, ideology, and identity and how players are positioned by the game. Bradford (2010) notes, "When young people play video games they do so as embodied subjects whose identities are shaped by the cultures in which they are situated, the circumstances of their lived experience, and the particularities of their dispositions, abilities and interests" (p. 54). This focus centers exploration on students' involvement with digital games as players, creators, and "readers," with the goal of critical reflection about practices of play. This consideration of play with known and unknown others can springboard into an examination of representations of self and others, of how these representations are constructed and interpreted through visual means and also through values, voice, and competencies as revealed through play.

Topics for exploration include analysis of how the player is positioned by the game, the ways texts seek to draw players into implied subject positions, and how they take up or resist that positioning. Curriculum dealing with this focus asks students to think through how they are positioned in digital games: How do games such as *Sid Meier's Civilization* (Microprose Software, 1991) position expansion and development? How is race and gender represented in the game? How are relations with other players framed by the ways that the game allows them to interact? Bradford (2010), for example, describes an ambiguous relationship with her avatar in *World of Warcraft*, characterized by a mix of identification invited through the second person form of address with which she is greeted and pragmatism, given her novice status and relative lack of skill within the game.

THE WORLD AROUND THE GAME

The primary concern of this focus is with the broader local and global contexts where game play takes place, and how the world around the game influences play. Areas for study include the exploration of a range of contexts for play, such as physical and virtual spaces, public and private settings, settings shared with others or experienced alone, differences in geographic locations and time zones in online gaming, and how context shapes relationships, interactions, and play. This focus also underscores contexts and influences such as marketing and globalization; the place and effect of advertising and convergence and participatory culture (Jenkins, 2006). Debates with students about media panics—addiction, "mind change" (see Metherall, 2011), violence—can be undertaken within this focus, allowing the exploration of the terms and assumptions underlying much of the reportage and an evaluation of the basis and evidence for these claims.

Paratexts have a particular bearing in this focus and may provide practitioners with a useful starting point for curriculum development. Consalvo's (2007; see also Newman, 2008) account of how the players' use of paratexts shapes game play also illustrates how player-designed paratexts contribute to the experiences of other players. Paratexts demonstrate the collaborative processes that take place in game play and, by cataloging the routes, combinations, and tactics available to the players, the complexity and detail of the digital game "text."

LEARNING THROUGH GAMES

Studies in this focus are qualitatively different from those in the other three foci, although like all four foci this focus overlaps with others, with curriculum and pedagogy likely to be spread across a number of areas. This focus is particularly concerned with the capacity of games to teach or impart information through what Bogost (2007) describes as "procedural rhetoric." It includes game-supported learning in curriculum areas, both through digital games specifically designed for education and the use of commercial, off-the-shelf digital games. Attention here is on both the specific curricular knowledge and understandings fostered through particular games, and on developing players' increased awareness of meta-cognitive strategies and processes. An important dimension here is the development of critical perspectives on both games and the social issues and problems they illuminate. Much of the "serious games" literature and research addresses this area, raising questions about the nature of curricular knowledge, the design features of games that enable specific kinds of understandings, the role of the teacher and the place of reflection in the spaces around games, constructions of learning and the learner, and the learner's relationship with the game.

Curriculum addressing this focus might trace rhetorical strategies across a number of digital games, starting with serious games that put forward a specific agenda and then using the recognition that digital games can have an agenda to examine the ideological assumptions of commercial off-the-shelf digital games. Teachers and practitioners could also highlight the different knowledges that quasi-educational games such as the *Sid Meier's Civilization* series allow players to engage with. On one level the games provide basic encyclopedia/Wikipedia style entries on various aspects of history from aqueducts to Leonardo's workshop. However, this is not the only literacy practice being developed, because the game also requires that the players develop a thorough understanding of the operation of its algorithm. It is in the latter area that teachers and practitioners can make the most useful intervention as the utility of these literacies is not readily apparent to students, unlike the encyclopedia entries which can be more readily accommodated into official forms of knowledge, yet are periphery to the literacies involved in the playing—and succeeding in—*Sid Meier's Civilization* series.

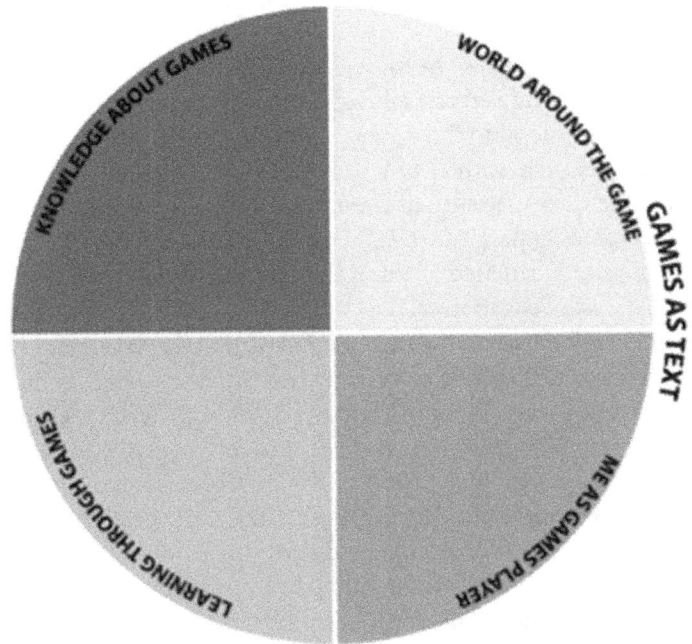

Fig 4.2. Games-As-Text.

THE MODEL IN COMBINATION

In linking together games and literacy in the way we propose, it is clear that significant commonalities, links, and overlaps exist between the two layers of the model. However, each layer also works individually. In both layers the constituent elements or foci are integrally related to each other, so that both within and between the layers the categories we introduce need to be conceived as mutually influential.

In any given iteration of the model, foci within and across both layers will interact in varying ways.

The model is intended to provide a framework for planning games-based curriculum and pedagogy, and arises from a mapping of characteristic features of digital games and game play. A number of elements are held in common. Key concepts across both layers are context, situatedness, and design. The importance of *context* and purpose in language learning and the role of context in shaping the construction of meaning have long been central tenets of English and literacy curriculum theory, with the view of literacy as socially situated practice well established in New Literacies scholarship, with respect to both older forms of literacy—reading, speaking, listening, and writing—and in new media and digital culture, including digital games (Gee, 2003; Lankshear & Knobel, 2007).

Situatedness also bridges the layers. Gee (2008a) notes that game play, like literacy itself, is primarily a *situated* form of knowledge. When developing literacy practices, students respond to the variance and demands of the particular situation, and situated factors such as their peer group, access to equipment, classroom, and teacher will shape the experience of learning as much as the material that is being learned. Digital gaming parallels this; the virtual experience of game play is always enacted in a physically situated location that may be characterized by affordances just as much as it is by constraints.

Design is a familiar term in the theorization of multimodal literacy (Kress, 2003; New London Group, 1996). In the proposed model, design embraces several crucial and related meanings and bridges across both levels, related to digital games conceived both primarily in terms of text and primarily in terms of action. The synthesis provided by Gee (2003, p. 49) between literacy and digital games foregrounds the centrality of design in both fields: "[in playing games] learning about and coming to appreciate design and design principles is core to the learning experience." As a term, *design* is both noun and verb; it describes the relationship between meaning-making elements on a screen or page and action—the process of designing as a creative activity, with multimodal literacy reconceptualised as *design*.

Yet there are important differences, too. Key among them is the recognition, in layer one, of those aspects outside a player's control and the active role that is played by the machine, the algorithms, and other elements of game play. The games-as-action layer maps the interrelationships in how digital games are played. This guide for developing curriculum mirrors students' out-of-school experiences of game play. The games-as-action layer insists strongly that digital games should not be conceived in primarily textual ways. The games-as-text layer differs in its text-based take on digital games and acts as a template for curriculum planning and pedagogy with digital games within contemporary curriculum guidelines.

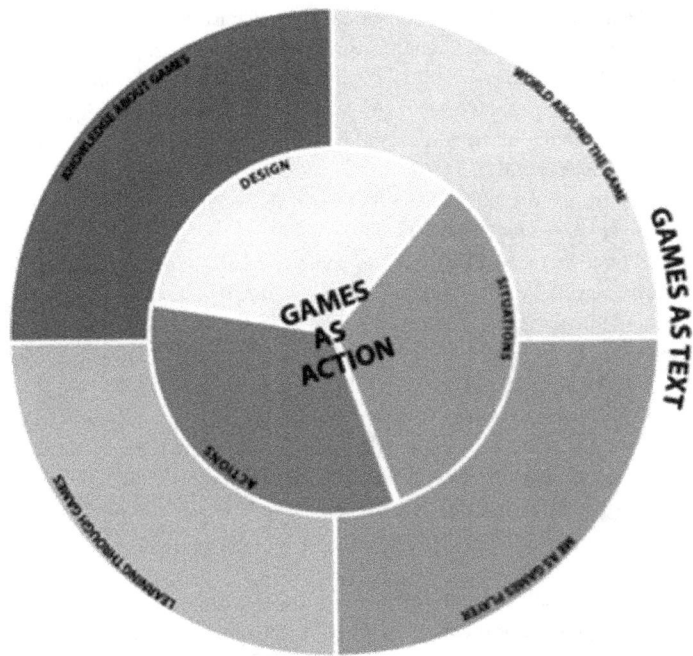

Fig 4.3. The Model in Combination.

It is our view that both layers are essential and that they speak to each other in multiple ways. Different contexts, classrooms, students, and curriculum mandates will result in the model being used to produce classroom activities that both respect those parameters and reflect young people's out-of-school experiences of digital games and game play.

REFERENCES

5th Cell. (2008). *Lock's quest* [Video Game]. Australia: THQ.

Aarseth, E. (1997). *Cybertext: Perspectives in ergodic literature*. Baltimore: Johns Hopkins University Press.

Amblin Entertainment. (2008). *Boom blox* [Video Game]. Australia: Electronic Arts.

Apperley, T. (2010). *Gaming rhythms: Play and counterplay from the situated to the global*. Amsterdam: Institute of Network Cultures.

Apperley, T., & Beavis, C. (2011). Literacy into action: Digital games as action and text in the English and literacy classroom. *Pedagogies 5*(2), 130–143.

Atkins, B. (2006). What are we really looking at? The future-orientation of video game play. *Games and Culture*, *1*(2), 127–140.

Beavis, C., & Charles, C. (2007). Would the "real" girl gamer please stand up? Gender, LAN cafes and the reformulation of the "girl" gamer. *Gender and Education*, *19*(6), 691–705.

Bioware. (2003). *Star wars: Knights of the Old Republic* [Video Game]. USA: LucasArts.

Bioware. (2009). *Dragon age: Origins* [Video Game]. Australia: Electronic Arts.
Bioware. (2010). *Mass effect 2* [Video Game]. Australia: Electronic Arts.
Blizzard Software. (2004). *World of Warcraft* [Video Game]. Australia: Blizzard Software.
Bogost, I. (2007). *Persuasive games: The expressive power of videogames.* Cambridge: MIT Press.
Bradford, C. (2010). Looking for my corpse: Video games and player positioning. *Australian Journal of Language and Literacy, 33*(1), 54–64.
Buckingham, D., & Burn, A. (2007) Game literacy in theory and practice. *Journal of Educational Multimedia and Hypermedia, 18*(3), 323–349.
Burn, A. (2005). Potter-literacy—From book to game and back again: Literature, film, game and cross-media literacy. *Papers: Explorations into Children's Literature, 14*(3), 5–17.
Coiro, J., Knobel, M., Lankshear, C., & Leu, D. J. (2008). Central issues in new literacies and new literacies research. In J. Coiro, M. Knobel, C. Lankshear, & D. J. Leu (Eds.), *Handbook of New Literacies Research* (pp. 1–22). Mahwah, NJ: Erlbaum.
Consalvo, M. (2007). *Cheating: Gaining advantage in video games.* Cambridge: MIT Press.
Durrant, C., & Green, B. (2000). Literacy and the new technologies in school education: Meeting the l(IT)eracy challenge? *Australian Journal of Language and Literacy, 23*(2), 89–108.
Flynn, B. (2003). Geographies of the digital hearth. *Information, Communication and Society, 6*(4), 551–576.
Galloway, A. (2006). *Gaming: Essays in algorithmic culture.* Minneapolis: University of Minnesota Press.
Games, I., & Squire, K. (2008). Design thinking in Gamestar Mechanic: The role of gamer experience on the appropriation of the discourse practices of game designers. In *Proceedings of the 8th International Conference for the Learning Sciences* (pp. 257–264). Utrecht: International Society of the Learning Sciences.
Gee, J. P. (2003). *What video games have to teach us about learning and literacy.* New York: Palgrave Macmillan.
Gee, J. P. (2008a). Learning and games. In K. Salen (Ed.), *The ecology of games: Reconnecting youth, games and learning* (pp. 21–40). Cambridge: MIT Press.
Gee, J. P. (2008b). Video games and embodiment. *Games and Culture 3*(3–4), 253–263.
Gee, J. P., & Hayes, E. R. (2010). *Women and gaming: The Sims and 21st century learning.* New York: Palgrave Macmillan.
Green, B. (1999). The new literacy challenge? *Literacy Learning: Secondary Thoughts, 7*(1), 36–46.
Gosling, V. K., & Crawford, G. (2011). Game scenes: Theorizing digital game audiences. *Games and Culture, 6*(2), 135–154.
Gutierrez, A., & Beavis, C. (2010). "Experts on the field": Redefining literacy boundaries. In D. Alvermann (Ed.), *Adolescents' online literacies: Connecting classrooms, digital media and popular culture* (pp. 145–162). New York: Peter Lang.
Halverson, E., & Halverson, R. (2008). Fantasy baseball: The case for competitive fandom. *Games and Culture, 3*(3–4), 286–308.
Hayes, E., & Games, I. (2008). Making computer games and design thinking. *Games and Culture, 3*(3–4), 309–322.
Hayes, E., & Gee, J. P. (2010). No selling the genie lamp: A game-literacy practice in the Sims. *E–Learning and Digital Media, 7*(1), 67–78.
Hsu, H., & Wang, S. (2010). Using gaming literacies to cultivate new literacies. *Simulation & Gaming, 41*(3), 400–417.
Hudson Soft. (1999). *Mario Party* [Video Game]. USA: Nintendo.
Intelligent Systems/Nintendo. (2010). *Wario Ware D.I.Y.* [Video Game]. Australia: Nintendo.

Jenkins, H. (2006). *Convergence culture: Where old and new media collide.* New York: New York University Press.
Jewett, C. (2008). Multimodality and literacy in school classrooms. *Review of Research in Education, 32*(1), 241–267.
Kress, G. (2003). *Literacy in the new media age.* London: Routledge.
Lankshear, C., & Knobel, M. (2007). *A new literacies sampler.* New York: Peter Lang.
Maxis. (1989). *SimCity* [Video Game]. USA: Brøderbund.
Maxis. (2000). *The Sims* [Video Game]. USA: Electronic Arts.
Metherall, M. (2011, July 14). Web weaves its effect on young brains. *The Age.* Retrieved from http://www.theage.com.au/technology/technology-news/web-weaves-its-effect-on-young-brains-20110713-1hdx9.html
Microprose Software. (1991). *Sid Meier's Civilization* [Video Game]. USA: MicroProse.
Mojang. (2009). *Minecraft* [Video Game]. Sweden: Mojang.
New London Group. (1996). A pedagogy of multiliteracies: Designing social futures. *Harvard Educational Review, 66*(1). Retrieved from http://wwwstatic.kern.org/filer/blogWrite44Manila Website/paul/articles/A_Pedagogy_of_Multiliteracies_Designing_Social_Futures.htm
Newman, J. (2004). *Videogames.* London: Routledge.
Newman, J. (2008). *Playing with videogames.* London: Routledge.
Nintendo (2008). *Mario Kart Wii* [Video Game]. Australia: Nintendo.
Obsidian Entertainment. (2010). *Fallout: New Vegas* [Video Game]. Australia: Namco Bandai Games.
OECD/CERI. (2009). *The new millennium learners: Main findings.* OECD Paris: Centre for Educational Research and Innovation (CERI), Directorate for Education, OECD.
Office of Educational Technology. (2010). *Transforming American education: Learning powered by technology.* Washington: U.S. Department of Education.
Pargman, D., & Jakobsson, P. (2008). Do you believe in magic? Computer games in everyday life. *European Journal of Cultural Studies, 11*(2), 225–244.
Pelletier, C. (2008). Gaming in context: How young people construct their gendered identities in playing and making games. In Y. B. Kafai, C. Heeter, J. Denner, & J. Y. Sun (Eds.), *Beyond Barbie and Mortal Kombat: New perspectives on gender and gaming* (pp. 145–159). Cambridge: MIT Press.
Peppler, K., & Kafai, Y. B. (2007). What video game making can teach us about learning and literacy: Alternative pathways into participatory culture. In A. Baba (Ed.), *Situated play: Proceedings of the Third International Conference of the Digital Games Research Association* (pp. 369–376). Tokyo: University of Tokyo.
Quantic Dream. (2010). *Heavy rain* [Video Game]. Australia: Sony Computer Entertainment.
Richards, J., & O'Mara, J. (in press). A blank slate: Using game maker to create computer games. In C. Beavis, L. McNeice, & J. O'Mara (Eds.), *Digital games: Literacy in action.* Adelaide: Wakefield Press.
Rockstar North. (2004). *Grand Theft Auto: San Andreas* [Video Game]. Australia: Rockstar Games.
Rockstar North. (2008). *Grand Theft Auto IV* [Video Game]. Australia: Rockstar Games.
Salen, K. (2007). Gaming literacies: A game design study in action. *Journal of Educational Multimedia and Hypermedia, 16*(3), 301–322.
Salen, K. (2008a). Towards and an ecology of gaming. In K. Salen (Ed.), *The ecology of games: Reconnecting youth, games and learning* (pp. 1–17). Cambridge: MIT Press.
Salen, K. (Ed.). (2008b). *The ecology of games: Reconnecting youth, games and learning* (pp. 1–17). Cambridge: MIT Press.

Sotamaa, O. (2010a). Achievement unlocked: Rethinking gaming capital. In O. Sotamaa & T. Karppi (Eds.), *Gaming as services: Final report* (pp. 73–81). Tampere: University of Tampere.

Sotamaa, O. (2010b). Play, create, share? Console gaming, player production and agency. *The Fibreculture Journal, 16*. Retrieved from http://sixteen.fibreculturejournal.org/play-create-share-console-gaming-player-production-and-agency/

Steinkuehler, C. (2006). The mangle of play. *Games and Culture, 1*(3), 199–213.

Steinkuehler, C. (2007). Massive multiplayer online gaming as a constellation of literacy practices. *ELearning 4*(3), 297–318.

Steinkuehler, C. (2010). Video games and digital literacies. *Journal of Adolescent & Adult Literacy 54*(1), 61–63.

Stevens, R., Satwicz, T., & McCarthy, L. (2008). In-game, in-room, in-world: Reconnecting videogames to the rest of kids' lives. In K. Salen (Ed.), *The ecology of games: Reconnecting youth, games and learning* (pp. 41–66). Cambridge: MIT Press.

Taylor, T. L. (2006). *Play between worlds: Exploring online game culture*. Cambridge: MIT Press.

Taylor, T. L. (2009). The assemblage of play. *Games and Culture, 4*(4), 331–339.

Ubisoft Montreal. (2009). *Assassin's creed II* [Video Games]. Australia: Ubisoft.

Walsh, C. S. (2010). Systems-based literacy practices: Digital games research, gameplay and design. *Australian Journal of Language and Literacy, 33*(1), 24–40.

Walsh, C., & Apperley, T. (2008). Researching digital game players: Gameplay and gaming capital. In Y. Xiao & E. Ten Thij (Eds.), *Proceedings of IADIS International Conference Gaming 2008: Design for engaging experience and social interaction* (pp. 99–102). Amsterdam: IADIS.

Walsh, C., & Apperley, T. (2009). Gaming capital: Rethinking literacy. In P. Jeffrey (Ed.), *Changing climates: Education for sustainable futures. Proceedings of the 2008 AARE*. Coldstream, Victoria: Australian Association for Research in Education (AARE).

Wardrup-Fruin, N. (2009). *Expressive processing: Digital fictions, computer games, and software studies*. Cambridge: MIT Press.

Westbrook, N. (2011). Media literacy pedagogy: Critical and new/twenty-first-century literacies instruction. *E-Learning and Digital Media, 8*(2), 154–164.

Zimmerman, E. (2009). Gaming literacy: Game design as a model for literacy in the 21st century. In B. Perron & M. J. P. Wolf (Eds.), *The video game theory reader 2* (pp. 23–31). New York: Routledge.

CHAPTER FIVE

Enabling Students to Be Effective Multimodal Authors

PAUL D. CHANDLER

INTRODUCTION

This chapter draws on the experiences arising out of a research project to develop students as effective 3D multimodal authors (Chandler, O'Brien, & Unsworth, 2009, 2010), referred to here as the 3D Multimodal Authoring Pedagogy (3DMAP) project,[1] involving 44 teachers and their classes. A set of lesson materials was prepared for these classes, and this chapter is based on my experience of developing those. The 3DMAP project involved particular software in particular classroom settings, and my intention in this chapter is to use that experience to inform the teaching of multimodal authoring more generally, which is important with the creation of multimodal texts now clearly featuring in the domain of literacy educators (e.g., ACARA, 2012). The following questions for discussion indicate some key issues taken up in the chapter:

1. What are some of the features of a classroom that embeds twenty-first-century understandings of literacy?
2. In what ways does knowledge of multimodal design elements help shape the pedagogy, curriculum, and assessment of multimodal authoring?
3. What is the nature of the relationship between teacher and student that is likely to best scaffold students as multimodal authors, and in what ways will this be evident in the teacher's activity in the classroom?

Walsh (2011) defines multimodality as "a study of the communicative process, particularly how meaning is communicated through different semiotic or meaning-making resources and in different social contexts" (p. 105). The emphasis in this chapter is the student as the originator, designer, and producer of such texts.

In the 3DMAP project "3D authoring" meant using computer software to do the kinds of things that would otherwise be done using live-action filmmaking. That is, the author must "construct" and "film" in a virtual space that involves considerations of length, breadth, depth, and the passage of time, and use the 3D space effectively to convey meaning. Authors/creators must take on various roles such as director, cinematographer, and location scout; they must select objects and locate them in a virtual 3D space and have ways of specifying their activity. The end result is video footage.

The core idea expressed in this chapter is that to effectively make meaning using any multimodal technologies involves not a grab bag of effects that seem to work, but embracing an organisational framework for systematic meaning-making. A suitable framework will not only identify *what* seems to work, but will systematically identify *why* and will provide a metalanguage to enable discussion and collaboration of the why and the what. "Grammatical design" is presented as that framework. Alongside that I identify the importance of teacher attitude, engagement, and deliberate action in structuring suitable learning experiences. We commence with an explication of "grammatical design."

GRAMMATICAL DESIGN

The use of the word *grammar* here is not in the sense of rules or a general sense of "proper English." Rather, as Collerson (1997) explains,

> a language like English (or indeed any language) offers a rich array of resources for making meaning, including words, other structures and the principles by which we select and arrange them to realise our purposes in using language. Grammar is the central organising system for all the meaning-making resources in a language, and it really consists of a series of options—a system of choices for making meaning. (p. 2)

In contrast to "traditional grammar," Halliday's functional grammar (Halliday, 1978, Halliday & Matthiessen, 2004)

> [begins] with the social context, because this is the basis for the functions of language and their associated meanings. A functional grammar accounts for how these are realised in texts through the choice of grammatical structures and vocabulary. (Collerson, 1997, p. 25)

Too often in the production of multimodal texts, teachers (possibly those who are not especially technologically literate) become excited when their students produce *anything*—and thus emphasize the *what* and the *how* of the production and overlook the *why*. To focus on grammatical design is to reemphasize the why, seeking to harness the resources available to make meaning for a particular social purpose (Unsworth, 2001).

In addition to the overall social purpose of a text, grammatical design helps us attend to how the various design elements (also referred to as *codes*) that are available can be combined with the conventions to make meaning, and thus focus on the how. In relation to still images—the framework on which ideas of the moving image can build—Kress and van Leeuwen (2001/2006) observe that "just as grammars of language describe how words combine into clauses, sentences and texts, so our visual 'grammar' will describe the way in which depicted people, places and things combine in visual 'statements' of greater or lesser complexity and extension" (p. 1). Thus the term *grammar* extends beyond the written word. Some design elements and conventions in relation to the mode of still images, as discussed by Anstey and Bull (2006), are shown in Table 5.1.

Table 5.1. Design Elements and Conventions in Still Images Combine to Make Meaning (Anstey & Bull, 2006, p. 108)

The design elements of	are combined through	the conventions of	to make meaning
• Colour • Texture • Shape • Form		• Balance among design elements • Layout (how attention is attracted and focused) • Vectorality (how the eye is led through the image)	

In the case of multimodal texts, the author needs to understand how linguistic, visual, spatial, gestural, and audio resources can be ordered and structured to make meaning. An explicit understanding of the design elements and conventions available and how these may be combined to make meaning is the cornerstone of what it takes to enable students to be effective multimodal authors. This is introduced for 3D multimodal texts in the following section.

To focus on grammatical design is to attend to the particulars of meaning-making, how the available modes are comprised and how they can be orchestrated to make meaning. Data from the 3DMAP project (Chandler, 2012, 2013) clearly indicate that the more specific the element, the less knowledgeable students claimed to be about it (compare a strong knowledge of genres with a poor knowledge of camera angles). The same seemed to be true for teachers. And so the first argument in favor of a "grammatical design" approach is that explicit understanding of how to orchestrate the design elements to make meaning is an important prerequisite for quality work, and that this does not come naturally.

A second reason for a focus on grammatical design is that teaching the systems of options for meaning-making gives students access to multimodal text analysis as a tool for critical multimedia literacy (Kellner & Share, 2007). To focus on the grammatical is to introduce a metalanguage incorporating terms such as *genre, social purpose, stage, design elements, conventions, color, line, balance, vectorality,* and so on—to have a common language to converse about the choices made, what alternatives might have been chosen, and the effects, therefore, of particular choices. A number of studies have demonstrated that explicit teaching of grammatical knowledge has benefited literacy development (Quinn, 2004; Schleppegrell, 2004; Torr & Harman, 1997; Williams, 2000). In the context of students' use of animation and digital video (Burn & Durran, 2006; Burn & Leach, 2004; Burn & Parker, 2003), when grammatical design was taught, students made sophisticated commentaries on their movie texts.

Having introduced the central theme of this chapter, grammatical design, and argued in favour of an explicit teaching of it, I now turn to describing the design elements available to the 3D multimodal author as a prelude to describing a pedagogy of 3D multimodal authoring.

GRAMMATICAL DESIGN APPLIED TO 3D MULTIMODAL AUTHORING

The author of 3D multimodal texts must orchestrate visual (still or moving image), linguistic (any handwritten or printed text which is present), audio (voice over or dialogue), audio (music and sound effects), spatial design, and gestural (body language, gesture, and choreography) modes. It is worth observing that teaching students to effectively orchestrate the full range of meaning in each of these modes is a deeply "literacy" experience and not necessarily the province of a literacy teacher alone, but could (and probably should) engage specialist expertise in a range of fields including music, drama, dance, and art.

While the focus of this chapter is to stress the *why* of multimodal authoring, in fact, the *what* can only be realized through particular tools. Furthermore, the *what* is shaped, to some extent, by the functionality and capabilities of the tool. Therefore, what this section does is to identify the design elements that are made possible within the 3D multimodal authoring environment Kahootz (Edgar, 2006; Maggs, 2008), but in a way that would readily transfer to other products currently in the marketplace[2] and attend to the systems of choices that are enduring. These systems of choices would also be applicable to the production of "video" texts through techniques such as live action filming, stop-motion animation, or claymation. Some resources and exemplars from the 3DMAP project are available at http://creatingmultimediatexts.com and other repositories and examples are available from http://www.muvizu.com (especially the "gallery" and "moguls" sections) and http://www.alice.org.

A 3D multimodal text is presented and developed as a series of *scenes*. The author selects one of many *worlds* (or *sets*) on which this scene is then further developed. It is possible to move through the world and thus choose a different *location* from the initial one. Furthermore, it is possible to re-colour and re-texture (i.e., *swatch*) elements of the chosen world. Indeed, it is possible to achieve some startling results, for instance, when what initially appears as lush grasslands can be re-colored to be a sparse desert. This can be complemented by effects such as those of *lighting* (with varying colour and direction) and *fog* (with varying color and intensity).

Each scene can be populated with a range of *objects*, which can be selected from the extensive built-in library. The object can be *resized*, have its *proportions* changed, and aspects of each object can be *re-swatched*. Thus, the author must choose how to populate the world, a task that embraces *set-dressing*, *props*, and *characters*. Included within this are decisions about how the objects are *physically positioned*, as it would be possible to have these (appear to) float in midair or be (partially) buried in the ground. Furthermore, there are choices related to the *arrangement* of these objects—showing a group of characters who are looking at each other to represent a conversation, for instance. Objects can be *animated*—that is, caused to perform built-in actions or move from one location to another.

In addition to adding visual objects to a scene, *audio* can be added. Some 3D multimodal authoring software products contain an extensive library of sound effects and the capacity for manipulation by specifying volume, pitch, echo, tremolo, and duration. The audio mode, therefore, is a design element alongside choice of world, physical positioning, swatching, etc.

From all of this, it is clear there are choices in relation to "creating the world"—design elements related to the following three categories of meaning:

- Setting and location (embracing design elements related to selection and swatching a set, identifying a location, adding various objects as set dressing, choosing lighting and special effects, and including background sound effects or music)
- Participant selection and construction (embracing design elements related to selection, swatching and sizing participants, and including dialogue)
- Arrangements and interaction of participants (embracing design elements relating to the positioning of participants, the eye lines, and gestures used)

Hallidayan linguistics (Halliday & Matthiessen, 2004) describes three systems of meaning through which the overall meaning of a text is constituted: representational/ideational, interactive/interpersonal, and compositional/textual. In the application of these ideas to multimodal texts, key references are Kress and van Leeuwen (2001/2006) concerning the still image, van Leeuwen (1996) concerning the moving image, and van Leeuwen (1999) concerning the auditory modes, and these are recommended to the reader for reference and extension reading.

The representational/ideational system is concerned with "communicating ideas related to the nature of events, the objects and participants involved and the circumstances in which they occur" (Unsworth, 2001, p. 18). The author needs to find ways of communicating to the viewer: What is it about? Who is it about? When did it happen? What does it say symbolically? "Creating the world" is principally associated with these systems of meanings. Halliday's work stresses that text is constructed for a social purpose and meaning-making conventions are socially constructed. For instance, black is the color of death in some cultures, whereas white carries that value in others; red conveys good fortune and joy in some cultures but does not have that same emphasis in others. When making decisions about re-coloring and swatching, the multimodal author needs to be aware of, and sensitive to, this level of detail in the codes used. Similarly, size, shape, proportions, clothing, and hairstyle of characters will communicate important information, but again care must be taken to avoid ambiguous interpretation. Whereas once a portly appearance may have signified wealth, it may now be interpreted as lack of health or disinterest in personal care. There are choices of colour, props, clothing, and location that will situate the text in a particular time of day, season, or era. Special effects such as fog can be used and may variously signify a spooky environment or evening closing in. Animation is also important to communicate certain meanings in this system: If the intention is to convey the meaning of "suddenly, a train rushed past, disrupting the quiet bushland," then the author might animate a train and some event such as a koala falling from a tree. Through the apparently simple acts of "creating the world" the visual language can richly communicate ideational meanings.

In addition to "creating the world," the author is engaged with making choices in relation to how that world is shown to the viewer. Five categories of meaning can be identified through which the viewing experience can be understood, arising from *camera use*. The categories of meaning relating to this are the following:

- Sequencing of information (design elements that influence the order and the pace in which the information is presented)
- Viewer stance (that is, decisions relating to point of view)
- Camera distance (that is, to convey meaning related to social distance, and the use of the camera to hide or reveal information)
- The angles through which the information is seen (vertical camera angles conveying meaning related to social power, and horizontal camera angles conveying meaning related to involvement)
- The movement of the viewer with respect to that which is viewed

The terminology used here is slightly awkward in parts (e.g., "the angles through which visual information is seen") but this is deliberately used to emphasize that it is how the viewer perceives the visuals that is ultimately significant; it does not matter whether the author has achieved this effect by moving the camera or moving the participants. This emphasizes a more general point, which is that a one-to-one relationship between software function and design element should not be inferred (as shown later in Table 5.2). While there may be a most obvious construction technique, in nearly every case there are multiple ways of attending to each design element.

From the Hallidayan perspective, it is through camera work that the nature of relationships between the participants in the text and the viewers of the text is established—the interactive/interpersonal systems of meaning (Unsworth, 2001). Through the camera, the multimodal author has ways of constructing social distance, social power, and the extent to which the viewer is onlooker or participant, and by moving and relocating the camera these relationships change over the course of the text. These systems of meaning are potentially even more interrelated and subtle than "creating the world." For example, one might elevate the camera to glimpse a train rushing toward the participants from a distant location, but to do so may simultaneously imply a change of power relationship with a participant on whom the camera was previously directed. Throughout the 3DMAP project, we could say that richness in use of the camera was less frequently found than how the world was constructed and populated. Yet technically the camera is quite easy to use. It may be that *idea* in the stories of middle years students tend to be somewhat "flat" and unsophisticated in relation to interpersonal meaning. Providing for interesting use of the camera offers a challenge to the multimodal author to develop a richness in the interpersonal meanings being communicated.

Beyond camera work there are other approaches to constructing interpersonal meaning, but they are frequently restricted because of the capacity of the software or the skill of the student. For instance, Kahootz provided no capacity to lip-sync visuals with audio, and almost no capacity for facial expression or for controlling the direction of gaze. The capacity for gesture—particularly to convey emotion (e.g., anger, frustration, disinterest)—was extremely restricted, and the ability for certain complex actions (such as the hand of a character to be realistically shown to clasp an object) is almost impossible to achieve.

The eight categories of meaning described above can be considered as describing the minimum systems of choices through which a 3D multimodal text can be constructed. None are optional. For instance, it is not possible to construct a text that is not located somewhere (though it may be in a somewhat nondescript locality, era, or time of day) and the camera must necessarily be operating at a particular distance and angle. No active decision in relation to viewer stance may well result in a text that is seen through the eyes of a distanced, dispassionate observer, but to the viewer this is nevertheless important. Through these eight essential categories of meaning, grammatical design focuses the author on making deliberate decisions. We should now move to a discussion of suitable means for teaching about the decisions involved in constructing meaning—a pedagogy of multimodal authoring—but first we make a brief excursion to address the third of Halliday's systems of meaning, that of the compositional/textual metafunction.

"Compositional/textual meanings are concerned with the distribution of the information value or relative emphasis among the elements" (Unsworth, 2001, p. 18). Of the three Hallidayan systems of meaning, this is probably the most difficult to introduce to young multimodal authors. In visual texts, the other two are primarily associated with either "construction work" or "camera work," whereas this one is developed in a more integrated manner requiring a range of design elements, emphasizing that design elements are not stand-alone technical competencies, but their deployment serves to make meaning in a number of domains simultaneously. Simplistically put, compositional/textual meaning embraces two concepts: first, what linguists call *modality*, which (again, simplistically) attends to "truth value from the point of view of the author" (consider the subtle difference between the statements *he caught the ball* and *it could be said that he caught the ball*). Second, *composition* is how the various elements are integrated into a coherent whole. Kress and van Leeuwen (2001/2006) discuss in detail the use of color to portray modality and in particular color attributes such as saturation, depth, illumination, brightness—attributes that are deliberate choices of the painter or photographer, but not necessarily available for the young multimodal author, given the state of development of the software. For instance, the deliberate choice of using a photorealistic figure in a cartoony landscape "says something" about the believability of either set or character.

In visual texts the idea of composition is possibly easier to grasp. First, it is suggested that there are socially constructed conventions associated with how participants are placed with respect to one another, such as the placement of one participant to the left or right of another carries certain meaning, as is deliberately placing an object or participant in the centre or the periphery of the screen. Second, there are also visual techniques that highlight certain participants rather than others (salience) and the use of devices to connect different elements together (such as dressing all members of a family in the same shirt, or showing a group of people as friends by locating them close to each other and facing each other).

Through the preceding discussion, I have used the notion of grammatical design to identify eight essential categories of meaning for 3D multimodal authoring, and related these to the three Hallidayan systems of meaning. Some gaps in the capacity of current generation of multimodal authoring software have been noted, with particular implications for conveying interpersonal meaning, process, and emotion. The underlying theme is that a multimodal authoring enterprise should be focused primarily on the systems of meaning rather than simply on the software function. I now move to discuss a pedagogy of multimodal authoring that is designed to engage learners with the software function, the design elements, and the conventions simultaneously.

A PEDAGOGY OF MULTIMODAL AUTHORING

By *pedagogy* I mean "the function, work or art of a teacher; teaching" (Pedagogy, 2009). It would be possible to treat each design element in turn, along with the relevant conventions and the software functions that may be used to realize these. In addition, it is also important to consider how authors might be helped to create texts independently. I will first describe the influences on a multimodal authoring pedagogy, and then proceed to describe a teaching approach for both circumstances.

Table 5.2. Sample Relationship Between Software Functions and Design Elements

Software Function	Design Element	Examples
Keypointing and animation	Movement of characters	Movement, gestures, posture, gaze
	Movement of objects	Background movements simply to create life and rhythm
Placing object/characters to compose a scene	Zoom	Long, medium, or close-up shots to show social distance between viewer and characters
	Point of view	Aerial, high, low, eye-level camera angles, such as to show the subjects' degree of power
	Framing	What is included or excluded in the shot and use of empty space
Colour and swatching	Setting and props	Backgrounds, foregrounds, 2D and 3D forms, colour, texture, material, weight, size, stability, shape, contrast, and symmetry
Camera movement	Zoom	Long, medium, or close-up shots to show social distance between viewer and characters
	Point of view	Aerial, high, low, eye-level camera angles, such as to show the subjects' degree of power
	Framing	What is included or excluded in the shot and use of empty space

INFLUENCES ON TEACHING APPROACHES

The design element approach emphasizes that authors/creators need to develop a repertoire of design elements and the corresponding social purpose(s) of these; software functions are not the focus of attention, but the means by which the design elements are realised. Furthermore, it can be observed that there is not necessarily one software function for each design element, nor one design element for each software function, as illustrated in Table 5.2.

Suitable teaching approaches must introduce different design elements and ways of achieving them, and support the learner in negotiating how new elements or approaches may be integrated with existing knowledge. The learning of software functions can't be ignored, as there are sequences of action involved in operating the software that must become both routinized and associated with particular design elements. The objective is to construct learning experiences that emphasize the deep learning of the *what* and the *why*, and at the same time provide opportunities to explore, practice, and routinize the *how*. These insights reinforce the desirability of giving separate attention to each design element (or, more likely, each category of meaning), realizing that there will be multiple ways to advance meaning within each category.

Several frameworks have been influential in shaping both the pedagogy of text creation and multimodal literacies more generally. These include the Learning by Design framework of Cope and Kalantzis (2009), the teaching/learning (or genre pedagogy) cycle of Rothery (Martin & Rose, 2005), and the "four resource model" (Anstey, 2002; Freebody & Luke, 1990). Rothery's teaching/learning cycle is built around the following three phases (though, like the others, more nuanced and detailed than can be described in a few lines):

- Deconstruction: learning experiences are provided so that the students become familiar with the purpose, overall structure, and linguistic features of the text type they will be writing/creating
- Joint construction: the teacher and the students work together to create another example of the genre based on suggestions from students
- Independent construction: responsibility for text construction is handed over to the students to write a text of their own

The Learning by Design framework is concerned with the educational process writ large, which is conceived as one where all students' learning ventures are centred in the use or production of meaningful texts. They describe four processes that guide the teachers' creation of teaching/learning experiences:

- Experiencing: use students' existing knowledge and also immerse students in new experiences
- Conceptualising: classify things, form concepts, define terms, and build generalizations

- Analysing: explore cause, effect, relationship, motives, and interests
- Apply: apply this knowledge to new situations

While these frameworks were never intended to be combined as a single pedagogical approach, overall we can take from them several guiding principles, not the least of which is that independent construction of a text does not emerge without a number of precursor teaching/learning activities that scaffold the student into being equipped for this task. A suitable scaffolding sequence might therefore include the following that are reflected in the VDDDR teaching procedure (described later):

- Using existing texts to inform further learning experiences (including texts prepared by students themselves)
- Deconstruction of existing texts (starting with identification of semiotic codes and moving to making inferences)
- The teacher and the students work together in joint construction as a form of modeling how texts are created and codes used
- Student independent construction of texts

The frameworks mentioned above also emphasize the importance of use of text for a "real" communicative activity and not "for practice," and this is reflected in the instructional sequences described below. They also emphasize a critical understanding of text. This is not explicitly developed any further in this chapter, but in the pedagogical strategies outlined below teachers have considerable freedom in the choice of text and the extent of deconstruction and analysis to enable the pursuit of a critical analysis. What is developed in the next sections are approaches to pedagogy at the level of detail of what teachers "do."

INTRODUCING LEARNERS TO DESIGN ELEMENTS THROUGH VDDDR

The teaching procedure described in Table 5.3 introduces learners to multimodal authoring through the systematic treatment of design elements embodying the scaffolding described above. It consists of the phases of View, Deconstruct, Demonstrate, Do, and Reflect and can be referred to by the acronym VDDDR. It is a teaching procedure in the sense described by Loughran, Berry, and Mulhall (2006)—it is "not something which is done to break up the normal routine, but chosen because it enhances student learning of the ideas under consideration" (p. 2). In particular, the intention is to allow considerable time for students to be using the software (the Do phase), enable "serious play" (Rieber, 2001), routinize the sequences of action involved in operating the software, and create the mental association between *how* and *why* (Vérillon and Rabardel, 1995). In this teaching procedure there is no joint construction because the whole class does not work on a common retelling—to do so becomes too laborious.

Table 5.3. Teaching Procedure for Exploring Each Design Element

	View	A short film clip, chosen deliberately to exemplify certain design elements and conventions[3]
	Deconstruct	Review and understand how meanings have been made using certain design elements/conventions
	Demonstrate	The teacher models construction of an element (using the software of choice) that uses those design elements/conventions to create meaning. Joint construction with the class.
	Do	Students use the software to create meaning using the design elements and conventions demonstrated
	Reflect and Represent	Consider how effective each effort has been at creating meaning using these design elements/conventions; students have the opportunity to (re)present their work to the class for critique and encouragement; the class is therefore able to learn from one another and from the consideration of "real" student texts
Repeat this process for several pieces of work, each taking no more than a lesson to complete, which are cumulative in their complexity and deliberately scaffolding the learning in meaning-making and technical skills.		

This teaching procedure is intended to be the pattern for a single lesson of about 45 minutes in duration. Attention is given to building up knowledge of one design element—how to do it, how it serves to make meaning, and conventions associated with it—as a unified learning event. As a rule of thumb, each phase is 5 to 10 minutes long, but with the most time (25–40 minutes) given to the Do phase. The teaching procedure can be used to introduce a specific design element (such as the conventions related to the use of sound effects to convey atmosphere and mood) or a wider category of meaning that would embrace multiple design elements; the level of delicacy would depend on the learning needs of the class.

An example of how VDDDR can be enacted by a teacher is as follows, drawing on the resources developed for the 3DMAP project.

View

- Explain that the focus is the development of the main characters in the story. Discuss the importance of character in a story and how the writer takes care to convey to the audience who the character is and what he or she is like. Encourage students to refer back to the examples screened in previous lessons as well as characters in favorite books, films, TV shows, and video games.

- View a brief video that illustrates effective development of character, such as the video entitled *Persuasion* on http://creatingmultimediatexts.com.

Deconstruct

- Discuss the "personality" of the characters, particularly focusing on how they look and the movements of each of the characters. How do these animations communicate the personality of a character? What could *tall* mean? What could *thin* mean? What might *short* and *round* say about a character?
- Color, size, and shape also can be used to create meaning about characters. Discuss the use of shape and size in books and animations to create meaning about a character.
- Discuss and explore how students can use size and shape to communicate the information they want the audience to know about their character.

Demonstrate

- Refer to a sample character profile. Consider carefully what each character is like—gender, age, personality traits. What will each look like to achieve this: what color, size, or shape?
- Demonstrate adding a character to a scene. Explore the object library to come up with ideas for suitable characters, place the character in the scene correctly, change the size and proportions appropriately, and change color/swatch appropriately.

Do

- Referring to their own character profile, which has been prepared in an earlier class, students select, place, resize, and swatch one or more characters to both include them in the scene and "describe what they are like" (e.g., gender, age, personality traits).

Reflect

- Students demonstrate their work to the class, describing why they chose the above and how these add to the telling of their story. Highlight students who have taken particularly innovative approaches.
- All members of the class make suggestions as to how pieces could be improved.
- Summarise with observations of what students have learned about constructing characters using visual elements and why you need to consider these when telling a story.
- Students complete a written reflection about what they learned and how they think it will help them as a multimodal author.

With this teaching procedure as a core, it is important to understand the context of the lesson sequence in which it is embedded. In the 3DMAP project, our assumption was that learners knew nothing about design elements and needed to progress to a stage that they would know enough to independently construct an entire text. They were introduced to all eight core categories of meaning along with a planning and production process, over the course of about 14 lessons. The sequence is that described in Table 5.3, which served the dual purpose of introducing each of the design elements and being a reasonable escalation of the complexity of technical skills in Kahootz. (If a different software environment is selected, the teaching sequence may need to be adjusted.)

Repeated use of the teaching procedure supports the three inter-related learning objectives: (1) extend students' repertoires of design elements, (2) develop students' understanding of how to realize these, and (3) develop students' understanding and use of metalanguage, in a sense, adding to the "kit bag" of resources that students can use in the composition of multimodal texts. Throughout a lesson sequence, it is vital that students be engaged with a "real text" used for "real communication." In the 3DMAP project, students worked on a retelling of a simple four-line nursery rhyme ("Little Miss Muffet"). They needed to creatively characterize Miss Muffet and the spider; to consider location, time of day, season, era; and to use the camera to portray the relationships between the characters and between the viewer and the character. A four-line piece offered more than enough engagement for 14 lessons, and indeed allowed for many creative and insightful retellings, which were real texts for the students.

A 14-lesson sequence, though, was too long to sustain concentration and interest. Certainly, a "practice piece" needs to be short—the culminating video may be 30 seconds or less in duration, and a four-line rhyme is more than long enough. A scope-and-sequence plan over several years is really required, and this emphasizes that multimodal authoring needs to be fully planned for in a school curriculum, not a particular teacher's hobby one year and forgotten the next. For certain activities, teachers could use a pre-prepared and nearly complete text, and students could re-version the text by manipulating a small number of design elements: suitable practice tasks do not need to be student-built from the blank canvas up. The challenge in creating a lesson sequence is not in the core teaching procedure but in working out what can be safely assumed or omitted, identifying the text on which students will work, the exemplars that will be used, and the depth to which critical and social analysis will be expected.

It is worth noting that the higher-achieving classes in the 3DMAP project had at least several sessions specifically learning the software—the *what* in isolation before the *what/why* in conjunction. We can't say if this is a necessary condition for success or a practical response by those teachers to their circumstances (e.g., "My class is scheduled for the computer lab—how can I use those times effectively in the weeks before we start our multimodal text?"). The VDDDR teaching procedure would not be the only strategy that a teacher would use to effectively introduce learners to software and the design elements.

INDEPENDENT CONSTRUCTION OF A MULTIMODAL TEXT

I now consider fashioning a unit of work in which students independently construct a multimodal text. This is different from the practice text described above because the student is responsible for all phases of the development, including the idea or storyline. Whereas in introducing design elements, the teacher was doing a lot, the focus here is more on what the students will do. Therefore, we need to consider (a) a suitable production sequence, (b) the scaffolding required, and (c) the role of the teacher.

In the 3DMAP project, the production sequence described in Table 5.4 was devised. Its creation was a matter of structuring the students' attention to the design elements in a sensible order while taking into account the realities of the software environment. In Kahootz, it was not possible to backtrack and change the "prototype world" once objects or characters had been added to it, and thus attention to location was an essential first stage. Similarly, the recording of narration was cumbersome if attempted either too early or too late in the process. So the details of a production process will necessarily vary, depending on the software used.

Table 5.4. An Instructional Sequence for 3D Multimodal Authoring

Lesson 1	Pre-production	Story idea, story outline, and character profile
Lesson 2		Scriptwriting
Lesson 3		Storyboarding
Lesson 3	Production	Location, setting, and mood
Lesson 4		Characters, objects, and props
Lesson 5		Acting and animation
Lesson 6		Adding narration
Lesson 7		Camera framing
Lesson 8		Camera angles
Lesson 9		Camera movement
Lesson 10	Post-production	Finalising the "first cut"
Lesson 11		Sound effects
Lesson 12		Titles, credits, music, and the "final cut"
Lesson 13	Finalising	A screening of all texts as a "film festival"
Lesson 14		Evaluation of student work

This production sequence, while it looks linear, should not be interpreted strictly in that manner. For instance, authors/creators might loop back and revise character profiles (pre-production) when they are actually implementing characters and objects (production). The sequence identifies with the phases of film-creation (pre-production, production, post-production), and this helps scaffold students through what is otherwise a lengthy sequence in which they may become lost.

Throughout this production process, it is important to consider what each lesson looks like and what the role of the teacher is. The teacher has the management and planning roles that set up the process, establish the task, and efficiently move the students through the various phases. In some lessons, students will work in a largely self-managed way. But in the lessons in the pre-production and production phases, the VDDDR teaching procedure can provide the basic framework. The teacher chooses a design element to focus on—perhaps one in which the students need some revision or consolidation. Through the phases of View, Deconstruct, and Demonstrate, the student knowledge of a design element is reviewed, the components of the "kit bag" re-assessed, and the metalanguage reinforced. In the Do and Reflect phases, the students apply themselves to the development of their text at whatever stage they are up to.

Experience with the 3DMAP project has suggested several features of the pedagogy that will facilitate the successful independent construction of a multimodal text. These are as follows:

- A *reality check*: For the project to be manageable within the confines of (say) 20 hours of classroom work, it will be quite brief (e.g., 60 seconds in length) and will not be of the same production quality as would emerge from a professional animation studio. Primary age students will invariably imagine that they can, in under 20 hours, produce something of the same quality and level of interest as a commercial short that will have taken thousands of hours of development. While they can produce interesting work, there is necessarily a quality difference. Students need to be shown examples of what is possible and be provided with clear advice as to what would represent quality (i.e., assessment tools—see below—are part of the classroom discourse). In addition, it will be helpful to have a *design brief* to help scope their intentions.
- A *design brief* could include the following, possibly presented as a checklist for students:

  o Be an imaginative narrative, a complete story
  o Be no longer than 60–90 seconds in length (not including titles and credits)
  o Be contained within a single page script
  o Have no more than three central characters
  o Keep dialogue to a minimum (use *show* as well as *tell*—don't use dialogue to "tell" everything)
  o Pay attention to timing of shots
  o Connect the viewer to one or more characters at different times throughout the story (attention to point of view and use of camera angles and social distance)
  o Make use of the 3D nature of the environment
  o Consider the audience and have appropriate content (e.g., G rating for violence)

- *The engagement of the teacher in the work of the student is critical.* I have observed teachers taking quite an arm's length approach to student work, more focused on discipline than content, and not being closely engaged with the compositional work of each student. In contrast, in another class the teacher was heard to critique a particular student's work in the planning phases along the following lines: *I told you not to have three characters—you had difficulty completing the first story with two, you need to be much more focused. Go back and revise your story.* This might seem like a fairly blunt approach to teacher-student relations, but it is illustrative of that teacher's close engagement with each student's work. It is not too extreme to suggest that, particularly for inexperienced students, the texts are nearly co-written and developed with the teacher, and it is the teacher's responsibility to progressively loosen the apron strings.
- *Other strategies for scaffolding* efficient and effective progress include:

    - Designate some "points of no return" in the production process. While backtracking may help students think through the complexity of the text they are producing, it can also result in unproductive revision cycles, where the student needs to move on to the next phase. For instance, once they have moved on to animation, that locks in all the phases prior to that.
    - Use a sign-off sheet at strategic stages to help scaffold student productive work. The student might work with a peer to critique their work to date, and when both are satisfied they sign off and then present to the teacher. A poster-sized sign-off sheet could be on display in the classroom.
    - Have a copy of the overall production sequence on display.
    - Immerse students in the metalanguage by placing definitions on display in the classroom.

There is a distinct type of activity in each phase of the overall production process. The VDDDR teaching procedure supports the learning of the design elements and the production phase. The post-production phase requires more goal-oriented work. I now turn to a detailed discussion of the pre-production (planning) phase.

THE PLANNING PHASE

It is perhaps obvious to state that a text starts with some kind of "idea in the head" that is then progressively elaborated and then finally realized in some tangible form (written word, multimodal text, etc.). Most of the preceding discussion has been concerned with either the building up of the "kit bag" of multimodal resources or facilitating effective realization of that idea. What we also need to be concerned with is how to generate that idea in the first place and then how to foster its development into a full text.

Idea generation, in this sense, is not something unique to multimodal texts, and is the business of the literacy teacher regardless of the modality in use. It can be helpful to provide students with some example stories to be read aloud to generate ideas and different perspectives. Students' ideas are shaped by the software environment and the education experience. If the software library presents students with 1,000 objects, but the first page is visions of farmyard animals, there will tend to be many stories written about such animals; if the exemplar texts used by the teacher in VDDDR embody themes of friendship, there will tend to be stories with this theme. We have seen numerous stories pay homage to texts in popular culture, featuring vampires, boy wizards, or exotic fish. So while showing examples of student-created work is essential (see "reality check" above) and helps to seed ideas, there are also limitations. Coming up with a good idea that is your own and that will sustain your work and interest over several weeks is absolutely crucial, and the engagement of the teacher with the student is perhaps as important at this point in the whole process as any. Just because there is a computer in the mix does not dilute the importance of the teacher bringing a full range of literacy strategies to bear on helping students crystallize a good idea in the first place.

In the 3DMAP project, story outlines, character profiles, script, and storyboard were used as planning tools, and these are presented in the Appendix. I prefer to think of these as "thinking tools"—an external activity helping nurture and structure one's thinking. It is also tempting to think of the planning phase (story outline, character profile, script, and storyboard) as sequential, but it could be that some to-and-fro between these is helpful in nurturing a good idea. Furthermore, there is the to-and-fro with the planning documents and software. Some teachers in the 3DMAP project sent their students on a reconnoitre of the scenes or characters available and asked their students to explore different camera angles; others kept their students off computers entirely. There is much scope for both individual experimentation and individual teaching styles. We certainly know that is necessary to help students be efficient in their work, and to not spend too much time with the software on work that they may then need to undo. This idea of needing to undo work may seem peculiar, but imagine using a word processor where you are unable to make modifications to the first paragraph once you have written the last. There are typically a range of technical inhibitions in the current generation of multimodal authoring software that one needs to be wary of. A teacher has an important role to guide the process in those practical ways.

Both storyboarding and scriptwriting deserve some separate discussion. First, storyboarding occupies a valued position as a planning and thinking tool in a range of communication genres within the school setting and many find that it is useful as it helps novice filmmakers know what they are doing. It is an import from the filmmaking industry, and there is probably considerable variation in the teaching community as to exactly what is meant by the term. In the 3DMAP project, *storyboarding* was the term used for planning the camera work: the distances, angles, and sequences of camera shots; without doing this, the whole text might be shot on one camera position. From observation in the 3DMAP project, it seems that students mentally conceive of their text as linear and complete—and so constructions such as filmic cuts need to be explicitly taught and planned. If a storyboard acts as a thinking tool to support these complex cognitive acts, it is valuable. The 3DMAP project has provided plenty of examples of students who don't refer to their planning documents during production, but if they fulfill a role as thinking tool, the extent to which they are used subsequently is not so important.

Scriptwriting is a different kind of planning document, as it contains the actual words of dialogue or narrative along with a director's actions and scene descriptions. In the 3DMAP project, it was necessary to continually exhort students to "show rather than tell." Possibly just because students are inexperienced, multimodal texts are often "words with illustration." It takes a lot of encouragement and persistence for the idea to cross modes and be expressed primarily visually. This is where the script and the storyboard can work together. Through the script, it can be seen exactly how much dialogue has been prepared, and through the "big print" of the script (film jargon for what is essentially the scene description) and the storyboard, how thorough the visual depiction is can be observed. The teacher can work with the student to recommend changes as necessary. The script itself should be prepared according to a particular format (see Appendix) and its finalisation should be the culmination of the "thinking" and the readiness to proceed to production. Students who have used the scriptwriting software celtx[4] have found that it has eased the process compared with handwriting a script in the correct format.

In summary, I feel able to make fairly good recommendations with regard to the pedagogy of learning the design elements and of scaffolding a production process, but less so in relation to the planning process, for which there are numerous possibilities for further enquiry, trial, and investigation. Consequently, within the context of keeping a reasonably tight rein on the efficient development of their students' texts, I would encourage teachers to experiment with how they use story outlines, character profiles, storyboards, and an iterative process with the software, along with other thinking tools and formats that they may devise.

This brings the discussion of viable classroom practices for multimodal authoring nearly to an end. A teaching procedure and instructional sequence have been described, and the importance of teacher engagement with the process of textual composition and the provision of scaffolding have been emphasized; we now move to the matter of assessment.

A GRAMMATICAL DESIGN APPROACH TO ASSESSMENT

A thorough approach to assessment of multimodal texts from the perspective of grammatical design is in its infancy (Chandler, Unsworth, & O'Brien, 2012). Certainly, an assessor (teacher or peer) can take the categories of meaning previously identified and apply a simple assessment by enquiring whether "the text makes meaning by attending to *[insert category of meaning]*" (refer to the eight categories of meaning identified above). The form of assessment could then be a written description, a high/medium/low ranking, or a point scale. To this list of categories of meaning it would be valuable to also add the following:

- An assessment of multimodality (the extent to which the various modes collaborate to make meaning)
- A recognition of the use of other media (e.g., on-screen credits, titles, etc.)
- A recognition of any technical innovation
- Whether the overall structure of the text is suitable

This approach to evaluation is fairly simple and user-friendly, but there are some inherent limitations. For instance, it is unclear exactly how to best handle multimodal collaboration; if a rating scale was used, is it reasonable to aggregate the score and present an overall total? Should each evaluation category be weighted equally? The intending-user of a rating scale may also reasonably wonder, "On what basis should different grades be awarded—where is the assessment rubric?" Such a device would be difficult to establish in a general-purpose way because the range of design elements and conventions is so vast. However, it would be possible for a teacher to establish a rubric to encompass the design-element attributes that might be expected, in the main, to be demonstrated in a short unit of work.

The main strength of a grammatical design approach to assessment is that it provides a structured basis for either a written or verbal exchange between teacher and student or student and student. As an example of assessment-as-learning, it can lead to identifying strengths, weaknesses, and possibilities of a text at a grammatical level, and thus lead to an increase in student multimodal capability and overall understanding of literacy concepts.

CONCLUSION

This chapter has been concerned with the pedagogy of multimodal authoring—the things a teacher does and the plans he or she might make to enable students to be effective multimodal authors. Guided by the theoretical perspective of grammatical design, teaching procedures, instructional sequences, and evaluation practices have been described. The explicit teaching of design elements (rather than software function) and of building a repertoire of design elements has been advocated. The lingering message is the importance of the teacher's attitude, engagement, and deliberate action. With this in mind, there are several recommendations I would make:

1) Software

- Consider the software available. Some of it is free, some of it is commercial; some of it is available for one operating system but not another; some of it makes heavy technical demands of a system, but other items will run on less capable equipment or require less technical expertise to install; some is designed for student use, other products are for more professional applications. There is no single piece of software that can be universally recommended, so it is essential to investigate carefully.

2) Class time and program

- Carefully consider the amount of time required to incorporate multimodal authoring into a class program. It seems it will always take more time than first estimated. For students with little background, to make a suitably nuanced and well-constructed video as short as 30 seconds represents a significant investment of time.
- Consider the place of a unit of work in relation to an overall scope-and-sequence of multimodal authoring.

3) Pedagogical approach

- Rethink the classroom so that the viewing/reading and writing/creating of multimodal texts are natural inclusions and that multimodal authoring is "mainstream" rather than "extra."
- Expect that an engaged, collaborative, and supportive approach will be required between the teacher and each student as they prepare multimodal texts.
- Approach multimodal authoring with the mindset of it being a literacy activity rather than an ICT activity.

4) Preparation

- Familiarize yourself with the multimodal design elements, both how to accomplish them technically and their meaning-making potential; be aware of key works such as Kress and van Leeuwen (2001/2006) and van Leeuwen (1996, 1999).

- Consciously identify and practice the delivery of teaching procedures that will effectively guide the students through the entire multimodal authoring process.
- Look for stimulating example texts that can be studied.

The pedagogy of multimodal authoring is something about which there are perhaps as many questions as answers. With the creation of multimodal texts clearly featuring in the domain of literacy educators (e.g., ACARA, 2012), this chapter has illustrated how literacy practices, particularly an emphasis on grammatical design, can apply to the teaching of multimodal as well as conventional texts, and has highlighted aspects of pedagogy about which there is growing certainty.

APPENDIX 1: SAMPLE STORY OUTLINE FOR A NARRATIVE

Title:		
Film genre		
Location		
Narrative stage	*Description of what happens*	*Narration*
Orientation/ Introduction		*Little Miss Muffet sat on a tuffet, eating her curds and whey.*
Event 1		*Along came a spider*
Event 2		*who sat down beside her*
Conclusion/ Resolution		*and frightened Miss Muffet away*

ENABLING STUDENTS TO BE EFFECTIVE MULTIMODAL AUTHORS | 101

APPENDIX 2: SAMPLE CHARACTER PROFILE

Name	Character description	Relationship with other character
Miss Muffet		
Spider		

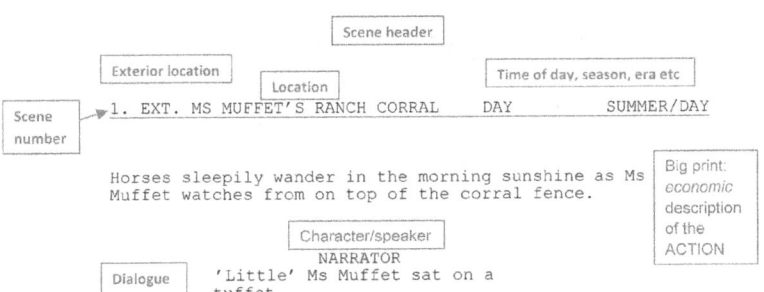

Fig 5.1. Sample Script, with Key Features Annotated.

APPENDIX 3: SAMPLE STORYBOARD FOR A SIMPLE NARRATIVE

	Shot 1	Shot 2	Shot 3	Shot 4
Narration:	Little Miss Muffet sat on her tuffet, eating her curds and whey	Along came a spider	who sat down beside her	and frightened Miss Muffet away.
Named:	Orientation	Event 1	Event 2	Resolution
Duration:	5 Seconds	5 Seconds	5 Seconds	5 Seconds
Camera movement, sound effects or other information:				

NOTES

1. The Australian Research Council Linkage Project "Teaching effective 3D authoring in the middle school years: multimedia grammatical design and multimedia authoring pedagogy" (LP0883563) was funded for 2009–2011. The Chief Investigators were Prof. L. Unsworth (Australian Catholic University) and Dr. A. Thomas (University of Tasmania), in partnership with, and also funded by, the Australian Children's Television Foundation.
2. Further examples of software of this type include Muvizu (http://www.muvizu.com/), Kids Movie Creator (http://www.kids3dmovie.com/en_01/Products.aspx), Alice and Storytelling Alice (http://www.alice.org), Moviestorm (http://www.moviestorm.co.uk/hub/australia), Reallusion (http://www.reallusion.com/), and Anim8or (http://www.anim8or.com).
3. Some suitable sites for clips include http://www.screeningshorts.org.uk, http://www.muvuzu.com, and http://creatingmultimediatexts.com
4. Available at no cost from http://celtx.com/

REFERENCES

ACARA. (2012). *Australian curriculum for English*. Retrieved from http://www.australiancurriculum.edu.au/English

Anstey, M. (2002). *Literate futures: Reading*. Coorparoo, Australia: State of Queensland Department of Education.

Anstey, M., & Bull, G. (2006). *Teaching and learning multiliteracies: Changing times, changing literacies*. Kensington Gardens, South Australia: IRA and the Australian Literacy Educators' Association.

Burn, A., & Durran, J. (2006). Digital anatomies: Analysis as production in media education. In D. Buckingham & R. Willett (Eds.), *Digital generations: Children, young people and new media* (pp. 273–294). Mahwah, NJ: Erlbaum.

Burn, A., & Leach, J. (2004). ICT and moving image literacy in English. In R. Andrews (Ed.), *The impact of ICT on literacy education* (pp. 151–179). London: RoutledgeFalmer.

Burn, A., & Parker, D. (2003). Tiger's big plan: Multimodality and the moving image. In C. Jewitt & G. Kress (Eds.), *Multimodal literacy* (pp. 56–72). New York: Peter Lang.

Chandler, P. (2012). What students know about multimodal authoring. In *Proceedings of the Australian Computers in Education Conference*. Perth, Australia: ACEC. Retrieved from http://acec2012.acce.edu.au/

Chandler, P. (2013). Middle years students' experience with new media. *Australian Journal of Education, 57*(3), 185–199.

Chandler, P., O'Brien, A., & Unsworth, L. (2009). Challenges in the development of a multimedia authoring pedagogy. Paper presented at the Australian Association for Research in Education (AARE) conference, Canberra. Retrieved from http://trove.nla.gov.au/work/153056540?q&versionId=166806572

Chandler, P., O'Brien, A., & Unsworth, L. (2010). Towards a 3D digital multimodal curriculum for the upper primary school. *Australian Educational Computing, 25*(1), 34–40.

Chandler, P., Unsworth, L., & O'Brien, A. (2012). Evaluation of students' digital multimodal narratives and the identification of high-performing classrooms. *Journal of Literacy and Technology, 13*(3), 80–127.

Collerson, J. (1997). *Grammar in teaching*. Newtown, NSW: Primary English Teaching Association.

Cope, B., & Kalantzis, M. (2009). "Multiliteracies": New literacies, new learning. *Pedagogies: An International Journal, 4*(3), 164–195.

Edgar, P. (2006). *Bloodbath: A memoir of Australian television*. Melbourne, Australia: Melbourne University Press.

Freebody, P., & Luke, A. (1990). Literacies programs: Debates and demands in cultural context. *Prospect: Australian Journal of TESOL, 5*(7), 7–16.

Halliday, M. A. K. (1978). *Language as a social semiotic: The social interpretation of language and meaning*. London: Edward Arnold.

Halliday, M. A. K., & Matthiessen, C. (2004). *An introduction to functional grammar*. London: Arnold.

Kellner, D., & Share, J. (2007). Critical media literacy is not an option. *Learning Inquiry, 1*, 56–69.

Kress, G., & van Leeuwen, T. (2001/2006). *Reading images: The grammar of visual design*. London: Routledge.

Loughran, J., Berry, A., & Mulhall, P. (2006). *Understanding and developing science teachers' pedagogical content knowledge*. Rotterdam: Sense Publishers.

Maggs, P. (2008, March). Kahootz 3.0: Developing software for the classroom. *Teacher*, 28–31.

Martin, J. R., & Rose, D. (2005). Designing literacy pedagogy: Scaffolding asymmetries. In J. Webster, C. Matthiessen, & R. Hasan (Eds.), *Continuing discourse on language* (pp. 251–280). London: Continuum.

Pedagogy. (2009). In *Macquarie Dictionary* (5th ed.). Sydney, Australia: Macquarie Library.

Quinn, M. (2004). Talking with Jess: Looking at how metalanguage assisted explanation writing in the Middle Years. *Australian Journal of Language and Literacy, 27*(3), 245–261.

Rieber, L. P. (2001, December). Designing learning environments that excite serious play. *Paper presented at the annual meeting of the Australasian Society for Computers in Learning in Tertiary Education, Melbourne, Australia.* Retrieved from http://www.nowhereroad.com/seriousplay/rieber-ascilite-seriousplay.pdf

Schleppegrell, M. (2004). *The language of schooling: A functional linguistic perspective.* Mahwah, NJ: Erlbaum.

Torr, J., & Harman, J. (1997). Literacy and the language of science in year one classrooms: Implications for children's learning. *Australian Journal of Language and Literacy, 20*(3), 222–237.

Unsworth, L. (2001). *Teaching multiliteracies across the curriculum: Changing contexts of text and image in classroom practice.* London: Open University Press.

van Leeuwen, T. (1996). Moving English: The visual language of film. In S. Goodman & D. Graddol (Eds.), *Redesigning English: New texts, new identities* (pp. 81–103). London: Open University Press.

van Leeuwen, T. (1999). *Speech, music, sound.* London: Macmillan.

Vérillon, P., & Rabardel, P. (1995). Cognition and artifacts: A contribution to the study of thought in relation to instrumented activity. *European Journal of Psychology of Education, 10*(1), 77–101.

Walsh, M. (2011). *Multimodal literacy: Classroom research and practice.* Newtown, NSW: Primary English Teaching Association.

Williams, G. (2000). Children's literature, children and uses of language description. In L. Unsworth (Ed.), *Researching language in schools and communities: A functional linguistic perspective* (pp. 111–129). London: Cassell.

FURTHER READING

Chandler, P. (2010). Not always as it first seems: Thoughts on reading a 3D multimodal text. *Literacy Learning: The Middle Years, 18*(1), 11–18.

de Silva Joyce, H., & Gaudin, J. (2007). *Interpreting the visual: A resource book for teachers.* Sydney: Phoenix Education.

Vincent, J. (2007) Writing and coding: Assisting writers to cross the modes. *Language and Education, 21*(2), 141–157.

CHAPTER SIX

The Image/Language Interface in Picture Books as Animated Films

A Focus for New Narrative Interpretation and Composition Pedagogies

LEN UNSWORTH

INTRODUCTION

The appearance of movie versions of established literary picture books is frequently highly celebrated within broad popular culture, as was the case, for example, with the movie *Where the Wild Things Are* (Jonze, 2009), based on Maurice Sendak's classic picture book (1962), the movie *Fantastic Mr. Fox* (Anderson, 2009), based on the picture book by Roald Dahl (1974), and the movie *The Polar Express* (Zemeckis, 2004), based on the well-known picture book by Chris Van Allsburg (1985). Like the original picture books, the movies attract a wide age-range of enthusiastic viewers among their audiences. This bridging of established literary culture with popular culture films provides the potential for a highly engaging pedagogic context in which teachers and children can together investigate the relationships between the books and movie versions of the stories. Through enjoyable learning experiences teachers can enhance students' appreciation of the interpretive possibilities of the story and how they may be similar and different in the different versions, while simultaneously developing the students' explicit understanding of how the meaning-making resources of image and language (as well as sound and music) are deployed to construct those interpretive possibilities. The release of the first *Shrek* movie (Elliott, 2001) drew attention to the different nature of the original picture book by William Steig (1990) from which the movie was derived but also provided opportunities to compare the original book with e-books that arose from the movie and to develop detailed comparative analyses of segments from these as a basis for classroom work (Unsworth, 2008a). The story of *The Little Prince* (de Saint-Exupéry, 2000a), which already exists in multiple versions (de Saint-Exupéry, 2000b; Donen, 2004), has similarly enabled comparative semiotic analyses as a basis for classroom work (Unsworth, 2006, 2008a) and will, no doubt, be given more impetus by the recently developed 52-episode animated television series (http://www.thelittleprince.com/tv-serie/).

While attention has been given to issues about children developing explicit knowledge of the meaning-making systems of language in terms of grammar, discourse, and genre (Locke, 2010; Macken-Horarik, Love, & Unsworth, 2011; Martin, 1993; Williams, 1993, 2005), recognition of the need for similar systematic understanding of how images make meaning is newly emergent in pedagogic research and practice (Cope & Kalantzis, 2000; Jewitt & Kress, 2003; Kress, 1997, 2000, 2003; Unsworth, 2001, 2002, 2008b). However, while there is a growing understanding of the need to reconceptualize comprehension in multimodal terms and to take account of the increasing ubiquity of digital multimodal texts, there remains a yawning chasm between the dominant monomodal paper media composition pedagogy practices in schooling and the rapidly increasing digital multimodal composition practices in the broader community (Chandler-Olcott & Mahar, 2003; Davies, 2006; Knobel & Lankshear, 2006; Thomas, 2007, 2008). Nevertheless, there are some programs of research and professional pedagogy development in digital multimodal composition in contexts of schooling (Burn & Durran, 2006; Burn & Leach, 2004; Burn & Parker, 2003), and new curricula such as the new national curriculum for English in Australia now require schools to address multimodal literacy in print and electronic media (http://www.australiancurriculum.edu.au/English/). The creation of digital animated movies is one dimension of multimodal digital authoring that is beginning to gain traction in schools. The government of the State of Victoria in Australia fostered this by providing 3D Animation Software called Kahootz (http://www.actf.com/education/kahootz) to all government primary schools in the state from 2008. Notwithstanding this, three years on, it would appear that few teachers and students demonstrate experience, expertise, or confidence in 3D multimodal animation authoring. However, an Australian Research Council-funded project is providing some indication that, given extensive and intensive support, teachers and students with little initial experience have been able to learn how to produce quite engaging original digital animated narratives (Chandler, O'Brien, & Unsworth, 2010; O'Brien, Chandler, & Unsworth, 2010). Digital animation software similar to Kahootz such as Moviestorm (http://www.moviestorm.co.uk), Muvizu (http://www.muvizu.com), Anim8or (http://www.anim8or.com), or Xtranormal (http://www.xtranormal.com/) is now easily accessible online, either free or at a modest cost, greatly facilitating the development of classroom work and enabling children to construct their own animated films on their desktop or laptop computer and upload them to the World Wide Web.

Learning to control the software takes some time but is relatively straightforward and seems tractable for most students in the upper primary/elementary school. What is new to most teachers and students is knowledge of camera and participant positioning options for constructing variation in social distance, inclusion/solidarity, power among characters and between them and the viewing audience, and options for the construction of variation in point of view. What is proposed here is that learning about the systems for meaning-making with moving images is not necessarily limited to those times when learning experiences are based on the use of 3D animation software, and that, in particular, the study of animated movies of literary picture books is one excellent additional context for developing such understanding as a resource for multimodal comprehension and composition. In 2011 Shaun Tan and Andrew Ruhemann received an Oscar at the Academy Awards for the best animated short film *The Lost Thing* (Ruhemann & Tan, 2010) from the original picture book by Shaun Tan (2000)—the movie can be viewed at http://www.traileraddict.com/clip/the-lost-thing/short-film. The book and movie versions are the same story, with the content being almost identical and with only modest changes in the verbal narration. Both versions use essentially the same minimalist depiction style of drawing characters—minimalist in the sense of not being realistic or naturalistic drawing but using simple dots and circles for eyes and not being concerned to have correctly proportioned head size or body parts—and the characters look much the same in the book and the movie. What is strikingly different is the deployment of the interpersonal aspects of the images constructing the interactive relationship between the represented participants and the viewer—particularly the social distance and the nature of the contact achieved by the gaze of the eyes of the characters directly at the viewer (Kress & van Leeuwen, 2001/2006)—as well as the difference in point of view (Painter, 2007; Painter, Martin, & Unsworth, in press; Unsworth, in press).

By comparing corresponding segments of the book and movie versions, students can learn how they can deploy the rudimentary animation software affordances available to them to create sophisticated depictions of affect and empathy in their own work and simultaneously develop a meta understanding of the systems of visual meaning-making for such purposes. Focusing on *The Lost Thing*, this chapter will illustrate such comparative analyses, showing how examination of a limited selection of basic meaning-making resources in images and their relationship with the language in the relevant story segments can yield key insights into how differences in interpretive possibilities are constructed in the book and movie versions. We will look at two contrasting categories of images: The first is where at least one character is directly facing the viewer so that the frontal plane of the viewer and the frontal plane of the character are parallel. The second category is where at least one of the characters has his or her back completely turned toward the viewer, but again with the frontal plane of the character and that of the viewer in parallel. In the case of the first category we will also note whether the character is looking directly at the viewer or not, and for both categories we will look at whether the image is a close-up, middle, or distant view. There are many other options for meaning-making in images that could be considered and that do occur in the book and the movie versions of *The Lost Thing*, but we will restrict the range here to those already noted for two reasons: First, they show what a powerful effect is achieved by the deployment of even such a limited range of resources. Second, even with basic animation software it is usually possible for students in their compositions to make the character face the viewer directly or to have the character with his or her back to the viewer. It is also usually possible to make the eyes look straight out at the viewer or to have them looking at something else (although sometimes this may necessitate having the head turned), and it is further usually possible to move the camera and/or the characters to have them appear close-up, at a middle distance, or remote.

IMAGES OF INCLUSIVE CONTACT

The construction of the viewer/character relationship in images has been explored by Kress and van Leeuwen (2001/2006). They have proposed a number of systems of visual meaning-making resources that construct such relationships. Here we will draw only on their systems of Involvement, Contact, and Social Distance. The system of Involvement is concerned with positioning the viewer to feel to a greater or lesser degree that he or she is involved with the depicted characters. The extent of involvement is influenced by the horizontal angle (Kress & van Leeuwen, 2001/2006, p. 133). If the depicted characters are presented facing us "front on," that is, the horizontal frontal plane of the viewer and that of the character are parallel, then we have a maximum sense of involvement with them as part of our own world. On the other hand, if the characters are depicted at an oblique angle, that is, the frontal plane of the viewer and that of the depicted character are not parallel, this has the effect of positioning the viewer to be more detached from depicted characters—to see them as "other." The greater the oblique angle the more detached is the viewer—in the extreme it is as if he or she is seeing the depicted characters "out of the corner of his or her eye."

In their system of Contact, Kress and van Leeuwen distinguish between an image where a depicted character gazes out at the viewer and one where there is no such gaze—either the character is looking elsewhere or there is no human or animal, or human-like or animal-like character with the equivalent of eyes that could look directly out at the viewer. Kress and van Leeuwen refer to images where the character gazes directly at the viewer as "demand" images, and where the image has no such gaze it is referred to as an "offer." Painter and her colleagues support the importance of distinguishing between these two types of images but take issue with the terminology used by Kress and van Leeuwen. For Painter and her colleagues (2014), the gaze of the depicted participant does not actually "demand" anything, but it does make interpersonal contact with the viewer; hence, they refer to such images simply as "contact" images. Where the depicted participants do not make eye contact with the viewer, the interactive role of the viewer is to observe the depicted participants and, hence, such images are referred to as "observe" images. The terminology of "contact" and "observe" images will be used in this chapter.

The system of Social Distance (Kress & van Leeuwen, 2001/2006) is realised by the "size of frame," which means that the depicted characters may appear as head and shoulders only, largely occupying the frame of the image, so that they appear close up to the viewer, or perhaps only their face or part of their face is visible, again largely occupying the frame, which makes them appear to be at a quite intimate social distance from the viewer. On the other hand, if the entire body of the depicted participant is visible, this positions the character as being further away from the viewer, and if the whole body depiction moves to the background of the image the depicted character may appear quite remote from the viewer. These extremes are commonly referred to as a "close-up" or "long shot" with "mid shot" indicating commonly accepted interactive social distance.

In the construction of images, choices are made simultaneously from the systems of Involvement, Contact, and Social Distance (in addition to other systems proposed by Kress and van Leeuwen [2001/2006] but not discussed here). The various combinations can result in different interactive relations with the viewer. For example, a close-up contact image with the frontal planes of the depicted character and the viewer parallel can construct a sense of closeness and intimacy, whereas if the parameter of social distance is changed to a "long shot" the impact of the "contact" dimension is greatly reduced.

REAR VIEW IMAGES

The "back view" is briefly discussed in one paragraph by Kress and van Leeuwen as "complex and ambivalent" with possible interpretations such as "maximally confronting," "trust," and "abandonment" (Kress & van Leeuwen, 2001/2006). But their discussion is only in the context of one photograph of the parents of one of the authors departing from his residence at the beginning of his university study. However, this brief discussion does emphasize the importance of the context and, by implication, the visual textual co-text in constructing the interpretive possibilities of the "rear view" image. What is not mentioned is the importance of the "back view" in relation to focalization (Genette, 1980). In the photograph, the parents with their backs to the camera were the "focalized," and in this case the possibility of their being "focalizing" characters did not arise. In studies of children's literature the "rear view" is important in establishing alignment between the reader and the point of view of the focalizing character (Painter et al., 2014; Unsworth, 2006). For example, in Anthony Browne's *Gorilla* (Browne, 1983) there are four back view images of Hannah alone, four of Hannah and the gorilla, and one of Hannah and her father (see Painter et al., 2014, for further discussion and examples of "back view" and focalization).

The option of "contact" is obviously not available for rear view images, but choices from other simultaneous systems such as social distance are. Such choices can significantly influence the interpretive possibilities of the "rear view" image. For example, if the image is a "close up" view it is likely that the rear view will construct the point of view as being "along with" the focalizing character depicted from the rear. On the other hand, if the image is a "long shot," depending on how remote the social distance is, it may be less likely that the point of view is regarded as being along with the character depicted from the rear and more likely that the character becomes the focalized with the point of view being that of the viewer unmediated by any viewpoint from inside the narrative.

THE BOOK AND ANIMATED MOVIE VERSIONS OF *THE LOST THING*: A FOCUS FOR COMPARISON

The original picture book version of *The Lost Thing* (Tan, 2000) and the animated movie (Ruhemann & Tan, 2010) tell a humorous and, notwithstanding assertions in the narration to the contrary, profound story about a boy who discovers a bizarre-looking creature while out collecting bottle tops at a beach. Having guessed that it is lost, he tries to find out who owns it or where it belongs, but the problem is met with indifference by everyone else, who barely notice its presence. Each is unhelpful; strangers and parents are unwilling to entertain this uninvited interruption to day-to-day life. Even his friend is unable to help despite some interest. In spite of his better judgement, the boy feels sorry for this hapless creature and attempts to find out where it belongs.

While there are many aspects of the two versions of this story that invite comparison and close analysis, in this chapter we will focus only on those episodes that in the movie include shots where the frontal plane of the depicted character is parallel with that of the viewer, suggesting maximum involvement. We will look at all of these shots where the character is facing the viewer and also the "rear view" shots. In the movie there is a total of nine such "front on" shots and five "rear view" shots. In the book there are no images, facing or "rear view," where the horizontal angle is such that the frontal plane of the viewer and that of the depicted character are parallel, so this means of positioning the viewer as involved with the characters does not occur in the book. Table 6.1 shows the six episodes that contain these nine front-on facing shots and five rear view shots in the movie.

Table 6.1. Fully Front-On and Rear View Images in *The Lost Thing* Movie

Episode	Images of maximum involvement		
	Front on		Rear view
	Contact	Observe	
Discovering the lost thing on the beach			1 mid
Asking for help to find where the lost thing belonged			1 long
Feeding the lost thing in the family shed	1 long 1 mid		
The Federal Department of Odds and Ends		1 long	1 mid
Saying goodbye to the lost thing	3 close	2 long	2 long
Coda: a weird, sad, lost sort of look	1 mid		

The pattern of occurrence of these images in the movie and their absence from the book is reflective of the expectation of *empathetic* engagement of the audience with the movie characters but a more detached *appreciative* engagement with the characters in the book. The next section will first briefly outline these different kinds of multimodal textual constructions of audience engagement. Following this, the episode segments from both the book and the movie indicated in Table 6.1 will be compared to show how the interaction of image and language in each case contributes to the construction of these different multimodal textual orientations to audience engagement.

THE IMAGE/LANGUAGE INTERFACE AND AUDIENCE ENGAGEMENT: APPRECIATION OR EMPATHY

While the narration of *The Lost Thing* is in the first person with several instances of direct address to the audience, the images in the book tend to keep the reader at a distance from the story events and characters. There are no images where the gaze of the characters is directed straight out from the image toward the reader, so there is no "contact" between the reader and the depicted characters in the book. There are also no images where the depicted characters are presented fully front on to the viewer, nor are there any images presenting a full "rear view" of the characters. Nearly all of the images are long distance views. Only three images are middle distance views and there are no close up views at all, so the social distance between the reader and the depicted characters is generally quite remote.

The Lost Thing is similar to many acclaimed picture books for younger readers, such as *Rosie's Walk* (Hutchins, 1968), *The Baby Who Wouldn't Go to Bed* (Cooper, 1996), *Come Away from the Water, Shirley* (Burningham, 1977), *The Snowman* (Briggs, 1978), and *Possum Magic* (Fox & Vivas, 1983/2004), which function as a kind of social commentary and deploy these socially distancing image choices, keeping the reader outside the story world to observe and learn from what goes on within it. Readers are not expected to build a personal relationship with the characters, or to feel moved or upset by the events of the story world. The appropriate reader stance is *appreciative*—one of relative distance as the story events are observed and lessons learned (Painter et al., 2014). In the picture books that they examined, Painter and her colleagues found that the non-realistic "minimalist" style of character depiction was a key signifier for the *appreciative* orientation appropriate to the picture books as social commentary.

On the other hand an *empathetic* reader stance entails readers being able to see themselves in the depicted character's role and to some extent being able to stand in the character's shoes. The generic drawing style contributes to the readers being invited to adopt this *empathetic* stance. Whereas the minimalist style is more iconic and stylised, focusing on happiness or sadness or anger, the generic style is more detailed, with the brush or pencil stroke based on the musculature of the human face, extending and nuancing the repertoire of emotions that can be depicted. Examples of the generic style include *Sunshine* (Ormerod, 1981/1983), *Uncle David* (Gleeson & Greder, 1992), *So Much* (Cooke & Oxenbury, 1994*)*, *An Evening at Alfie's* (Hughes, 1984), and many images in Anthony Browne's books, such as *Piggybook* (1986/1996), *Zoo* (1994), and *Into the Forest* (2004). But in the movie version of *The Lost Thing* the minimalist drawing style of the book is largely retained, and yet the reader stance that is invited is much more of the empathetic. In discussing the story episodes noted in Table 6.1 it will be seen that what contributes strongly to achieving this is the interaction of the language with the combination of choices of social distance with rear view or frontal images and contact or observe choices with the latter.

Discovering the Lost Thing and Asking for Help

The first two episodes listed in Table 6.1 each contain one of the images in the category of maximum involvement that we are examining. Both are rear views. The first is a mid distance view showing the boy's back and head only in the foreground as he says:

Nobody else seemed to notice it was there.

THE IMAGE/LANGUAGE INTERFACE IN PICTURE BOOKS AS ANIMATED FILMS | 113

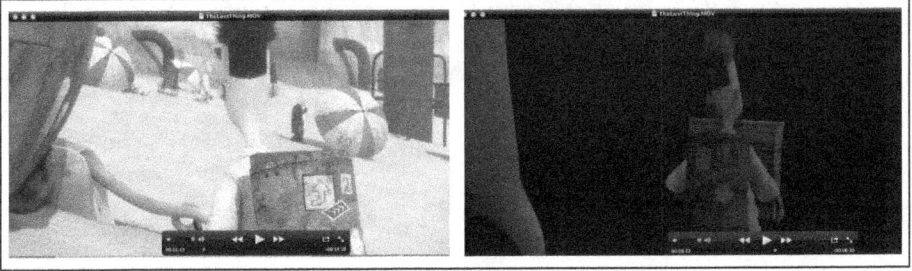

Fig 6.1. Rear View Mid Shots in *The Lost Thing* Movie.

This mid distance rear view image (shown on the left of Figure 6.1) clearly positions us along with the point of view of the boy as he says this, and we see from almost the same perspective what he sees on the beach, except that we see a mid to close rear view of him as well. The image reinforces the effect of the verbal "Nobody else…" in drawing attention to the boy's perspective and inviting empathy with him. This does not occur in the book. The narration is the same, but it is positioned above a large image on the second double-page spread, which is an observe image showing in the foreground all of the upper body of the boy, apart from his legs. The oblique angle shows the boy from the slightly rear, right profile on high steps sloping gradually down to the beach, and looking out to a distant view of the beach on which can be seen the small distant depiction of the lost thing and small depictions of people. That the narration is coupled with such a view may well also emphasize the singularity of the boy's noticing the lost thing from such a distance while those in proximity to it on the beach are not noticing, but the point is that this image/language coupling does not invite empathy with the boy in the way that the coupling of the narration with the mid distance rear view image does in the movie.

The long distance rear view in the movie in the second episode from Table 6.1 does not have the same effect. It occurs very briefly following the narration:

I asked a few people if they knew anything about it…

At the moment we see the rear view of the boy, we see the whole length of his body taking up only about one third of the frame so he appears quite far away. The long distance in this case seems to diminish the empathetic impact of the rear view and the boy is seen more as the focalized than the focalizer. However, there is perhaps somewhat more alignment with the boy in the movie as a result of this fleeting rear view, compared with the double page spread in the book where four separate vertical panels of illustration taking up the full length of the page accompany the narrative text, which is positioned below the second panel:

I asked a few people if they knew anything about it, but nobody was very helpful.

The first panel is a bird's eye view, from a great height, of the boy and the lost thing on the beach. The remaining three large panels show long distance observe images of the lost thing and the whole body of the boy in profile positioned as interacting with different characters in the distance. These images strongly maintain the more distanced appreciative, rather than empathetic, relationship.

Feeding the Lost Thing

In the book the feeding episode is shown visually in an image on the left hand side page as a long distance observe view of the full body of the boy standing on top of the ladder leaned up against the fully depicted lost thing. Below this image at the bottom of the page the following narration occurs:

> I hid the thing in our back shed and gave it something to eat, once I found out what it liked. It seemed a bit happier then, even though it was still lost.

In the movie this narration about feeding the lost thing after finding out what it liked is omitted. We see the boy climb the ladder and the two contact images occur during this move—first of the boy looking up from the bottom of the ladder holding a box of food and then looking out from the top of the lost thing as he feeds it. This is the first occasion in the movie when the gaze of the boy is directly out toward us as viewers. It is the first contact image with maximum involvement due to its being a parallel frontal view. The first of these two contact images, at the bottom of the ladder, is a long view where we see the full length of the boy from a high angle and he is looking straight up at us. The second contact view is mid distance at the eye level as we see the boy looking straight out at us after he has climbed the ladder to the top of the lost thing. So not only is the boy making contact with us, but he has moved closer and to the same horizontal level. The combination of maximal involvement through a parallel frontal angle, contact, and close social distance increases our engagement with the boy. The narration omitted from the movie is not required as the movie shows rather than tells how the boy finds out what the lost thing likes and shows his feeding the lost thing, with the music and the warm bright ambient colours emanating from the lost thing communicating positive emotion. What is achieved visually is the building of further empathy with the boy.

The Federal Department of Odds and Ends

In the book the image depicting the arrival at "the tall grey building" is an oblique high angle "bird's eye view" of the boy and the lost thing as miniscule figures at the foot of the building. The narration in the book and the movie is the same:

> We arrived at a tall grey building with no windows.

In the movie, after a similar bird's eye view of the lost thing and the boy walking to the entrance of the building, the arrival depiction becomes an image with the maximal involvement parallel frontal angle, long distance observe view of the boy and the lost thing standing beside each other and facing the viewer but with the boy's eyes looking slightly upward and to the left into the building. Although this is not a contact image, it is the first time the frontal plane of the viewer has been in parallel with the frontal plane of both the boy and the lost thing simultaneously. Hence the involvement with both characters as a pair is greatest here. While the language and the actual events are the same in both versions of the story, the visual representation in the movie is designed to effect increased involvement of the viewer.

In the movie the mid distance rear view of the boy in the Department of Odds and Ends occurs just before the small creature touches him and warns him not to leave the lost thing in the department and gives him a card with a sign on it. The following is the narration in the movie at this point:

> I was looking around for a desk, when I suddenly felt something touch my elbow.

The boy is touched on the elbow from behind and, at this mid distance view, with the upper body of the boy and the rear of his head in view, it is the case that the viewer feels some empathy with the boy knowing he is about to be startled from behind. In the book, however, this scene is depicted as an oblique long distance observe view with the full body of the small creature, the boy, and the lost thing all visible, and the creature passing the card to the boy on his right hand side. The narration in the book reads:

> I was looking around for a pen when I felt something tug the back of my shirt.

The narration in the book and the movie are only inconsequentially different. Verbally, there is strong inferred alignment with the character of the boy as the audience empathizes with being unexpectedly touched from behind. But in the movie the rear image of the boy intensifies this empathy whereas in the book the oblique distance observe view in the image diminishes the empathetic impact of the narration and moves the overall reader stance at this point to one of appreciation.

Saying Goodbye: Indifference, Involvement, and Intensification

In the book one image depicts the parting of the boy and the lost thing. Above the image on this page the text reads:

> I didn't know what to think, but the lost thing made an approving sort of noise. It seemed as good a time as any to say goodbye to each other. So we did.

Below this text the image is a long distance observe view of the boy and the lost thing in profile, facing each other, gesturing a goodbye wave to each other with both hands/"tentacles" extended forward. And then at the bottom of the page is the single line:

> Then I went home to classify my bottle-top collection.

Notwithstanding the first person narration, the nature of the image and the language chosen maintain the sense of detached viewer observation—very much an *appreciative* stance. There is a complete lack of verbal commitment to any emotional involvement in the departure, and the image also indicates a fairly routine, unemotional waving gesture, while the final line of text on the page implies emotional indifference to the encounter with, and departure from, the lost thing. It is interesting to compare this not only to the treatment of the departure itself in the movie but also to the way in which this episode in the movie portrays a kind of culminating visual construction of the growth of companionship and emotional connection of the boy to the lost thing.

Half of all the images of maximum involvement in the movie occur in the episode where the boy and the lost thing are saying goodbye, as shown in Table 6.1. The seven such images in this episode include contact, observe, and rear view images. Each of these categories occurred separately, in turn, in the previous episodes, but all categories combine only in the "saying goodbye" episode.

Fig 6.2. Saying Goodbye Silently in the Movie Version of *The Lost Thing*.

The contact images are close up views of the boy's shoulders, neck, and head looking straight out at the viewer (Figure 6.2, top left), as the door of the strange creature's sanctuary opens. These are the first such close up contact images with maximum involvement, as, in the earlier episode, the contact moved from long view to mid view only. Not only is the contact shift to a close up view, but also there are three such close up views in this episode. Hence the "saying goodbye" episode visually intensifies this more intimate contact with the boy.

After the first two such contact views, we see the two long distance observe images showing the boy and the lost thing beside each other facing out toward the viewer, but with the boy's gaze somewhat upward rather than directly at the viewer, as they look through the door to the strange creature's sanctuary (Figure 6.2, top right). These images of maximum involvement of the viewer with the boy and the lost thing together reflect the similar image from the previous episode when they are about to enter "the tall grey building." But in this "saying goodbye" episode we have two such views, again intensifying through repetition the emphasis on maximum viewer involvement with the boy and the lost thing together.

In the movie the entire "goodbye" scene is conveyed only through the images and there is no narration at all. The narration accompanying the corresponding story segment from the book, which was quoted above, is omitted from the movie. The parting of the boy and the lost thing is depicted minimally in the book through the one observe image of the boy and the lost thing in profile facing each other and waving goodbye. What is described in the previous paragraph here indicates the greater visual commitment to the depiction in the movie of the actions that occurred immediately prior to this scene. There is also greater commitment in the movie to the actions that occurred immediately following this common "waving" scene. This is where we see in the movie the full rear view of the boy parallel to the frontal plane of the viewer with the boy facing the door of the sanctuary as the lost thing departs through it (Figure 6.2). In this case, although it is a long distance view, the rear view image does indeed position the audience view along with that of the boy. Engagement with him is increased through this distance rear view image because of the impact of the intensified involvement and contact images that have preceded this scene. The camera lingers on this rear view of the boy for some seconds, and as the sanctuary door closes, the boy's head is tilted to one side so that he can maintain his view though the remaining opening (Figure 6.2). This second rear view with the head tilted also intensifies the involvement and empathy of the viewer with the boy.

Coda: A Weird, Sad, Lost Sort of Look

The last close up contact image of the boy in the movie occurs as he appears, presumably some years later, travelling home from work in the tram, and reflecting on the earlier encounter with the lost thing. The narration is identical in the book and the movie:

> I still think about that lost thing from time to time. Especially when I see something out of the corner of my eye that doesn't quite fit. You know, something with a weird, sad, lost sort of look.

Just as the narration comes to the final words, "a weird, sad, lost sort of look," the character turns around to face the camera and looks out, making contact with us as the viewers. This provocative coupling of image and language obviously raises questions about who has the "weird, sad, lost sort of look," and in a manner that maximizes the involvement of the viewer. In the book this powerful provocation does not emerge. The previous page is a long distance view of a tram, and although the characters inside are small, one is recognizable as the boy in this story. Hence the image on the same page as the narrative text above, which is a view from inside the tram of an odd orange creature with a light bulb for a head on the station, could be regarded as being seen from the boy's point of view as a passenger in the tram, but we do not have actual contact with the boy in this segment of the book, maintaining the consistent distancing of the reader from direct involvement with the characters throughout the book.

INTERPRETIVE POSITIONING THROUGH THE IMAGE/LANGUAGE INTERFACE: FROM COMPREHENDING TO COMPOSING

What is clear is that in the movie version of *The Lost Thing* the viewer is positioned differently in relation to the interpretation of the story events from the reader of the original picture book version of the story. This repositioning is achieved through a range of narrative movie techniques which cannot all be addressed in the space available here. What has been discussed reflects the fact that fundamentally the characters and events remain essentially the same in both versions of the story. Changes to the language of the narration are minimal and, arguably, for the most part inconsequential. The most common variation in the narration is the omission of some of the language as the story events are shown visually and do not need also to be told. In the showing rather than telling there is frequently greater commitment to detailing prior and subsequent actions to those depicted in the static "snapshot" images in the book. While this has not changed the substantive events of the story as related in the book, it has allowed an enhanced visual depiction to convey more of the characters' interpersonal perspectives on the events. In this chapter we have seen that this infusion invites more of an alignment of the viewer with the feelings and experiences of the boy as depicted in the movie. This invitation to a more empathetic stance in relation to the movie is largely achieved by varying a range of meaning-making parameters of the images while essentially maintaining the minimalist depiction style. A comprehensive discussion of the variation of these visual parameters has not been possible here. Moreover, a deliberate decision was made to limit the discussion to a few simple image representation choices that could most easily be adopted by upper primary school children in their animated story composition using now commonly available and easily accessible software. Only four aspects of image representation were addressed: maximum viewer/character involvement through parallel frontal planes; rear/front view; social distance (close-up, medium, distant); and contact/observe. The brief account in this chapter has outlined how these resources have been deployed prosodically to contribute to intensifying the empathetic orientation of the movie to the character of the boy. Experience in researching the initiation of teachers and students into digital animated narrative movie making suggests that while movie making affordances such as different camera angles and close-up or distance shots are either well-known or awareness is quickly acquired, what is essential is to build an understanding of how such affordances can become resources for constructing a variety of views or interpretive stances in relation to narrative events and to acquire, over time, explicit comprehensive knowledge of the systems of meaning-making within images and a common metalanguage for describing and discussing them. As students develop greater explicit knowledge of how semiotic resources of image and language make meaning independently and in collaboration, they will be better equipped to discern the interpretive possibilities of the multimodal texts they encounter and also to deploy such resources in constructing the interpretive possibilities in the multimodal texts they compose. Animated movies of well-established picture books such as *The Lost Thing* can provide a most enjoyable context for students and teachers in pursuing systematic development of multimodal comprehension and composition in the English classroom.

REFERENCES

Anderson, W. (2009). *Fantastic Mr. Fox* [Motion picture]. [Produced by W. Anderson, S. Rudin, A. Abbate, & S. Rales]. United States: 20th Century Fox.
Briggs, R. (1978). *The snowman*. London: Hamish Hamilton.
Browne, A. (1983). *Gorilla*. London: Julia MacRae.
Browne, A. (1986/1996). *Piggybook*. London: Julia MacRae.
Browne, A. (1994). *Zoo*. London: Random House.
Browne, A. (2004). *Into the forest*. London: Walker Books.
Burn, A., & Durran, J. (2006). Digital anatomies: Analysis as production in media education. In D. Buckingham & R. Willett (Eds.), *Digital generations: Children, young people and new media*. Mahwah, NJ: Erlbaum.
Burn, A., & Leach, J. (2004). ICT and moving image literacy in English. In R. Andrews (Ed.), *The impact of ICT on literacy education* (pp. 151–179). London: Routledge.
Burn, A., & Parker, D. (2003). Tiger's big plan: Multimodality and the moving image. In C. Jewitt & G. Kress (Eds.), *Multimodal literacy* (pp. 56–72). New York: Peter Lang.
Burningham, J. (1977). *Come away from the water, Shirley*. London: Cape.
Chandler, P., O'Brien, A., & Unsworth, L. (2010). Towards a 3D digital multimodal curriculum for the upper primary school. *Australian Educational Computing, 25*(1), 34–40.

Chandler-Olcott, K., & Mahar, D. (2003). "Tech-saviness" meets multiliteracies: Exploring adolescent girls technology-related literacy practices. *Reading Research Quarterly, 38*(3), 356–385.

Cooke, T., & Oxenbury, H. I. (1994). *So much*. London: Walker Books.

Cooper, H. (1996). *The baby who wouldn't go to bed*. London: Doubleday.

Cope, B., & Kalantzis, M. (Eds.). (2000). *Multiliteracies: Literacy learning and the design of social futures*. Melbourne: Macmillan.

Dahl, R. (1974). *Fantastic Mr. Fox*. Harmondsworth: Puffin.

Davies, J. (2006). Escaping to the borderlands: An exploration of the Internet as a cultural space for teenaged wiccan girls. In K. Pahl & J. Rowsell (Eds.), *Travel notes from the new literacy studies* (pp. 55–71). Clevedon: Multilingual Matters.

de Saint-Exupéry, A. (2000a). *The little prince*. London: Penguin.

de Saint-Exupéry, A. (2000b). *The little prince* (CD ROM). Tivola.

Donen, S. (Writer). (2004). *The little prince*. Canada: Paramount Home Video.

Elliott, T. (Writer). (2001). *Shrek* [Movie]. Glendale, CA: Dreamworks.

Fox, M., & Vivas, J. (1983/2004). *Possum magic*. Adelaide: Omnibus.

Genette, G. (1980). *Narrative discourse: An essay in method*. (J. E. Lewin, Trans.). Ithaca, NY: Cornell University Press.

Gleeson, L., & Greder, A. (1992). *Uncle David*. Sydney: Ashton Scholastic.

Hughes, S. (1984). *An evening at Alfie's*. London: Bodley Head.

Hutchins, P. (1968). *Rosie's walk*. Harmondsworth: Penguin.

Jewitt, C., & Kress, G. (Eds.). (2003). *Multimodal literacy*. New York: Peter Lang.

Jonze, S. (Writer). (2009). *Where the wild things are* [Motion picture]. Produced by T. Hanks, G. Goetzman, M. Sendak, J. Caris, & V. Landay. United States: Warner Brothers.

Knobel, M., & Lankshear, C. (2006). Weblog worlds and constructions of effective and powerful writing: Cross with care, and only where signs permit. In K. Pahl & J. Rowsell (Eds.), *Travel notes from the new literacy studies* (pp. 73–92). Clevedon: Multilingual Matters.

Kress, G. (1997). Visual and verbal modes of representation in electronically mediated communication: The potentials of new forms of text. In I. Snyder (Ed.), *Page to screen: Taking literacy into the electronic era* (pp. 53–79). Sydney: Allen and Unwin.

Kress, G. (2000). Multimodality. In B. Cope & M. Kalantzis (Eds.), *Multiliteracies: Literacy learning and the design of social futures* (pp. 182–202). Melbourne: Macmillan.

Kress, G. (2003). *Literacy in the new media age*. London: Routledge.

Kress, G., & van Leeuwen, T. (2001/2006). *Reading images: A grammar of visual design* (2nd ed.). London: Routledge.

Locke, T. (Ed.). (2010). *Beyond the grammar wars: A resource for teachers and students on developing language knowledge in the English/literacy classroom*. London: Routledge.

Macken-Horarik, M., Love, K., & Unsworth, L. (2011). A grammatics "good enough" for school English in the 21st century: Four challenges in realizing the potential. *Australian Journal of Language and Literacy, 34*(1), 9–23.

Martin, J. R. (1993). Genre and literacy—modelling context in educational linguistics. *Annual Review of Applied Linguistics, 13*, 141–172.

O'Brien, A., Chandler, P., & Unsworth, L. (2010). 3D multimodal authoring in the middle years: A research project. *Synergy, 8*(1), 1–5.

Ormerod, J. (1981/1983). *Sunshine*. Harmondsworth: Penguin/Puffin.

Painter, C. (2007). Children's picture book narratives: Reading sequences of images. In A. McCabe, M. O'Donnell, & R. Whittaker (Eds.), *Advances in language and education*. London: Continuum.

Painter, C., Martin, J. R., & Unsworth, L. (2014). *Reading visual narratives: Image analysis of children's picture books*. London: Equinox.

Ruhemann, A., & Tan, S. (Writer). (2010). *The lost thing* [Short film]. Richmond Australia: Madman Entertainment.

Sendak, M. (1962). *Where the wild things are*. London: Bodley Head.

Steig, W. (1990). *Shrek*. New York: Michael Di Capua Books.

Tan, S. (2000). *The lost thing*. Sydney: Hachette.

Thomas, A. (2007). *Youth online: Identity and literacy in the digital age*. New York: Peter Lang.

Thomas, A. (2008). Machinima: Composing 3D multimedia narratives. In L. Unsworth (Ed.), *New literacies and the English curriculum: Multimodal perspectives*. London: Continuum.

Unsworth, L. (2001). *Teaching multiliteracies across the curriculum: Changing contexts of text and image in classroom practice*. Buckingham, UK: Open University Press.

Unsworth, L. (2002). Changing dimensions of school literacies. *Australian Journal of Language and Literacy, 25*(1), 62–77.

Unsworth, L. (2006). *e-literature for children: Enhancing digital literacy learning*. London: Routledge.

Unsworth, L. (2008a). Comparing and composing digital re-presentations of literature: Multimedia authoring and meta-communicative knowledge. In L. Unsworth (Ed.), *New literacies and the English curriculum* (pp. 186–212). London: Continuum.

Unsworth, L. (2008b). *Multiliteracies and metalanguage: Describing image/text relations as a resource for negotiating multimodal texts*. In D. Leu, J. Corio, M. Knobel, & C. Lankshear (Eds.), *Handbook of research on new literacies* (pp. 377–405). Mahwah, NJ: Erlbaum.

Unsworth, L. (in press). Point of view in picture books and animated film adaptations: Informing critical multimodal comprehension and composition pedagogy. In E. Djonov & S. Zhao (Eds.), *Critical multimodal studies of popular culture*. London: Routledge.

Van Allsburg, C. (1985). *The polar express*. London: Andersen.

Williams, G. (1993). Using systemic grammar in teaching young learners: An introduction. In L. Unsworth (Ed.), *Literacy learning and teaching: Language as social practice in the primary school* (pp. 197–254). Melbourne: Macmillan.

Williams, G. (2005). Grammatics in schools. In R. Hasan, C. Matthiessen, & J. Webster (Eds.), *Continuing discourse on language: A functional perspective* (Vol. 1, pp. 281–310). London: Equinox.

Zemeckis, R. (Writer). (2004). *The polar express* [Motion picture]. [Produced by R. Zemeckis, G. Goetzman, S. Starkey, & W. Teitler]. United States: Warner Brothers.

CHAPTER SEVEN

Using Focalisation Choices to Manipulate Audience Viewpoint in 3-D Animation Narratives

What Do Student Authors Need to Know?

ANNEMAREE O'BRIEN

INTRODUCTION

Pennie and Beth[1] are at a computer working on the final scene in their digital three-dimensional (3-D) animation. It is a retelling of an Australian Aboriginal dreaming story, "How the Sun Was Made." As they talk about the design of meaning in their narrative, the girls frequently refer to what they want their viewer to know. They have paid careful attention to the choice and adaptation of characters and objects to suit their purpose, and to use of colour and lighting to establish mood, setting, and time of the story. The animation is a series of long to mid shots that position the viewer at a distance from the characters and the action—until the final shot. This is undoubtedly the most effective part of the story and it is clear the girls have considered their viewer's position in relation to what is happening on the screen. In this beautifully composed moment, the viewer is finally in close, positioned just behind a group of animals, with everyone looking directly at the salient object, the rising sun in the distance. As Beth explains:

> We want the people's attention to go onto the sun and the animals are going to be kind of pushing you there. Pointing you there.... It kind of gets your attention to look too. Kind of pointing, that way. (Pennie and Beth, Interview 1)

This revelatory moment was the impetus that shaped the research discussed in this chapter. It showed that while Pennie and Beth instinctively understood that they could position the viewer to see something in a particular way, they were unable to clearly articulate what they were doing, or that the same understanding of viewer perspective could also be applied to each of the other shots in their animation. Beth and Pennie did not have a grammatical knowledge of how this meaning-making process works in the moving image context or the metalanguage to talk about it.

This insightful interaction also suggested that if students had explicit knowledge about how the viewer can be "pushed" or positioned in different ways to see the characters and action, they could more purposefully design meaning in their multimodal narratives using the moving image tools available to them.

The purpose of this chapter is to identify what student authors need to know to be able to manipulate viewer position at different times throughout their animation narratives and how they can do it. This is approached through *focalisation* theory—authorial choice of viewer/reader perspective. Choices about focalisation or *who* sees *what*, *when*, and *how* enable the author to create and shape character relationships within a narrative and to manipulate the external viewer's position and affiliation with characters as the story unfolds, adding colour, richness, and emotional layers to storytelling. To do this, we need to identify how these focalisation meaning choices can be expressed or *realised* using the available modal resources. In the context of 3-D animation, the focus here is how *moving image* resources provide opportunities for creative and insightful ways of bringing this meaning into being.

This work is situated within a sociocultural theoretical frame of reference that supports the spotlight on authorial "choice," defined by *semiosis* or the "act of *meaning*"[2] itself, and the process of *realising* this *meaning*. This is informed by social semiotics (Jewitt, 2009; Kress, 2010; van Leeuwen, 2005a) and systemic functional theory (SF theory) that has emerged from Halliday's (1973, 1978) pioneering work in systemic functional linguistics (SFL). This socially responsible account of semiotic systems and the process for realising meaning through the choice of apt moving image semiotic resources informs this early development of an inventory or grammatical "tool kit" identifying the focalisation options for varying viewer stance in relation to characters and events to develop interpersonal relationships. This "tool kit" is not presented as orthodoxy, but as a socially shaped, adaptive, dynamic resource framed by the following questions:

- What are the possible focalisation options for constructing different viewpoints within a narrative through which the viewer experiences the story?
- How can focalisation choices be used to design interpersonal relationships between characters in the story, and between characters and the viewer?
- How can we describe the meaning-making resources of moving image for constructing audience viewpoint in animated narratives?

Key focalisation choices available to the author to manipulate interpersonal relationships are identified, along with the semiotic systems from which moving image, meaning-making choices can be made. The intention is to provide an account for users as both readers and producers of multimodal texts of how these design resources can be deployed in constructing viewer perspective. I then provide a brief commentary on how this work can inform literacy practice in apprenticing young animation authors into designing meaning through attention to viewer stance.

3-D ANIMATION AND THE MOVING IMAGE MODE

Creating an animation is a complex simultaneous process of orchestrating the distribution of meaning across a dynamic combination of multiple communication modes including visual, sound, gesture, spatial, and linguistic (Cope & Kalantzis, 2000; New London Group, 1996). In light of this complexity, this work just looks at the moving image mode in realising focalisation choices within the broader multimodal context.

Moving image resources do much of the initial "heavy lifting" in communicating meaning in a 3-D animation, carrying a greater part of the "functional load" across the semiotic resources (Jewitt & Kress, 2003). The machinima-style animation software[3] used in this study comes with asset libraries of visual digital resources including 3-D characters, objects, settings, and tools to adapt how they look, along with virtual camera tools, editing tools, and audio assets. It is an example of emerging digital 3-D styles of animation, where the animator can move the camera around and through 3-D objects in a 3-D virtual space.

MOVING IMAGE SEMIOTIC RESOURCES

Moving image is defined here as the depiction of action and movement occurring over time and space. Burn and Parker (Burn, 2013; Burn & Parker, 2001, 2003) identify two framing devices or operational capabilities that orchestrate meaning with the moving image: *spatial framing* and *temporal framing*. Spatial framing is the work of the moving image camera that records how we see space and subjects. Motion is created through the movement of characters and objects through space, recorded by the camera. Temporality is created by linking sequences of moving images through editing to shape time and duration. These semiotic resources of camera initiated movement, character initiated movement and a combination of both (Kress & van Leeuwen, 2006, p. 261; van Leeuwen, 2005b, p. 86–87) in conjunction with shot framing and shot sequencing through editing work together to shape time and space.

MOVING IMAGE AND CAMERA

Camera movement and character movement through the virtual 3-D space over time are central to this animation process and to the design of viewer stance. Here, we look at how moving image resources can be used to make considered choices about what is seen by whom, and how it is seen. This meaning can be realised through choices made by the filmmaker about direction of acting and camera, use of camera tools for shot framing, shot angles, shot distance, and camera movement. These resources enable the author to animate virtual characters and objects and show them moving through the space. The virtual camera can dolly, pan, zoom, and tilt; it can be attached to subjects and objects and move with them, for example, positioning the viewer to fly as a bird or zoom through a virtual space.

MOVING IMAGE AND EDITING

The temporal affordance of moving image is created through the process of shot sequencing called editing, which transforms a series of separate images into a moving image sequence taking place over time. A film is usually made up of an ordered sequence of shots. A shot is technically defined as "one uninterrupted image" (Bordwell & Thompson, 2010, p 494); it is "the time in which a camera runs without interruption" (Kuhn, 2009, p. 262). A scene is a sequence of shots "in the one time and space" (Bordwell & Thompson, 2010, p. 493). A sequence of associated scenes makes a film.

Linking sequences of shots together enables the animator to manipulate viewer perspective in relation to particular characters at different times in the narrative. This process is particularly evident in the widespread use of the shot-reverse (or action-reaction) shot system in film and animation. Here, in a context with two characters, a conversation, for example, the viewer first sees from one character's perspective (the action) and then from the other speaker's perspective (the reaction) in the following shot.

FOCALISATION

Attention to focalisation choices enables the storyteller to choose a particular way of seeing things, but it is a tricky concept for students (and their teachers), and for good reason. The terminology related to reader/viewer position is slippery theoretical territory where terms such as *point of view*, *perspective*, *slant*, and *stance* have many nuances.[4] The term *focalisation* was introduced by narratologist Gerald Genette

([1972] 1980) as a replacement for *perspective* and *point of view*, and developed further by Bal (1981, 2009) in the context of text analysis. Focalisation also, however, offers a valuable conceptual and semantic precision that can be used by authors in producing meaning.

THREE COMPONENTS OF FOCALISATION

The semantic precision of focalisation enables us to talk about how an author can draw on three concurrent, interrelated components of a *focalisation* event: the *focaliser* is who the viewer is spatially positioned to see as; the *focalised* is the subject or what is seen; and *focalising* is the act of seeing—the way the focaliser sees the focalised. These authorial choices of *who* sees, *what* is seen, and *how* it is seen characterise the theoretical approach to focalisation in this work.

Who are the participants in this focalisation process? Kress and van Leeuwen (2006) identify two categories of text "participants"—internal and external. The internal text participants are the depicted characters or subjects; external text participants are the reader/viewer and the author. The author is able to use focalisation resources to orchestrate the position of the viewer participant in relation to the characters and events within the narrative. Through focalisation choices, the author can draw the reader's/viewer's attention to a character and to highlight the character's experience at a certain point in the narrative. Focalisation can be variable, shifting between the viewer and the depicted characters, and between characters. Focalisation makes possible "the most important, most penetrating, and most subtle means of [viewer/reader] manipulation" (Bal, 2009, p. 116).

DESIGNING INTERPERSONAL RELATIONSHIPS

How can the animation author use focalisation choices to construct interpersonal relationships between these text participants? The process enabling this comes from SF theory based on Halliday's (1973, 1978) work with systemic functional linguistics, which sees meaning as shaped by the two basic tenets: function and system. Function is theorised as *register theory* that in moving image concerns the relationship between the *function* of the moving image communication mode (the text) and the *context* of its use. System is about identifying and organising knowledge about meaning-making resources into a *system network* to make specific knowledge of the meaning systems visible. A system network is used below to develop a systemic framework mapping and organising knowledge about meaning choices for focalisation using moving image resources.

REGISTER THEORY AND METAFUNCTIONS

Register theory describes the functions or purposes of a communication event of any sort in terms of three universal meaning variables: *field*, *tenor*, and *mode*, which work simultaneously to make meanings (Halliday & Hasan, 1985). Register is made up of the combination of the field, tenor, and mode vectors of meaning, with a systematic relationship between them. In each of the Register vectors, meaning is enacted through an associated metafunction (Halliday, 2004; Halliday & Hasan, 1985; Martin, 2011). *Field* presents the subject matter and the represented reality: the world, the characters, and their actions and reactions as expressed through the *ideational* metafunction. *Tenor* concerns the social positioning or status in the relationships between the participants in the communicative event, relations negotiated in relation to power, and degree of affect and affiliation. Tenor is realised through the *interpersonal* metafunction. *Mode* is organisation of the information flow shaped by the medium chosen to deliver this meaning and realised through the *Compositional* metafunction.

INTERPERSONAL MEANING

The *interpersonal* metafunction, the function for creating relationships and the social meaning of interactions between the text participants, is where the author can establish feelings, attitudes, power relationships, and credibility. Painter and Martin (2011) divide the interpersonal metafunction into two subsystems of meaning, *affiliation* and *affect*. They argue that the design of interpersonal relationships serves to enact and express the *affiliation* or relationship alignment between the participants and the *affective* or emotional feeling between the participants (p. 133).

In this research context, the interpersonal focus is narrowed to just the development of affiliation or relationship alignment between the interactive text participants and how this can be achieved through focalisation choices. These choices are realised using the available moving image semiotic resources.

INTRODUCING THE SYSTEM NETWORK

This section describes an inventory of moving image resources for constructing affiliations between text participants through focalisation, the manipulation of viewer stance. It names and maps the available semiotic systems and describes the semiotic resources and their *semiotic potential* or the kinds of meanings each affords. This knowledge of the possible moving image semiotic resources for focalisation can then be made visible to users.

What is seen on the screen and how it is seen is shaped by authorial choices that can be intuitive or deliberate. Knowing what the available focalisation choices are means animation authors can choose strategically from the alternatives available. Access to this knowledge means authorial choices about use of focalisation are more likely to be considered ones.

METALANGUAGE

These systems of focalisation options also provide a metalanguage of grammatical design, a shared language for teachers and students to talk about how focalisation can be designed and varied. Studies have shown that access to a shared metalanguage enables students to make noticeably more sophisticated, precise commentaries on their own movie texts (Burn & Durran, 2006, pp. 282–283) but that, as yet, few of us have a shared language that can "capture the production logic of innovative digital media design" (Sheridan & Rowsell, 2010, p. 22). Care, therefore, has been taken with the naming of the options here to facilitate use of a shared metalanguage with middle years students for talking about focalisation choices and the ways in which moving image semiotic resources work to realise these choices.

SYSTEMS

The organisation of *semiotic resources* for moving image focalisation draws on Halliday's (Halliday & Hasan, 1985) system networks. This taxonomic inventory describes the available semiotic choices. Opposition is the primary category in any system network as shown in Eggins's (2004, p. 198) example in Figure 7.1. As an example, the choices within the main course of a meal are set out as a system network to show the basic system conventions. This is a map of the logical choices available in one particular circumstance.

This network demonstrates how a choice of options means the user can create several alternative main courses. Choices are arranged in a series of graded oppositions that require a decision at each level. Beginning on the left, the curly bracket indicates simultaneous choices—from both the protein and greens components of the meal. This example then follows choice of greens to show how the delicacy of choice increases further into a system. The square brackets offer either/or choices. In a more complex network, each of these meaning options has identifiable *realisations*, statements describing the general characterisation of the meaning potential involved, specifying how the option is realised as seen in Figures 7.2 and 7.3.

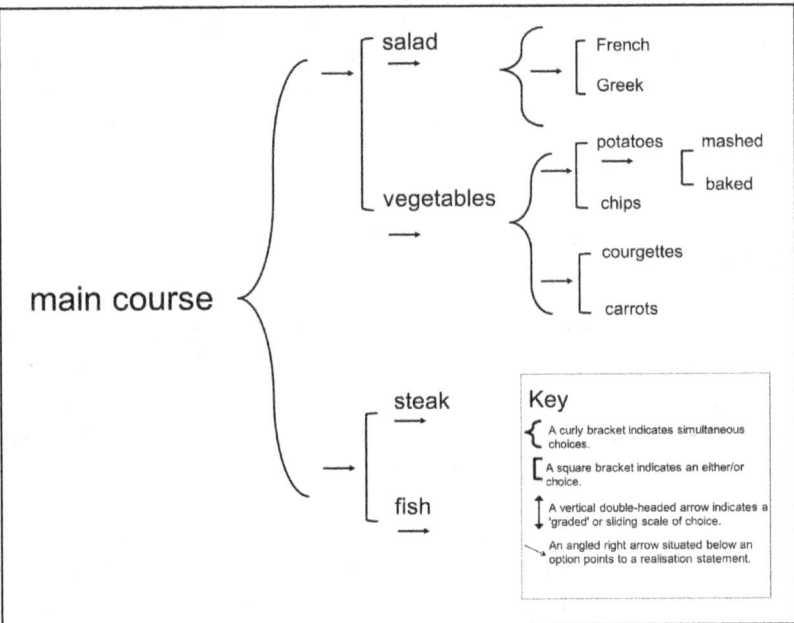

Fig 7.1. Example of part of a system network and explanation of symbols, reproduced from Eggins (2004, pp. 196–198).

FOCALISATION SYSTEM NETWORK

This Focalisation[5] system is designed to identify possible viewer/character affiliation options in this 3-D animation production context. Establishing affiliation between the viewer and a character concerns how the viewer is positioned to align with a particular character or characters across the overall film. Such affiliations can be timely and variable. Focalisation choices enable the user to construct and manipulate these interpersonal interactions. These choices are realised or enacted using the available moving image semiotic resources through the interrelated resources of camera and character initiated movement, in conjunction with shot framing and editing. Through these choices, interpersonal relationships between the participants in a moving image text can "change in front of our eyes" within or across shots (van Leeuwen, 2005b, p. 87).

There are three simultaneous initial entry points into this interpersonal, moving image Focalisation network as seen in Figure 7.2: the Focaliser system (choice of who sees); the Focalised system (choice of what is seen); and the Focalising system (choice of how it is seen). Meaning is achieved by a simultaneous combination of these semiotic design elements as these options work together, either in a complementary or contrasting way. There are multiple pathways through the system, and like the different potential meals in the example above in Figure 7.1, a story too can be "told" in different ways.

While the micro focus in this work is the construction of interpersonal meaning through focalisation in a single shot, or across two or more associated shots in a sequence as they work together to develop a relationship between the focalisation participants, it is the cumulative effect on the overall design of the narrative that counts.

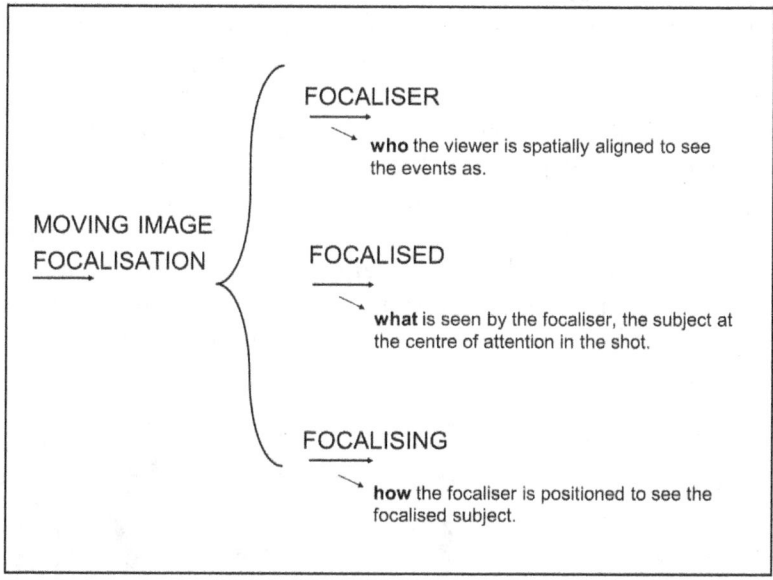

Fig 7.2. The primary oppositions in a Focalisation system network.

RESEARCH METHOD AND EXAMPLE

This system network has developed through a dynamic mix of theory and practice. Early examples of student use of focalisation resources are used to illustrate this final design of the network, in particular the work of one student, 11-year-old Riley.

Riley responded to an introductory lesson introducing explicit grammatical design information about viewer stance by applying it in innovative ways in a retelling of the nursery rhyme "Humpty Dumpty." At the time, Riley's class was participating in a series of lessons to develop knowledge and application of multimodal semiotic design in conjunction with how these meanings could be realised through the software affordances, including camera movement and character movement.

During this process, I worked with the class teacher to introduce students to point of view through a View, Deconstruct, Demonstrate, Do, and Reflect pedagogic cycle (Chandler, O'Brien, & Unsworth, 2010), discussing examples and experimenting with different options. Students were encouraged to think about what these possible alternatives contributed to the telling of their story in terms of interpersonal relationships between the viewer and the depicted character.

As seen in the screen shots in Figure 7.3, Riley's Humpty story is set in a medieval context. The title shot shows the egg sitting on the bridge. Shot one is from Humpty's point of view, as he wags his legs surveying the scene before him. In shot two, we see Humpty falling off the bridge. In shot three, the King's men (knights) gather round. Shot four shows Humpty in a coffin when a weeping hen arrives and peers in. The various drafts of Riley's work show that he tried a number of focalisation options for some shots before making a final decision. This student's creative and thoughtful decisions about viewer affiliation in each shot and across the story became the catalyst for demonstrating to students how viewer position could be manipulated for narrative purposes and in particular for influencing the way the viewer related interpersonally to the depicted characters.

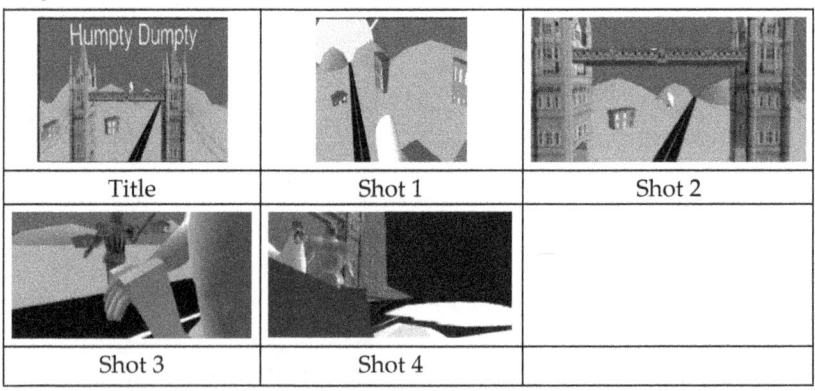

Fig 7.3. Shot sequence from Riley's "Humpty Dumpty" retelling.

CHOICE OF FOCALISER

Focalisation knowledge enables the animation author to make informed choices about who sees, what, and how at every stage in designing their film. The Focalisation overview in Figure 7.4 shows how these moving image options work together, with the simultaneous choice of Focaliser (who sees), Focalised (what), and Focalising (how).

USING FOCALISATION CHOICES TO MANIPULATE AUDIENCE VIEWPOINT | 133

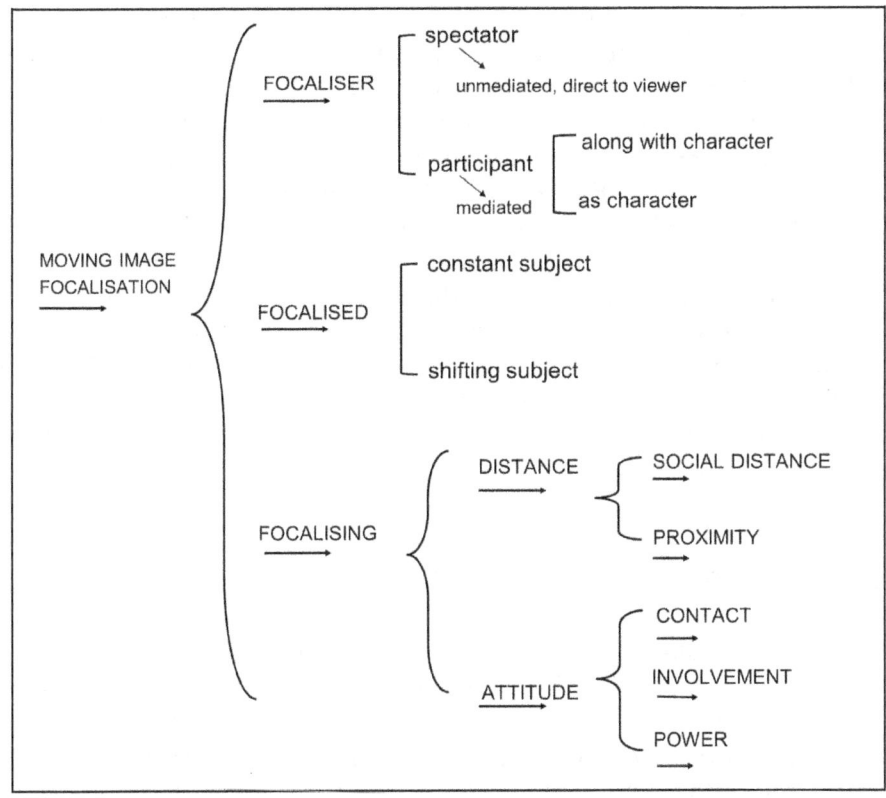

Fig 7.4. The primary oppositions in a moving image Focalisation design network.

The Focaliser entry point offers two either/or choices as shown in Figure 7.5. The viewer can be positioned to see the action directly or to "see" vicariously via a character.[6] Painter, Martin, and Unsworth (2013) categorise these two options as "mediated" (vicarious) focaliser and "unmediated" (direct) focaliser and the design of this section of the network draws on their work.

UNMEDIATED FOCALISATION

Unmediated or "direct as viewer" choice means the camera can position the viewer anywhere in relation to the action and characters, with no intermediary. The viewer is positioned to see the focalised subject from outside the story world. Using the terms *external spectator* or *external observer* seems to make this outsider viewer position clearer to students. As it is unrelated to any character within the story, this focalisation position does not have to look "natural" and makes possible the occasional use of creative but improbable shots.

The first example in Figure 7.5 from the title shot of "Humpty Dumpty" (Figure 7.3) is an unmediated view of Humpty sitting on the bridge. Interpersonally, the distance between the unmediated viewer and the remote character could be seen to create a sense of aloofness between the viewer and the subject. This type of distant unmediated focaliser is often the default shot position in student filmmaking, as evident in Pennie and Beth's Dreamtime story discussed earlier. Typically this is the default focaliser position because students do not know how or why they could use alternative focalisation choices. Riley's animation would be far less interesting to watch if the rest of the shots were to be like this. In this shot, however, we also need to consider that interpersonal meaning isn't the only meaning system at work. From an ideational perspective, this unmediated shot provides essential plot information as it shows Humpty's fall; and compositionally, Humpty is positioned in the middle of the shot with waving white legs to draw the viewer's attention.

MEDIATED FOCALISATION

The opposing Focaliser option provides more innovative potential for manipulating interpersonal meaning. The "mediated" focaliser option offers the author two either/or choices to enable the viewer to participate briefly in the story world—either *along with* a character, or through identification *as* a character (Painter et al., 2013).

ALONG-WITH-CHARACTER FOCALISATION

Positioning the viewer to see events along with the character aligns the viewer close behind or alongside a character. Here, the viewer can see part of the character's body and also sees what the "aligned character" sees (often called an "over shoulder" shot). There are two examples of this choice of focaliser in Riley's Humpty story. In shot 2 (Figure 7.3) the viewer is positioned at the elbow of one of the knights (a King's soldier); but although we are closely aligned with this character, we cannot see his face. We can see along with this character, as we can clearly see what he is looking at. In shot 4 (Figure 7.3), the viewer is positioned alongside Humpty in the coffin, and again we can only see part of Humpty. The hen peering in is the focalised subject, offering a point of shared visual interest. This shared perspective affiliates the viewer with the aligned character, but without entirely losing our external spectator perspective. More generally, this option allows for affiliation without complete identification.

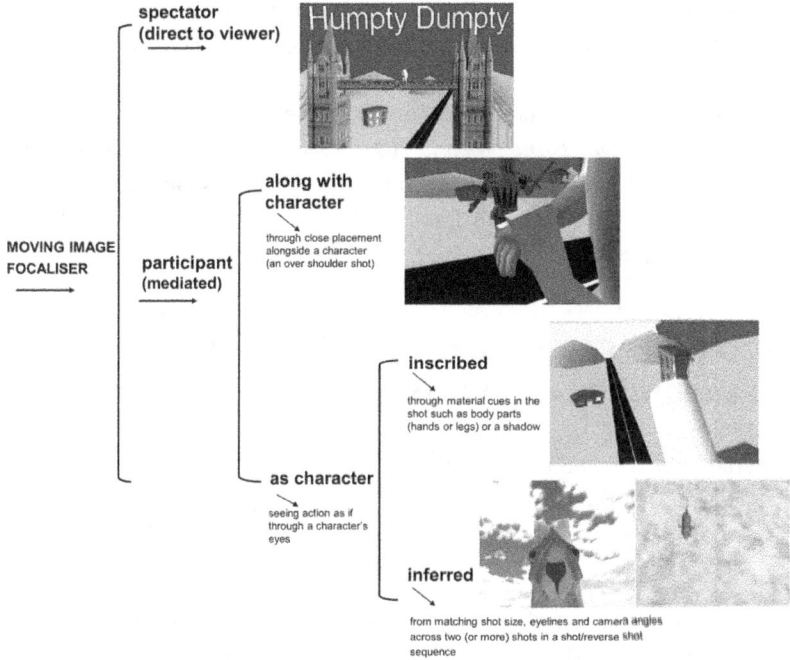

Fig 7.5. The primary oppositions in a moving image Focaliser system (after Painter et al., 2013).

AS CHARACTER FOCALISATION

The viewer is positioned "as a character" within the story when seeing the events from the character's exact spatial position. This first-person option is realised through positioning the camera approximately where the character's eyes would be, showing what this character would see. Called a "point of view" shot, it creates a completely shared perspective between the viewer and the character. This position can give the viewer "an exaggerated sense of intimacy" with the character (van Sijll, 2005); and as Verstraten (2009, p. 90) notes, this option can logically be used to privilege the point of view character's position in telling the story, and encourage strong viewer affiliation with this character's vision or situation.

A first-person perspective is used to enable the viewer to experience story events directly and also focuses absolute attention on the subject of the shot. In filmmaking, bringing story events close can be an intense and emotionally draining experience for the viewer, so this first-person perspective is generally used strategically (van Sijll, 2005) to maintain a balanced emotional rhythm. In contrast, first-person "shooter" video games use this first-person perspective much of the time, creating a dramatic, action-packed, emotional roller coaster experience for the player (Galloway, 2006).

In terms of metalanguage, many students in the study were already familiar with the term *first-person point of view* from game playing experience, and from first-person point of view work with print texts. As a consequence, the term *first-person point of view* was commonly used in the classroom to describe the "as character" focaliser perspective.

INSCRIBED OR INFERRED? REALISING "AS CHARACTER" OR FIRST-PERSON FOCALISATION

Focalising "as character" can be realised two ways: meaning can be *inscribed*, or it can be *inferred* (Painter et al., 2013).

Inscribed Meaning

Meaning can be inscribed in the shot through the use of material or physical cues such as hands or feet or a shadow in the shot as they would be seen by the character. This information clearly shows the character is spatially positioned exactly where the camera is. As seen in Figure 7.5, the "as character" example positions the viewer as Humpty, inscribed by the physical cue of the swinging legs in the front of the shot. Inscribing a first-person perspective in film also often relies on resources from other modes, for example, the focalised subject beckoning to the camera or speaking directly to the camera, or the sound of footsteps in combination with the camera moving toward something.

Inferred Meaning

Inferred meaning is where information in one shot sets up the context for the viewer to understand whose point of view is the focus of the following shot. For example, a character shown looking around or at the camera in shot A, followed by a shot of something (for example a key) in shot B (or vice-versa), enables the viewer to assume that the subject of shot B is what the character in shot A sees, and that we are now seeing "as this character." Murphet (2005, p. 91) calls this *associative* focalisation, where inferred meaning enables us to associate the perceptions created across a sequence of shots as they fuse into a "single complex image in the mind" (p. 91).

Inferred meaning is realised through a "shot-reverse shot" film editing technique. Matching shot size, eyelines, and camera angles across two (or more) shots visually "stitches" (Macken-Horarik & Andoniou, 2007, p. 372) shots of focaliser and focalised together in fabricating a strong "spatial continuity" that generates a realistic assumption that subject must be near the focaliser and sharing the same "semantic-perceptual space" (Eder, 2006, p. 71). This technique is vital to the development of interpersonal relationships in moving image texts and is well ingrained in our viewing behaviour as demonstrated in early twentieth-century Russian filmmaker Lev Kuleshov's famous montage experiment. Kuleshov took a series of shots of people's faces from different times and places and edited a sequence where each face was followed by a shot of random event or subject. By matching eyelines and camera angles between each face and the following event, he was able to construct a logical film narrative in which the audience automatically assumed the events and characters were in the same time and space. As McQuire (1998) concludes: "what began as a *trick effect* gravitated to constitute the very fabric of cine-realism—at least when performed within certain parameters" (p. 79).

CHOICE OF FOCALISED SUBJECT

Choice of focalised subject works in conjunction with choice of focaliser to establish affiliation between the viewer and characters, and between characters. In a mediated viewer position where the viewer is positioned as or alongside a character, attention is on what—the things and people—the focalising character is looking at. This is evident in Riley's Humpty (Figure 7.3) where in shot 1, through Humpty's eyes, we see the character's world as he looks around from the bridge. In shot 3, the viewer is aligned with the knights as we are positioned close alongside one knight looking at another. Again, in Riley's final Humpty shot, the viewer is positioned alongside the broken Humpty inside his coffin, and the subject focus is shared as we look up to the focalised subjects as they peer in.

Seeing one character as the subject more often than others can also be effective in developing the focaliser's affiliation with this character. Viewer/character affiliations can be manipulated through degrees of emphasis or "focus" on a character as the subject (Chatman, 1980, 1986; Nunning, 2001, p. 216), which can be used to encourage stronger empathy with the fate of this character. This means that even if we don't ever see things from the character's literal perspective, the viewer can still share a strong affiliation with the character and we can feel that we share the character's point of view through the interest-focus on this character as the subject of shots (Chatman, 1986, p. 190). In summary, although in some situations focalising as a character can give the most complete identification with the character, this is always influenced by the subject of the shot and in the context of any previous development of affiliation.

FOCALISED SUBJECT AND MOVING IMAGE SEMIOTIC RESOURCES

The author can choose to have a constant subject in the shot or use the available moving image options to change the subject within the shot. This can be done through movement initiated by the camera, the character, or both (see Figure 7.4).

Changing the subject within a shot is a powerful technique as it destabilises perceptions of who or what the focaliser (mediated or not) is being affiliated with in the shot. The use of character initiated movement to change the focalised subject is used with great effect in the last shot in Riley's Humpty. In shot 4 (Figure 7.3) the viewer is positioned inside the coffin alongside the broken egg, looking out at a knight (the focalised subject). Any perceived affiliation between the knight and the focaliser alters when unexpectedly a hen walks into the shot—closer to the coffin and in front of the knight. The focaliser's attention is now riveted on the hen as a single tear runs down her face; metaphorically, the knight fades into the background. The closing lid of the coffin breaks this visual connection with the characters outside, and the viewer is alone with Humpty inside the coffin. The viewer's affiliation with the focalised subjects changed with the movement of the characters and with the shutting of the coffin lid.

Camera movement can also be used to play with the viewer's perceptions of the subject. The technique of having the camera follow a character for a short time in a busy scene and then suddenly swapping to a different character is sometimes seen in the opening shots of films. The viewer is left trying to makes sense of who or what is important in the shot as it is impossible for the focaliser to create any affiliation with these changing characters.

FOCALISING CHOICES

The other simultaneously occurring powerful choices within this tripartite focalisation system concern how the relationship between the focaliser and the focalised can be portrayed using the available focalising system resources (Figure 7.4). *Focalising* choices determine the nature of affiliations between the *focaliser* and the *focalised*, either in a single shot or over a sequence of associated shots. The three Focalising systems here, Distance, Contact, and Attitude (Figure 7.4), are derived from Kress and van Leeuwen's (2006) principal "still image" social meaning systems for analysis and description of the interactive relationships between the focaliser and the depicted subject. I have adapted and extended these systems to work specifically with the production and analysis of moving image animation narratives as these "how" choices enable the nature of focaliser/focalised subject interactions to change constantly within a single shot as well as across shots.

The Distance system also draws on recent work by Painter, Martin, and Unsworth (2013) to include Proximity as a parallel system (Figure 7.6). Social Distance concerns degrees of distance between the viewer and the depicted characters via both mediated (as character and alongside) and unmediated (direct as viewer) focaliser choices, looking at how closely the focaliser is positioned in relation to the subject. Proximity concerns the perceived distance between the depicted characters framed within the shot, how close together or how far apart they appear in the shot.

SOCIAL DISTANCE SYSTEM

What does distance or closeness between participants contribute to development of relationships and to the telling of the story? Kress and van Leeuwen's (2006) Social Distance system for still images describes how size of shot frame can be used to spatially manipulate relationships through a social interpretation of distance separating people, places, or things. Social distance is based on Edward Hall's (1966) theory of how in our everyday interactions with other people such as close family, intimate partners, friends, acquaintances, and strangers, we each carry an "invisible set of [personal] boundaries" beyond which we are only comfortable to let certain people in (p. 124). Others coming into this space can elicit feelings of social discomfort depending on how well we know them and what we feel about them. As portrayed in Figure 7.6, social distance is a sliding scale between intimate and remote with many graduations, and it is important in establishing the nature of interpersonal relationships and affiliation in a moving image text.

Choice of social distance is important in every shot, encouraging or discouraging the viewer in forming affiliations with the characters. Social distance is realised by shot size, which determines how much of the subject is seen. Social distance is discussed through examples from "The White Dove," a 3-D animation narrative by Year 6 student Lara in Figure 7.6. An extreme close-up of part of a face such as the eyes, or a close-up showing the head and shoulders of the character, situates the interaction between character and focaliser within a close, intimate personal space. It creates an imaginary intimacy. A mid-shot showing two characters from the waist up suggests friendship or a close social relationship. The more we can see of a character's whole body in the surrounding, the greater the sense of social distance. Long shots can be used to create a sense of public or stranger distance, serving to keep the viewer at arm's length from any emotional connection to the characters and the events in the story.

As in any real life interaction, the focaliser will usually feel comfortable seeing characters they have an affiliation with at a close social distance, for example, a close-up of the main character's face. Placing the focaliser socially in close proximity to the character can be deployed to create an affinity between the focaliser and the character. This is possible because the intensity of the emotional affiliation with the subject increases exponentially in direct relation to the degree of encroachment into the focaliser's perceived intimate social space (Kress & van Leeuwen, 2006; Painter et al., 2013). This use of personal social space can also be designed as a negative interaction, for example, a close-up of the villain in the story could create a feeling of fear or unease as it invades the viewer's personal social space.

Social distance is also a useful resource in setting up associative focalisation relationships through changes in social distance across a shot sequence. For example, cutting from a wide shot showing people in the distance to a close-up shot of one face in the group serves to connect the focaliser more strongly to this character for the moment than the others in the shot.

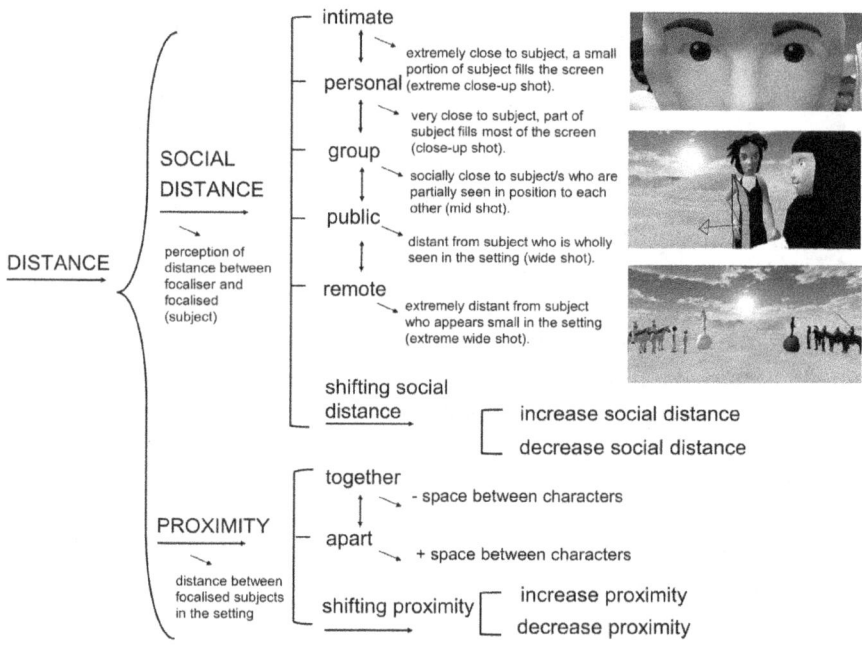

Fig 7.6. The primary oppositions in a Distance system.

Character initiated movement can manipulate social distance because "as the distance changes, so will the viewer's imaginary relation to the people, places and things shown" (van Leeuwen, 2005b, p. 88). The subject can move closer to the camera, coming into the focaliser's personal space to increase imaginary intimacy with the focaliser (or fear if it is a threatening character or action) or move further away from the camera to increase social distance.

Change in social distance can also be camera initiated as the camera can zoom out or zoom in to move the focaliser toward or away from the focalised subject, visibly changing the social distance and the associated emotional connections within a shot. For example, the unmistakable emotion in a close-up quickly disappears when the camera pulls out to a more distant view.

PROXIMITY

The parallel system of PROXIMITY, working in conjunction with Social Distance, is also a useful affiliation tool for the author to develop and portray relationships between the depicted characters. In positioning characters in a shot, one of the choices the author makes is about the subjects' (implied) physical closeness to each other and what this proximity choice might tell the viewer. Focaliser knowledge of proximity is dependent on how much can be seen framed in the shot. A long shot or mid-shot will give more information about proximity in a single shot, whereas close-ups may be used to create close proximity through associated shot-reverse shots.

Based on social distance, characters shown positioned close together can indicate social familiarity. Or, characters can be positioned apart, where the degree of space between the depicted characters can range from negligible to vast, signalling a corresponding increase in distance in the character's relationships with each other.

The long shot in Figure 7.6 is an interesting combination of two aspects of proximity. The light coloured characters on the left are positioned close to each other in a tight group, as are the dark coloured characters on the right. The bunching of characters together within each group indicates group affiliation. However, the space shown between the light and the dark groups in the shot also signifies important narrative information about the interpersonal interaction between the two groups. The large space between suggests a lack of affiliation between the two groups.

Character movement can be used to shift this perception. If, for example, in this shot the groups move toward each other and mingle, the meaning changes. Such an intermingling could indicate friendship, or hostility if it is a battle scene—depending of course on information from other modes such as facial expressions, body language, sound effects, and music.

In other examples, based on Kuleshov's experiment, shot–reverse shot sequencing can be also used to construct a close proximal relationship between characters not even in the same place. For example, a telephone conversation can be visually constructed through a shot-reverse shot sequence of close shots of each of two characters on the telephone, establishing a pseudo but still effective sense of close proximity between them.

The camera and the character can also move together to shift social proximity. Verstraten (2009) illustrates this through the following scenario: if a character walks menacingly toward the focaliser and the camera moves back indicating the focaliser is backing away, this quickly establishes a relationship based on the focaliser's fear of the approaching subject. If, however, the camera remains still, positioning the focaliser as stationary and holding ground as the menacing character approaches, it constructs a different relationship. This time the focaliser is portrayed as brave or perhaps unafraid of the approaching character.

CONTACT SYSTEM

The system of Contact as shown in Figure 7.7 concerns focaliser–focalised connection through direct eye contact or gaze or no contact. There are no graduations. The author can position the depicted subject's gaze to create direct (imaginary) eye contact with the focaliser, or not.

What can the contact system contribute to the design of interpersonal relationships? The "no contact" option is more common in a narrative film text, as it creates an illusionary barrier between what is real and what is imaginary—implying the characters don't know they are being looked at. "No contact" may be used strategically by the author to keep the viewer at a distance from the internal story world.

In contrast, direct contact is a powerful direct address to the focaliser, described by Kress and van Leeuwen (2006) as a "demand for attention" (p. 120). Direct contact can be used to increase the focaliser's mediated or unmediated affiliation with some depicted characters. In an unmediated context, direct contact from a depicted character to the viewer breaks the "fourth wall," the boundary separating the imaginary world from the real world, to explicitly acknowledge the viewer's presence. Direct contact is a one-way process, with the character inviting the viewer's involvement in this fictional world, and can be used to heighten identification or empathy at key moments in the story (Painter et al., 2013). The use of such close direct contact (shown in the direct contact shot example in Figure 7.7) at a pivotal narrative moment can align the viewer with this character, creating a sense of affiliation through the illusion she is interacting directly to you.

Within the moving image Contact system, temporal and movement resources can enable gaze to shift in various ways during a single shot and for different lengths of time. Shifting gaze can be realised through use of camera movement or character movement, but contact only occurs when the character is directed/animated to look at the camera. "Contact" can be dynamicised through character movement where the focalised character/subject can initiate or break contact, where the focalised character can be directed/animated to look toward the camera and then turn away or avert their gaze. Opportunity for contact can also be initiated through camera movement where the camera can move the focaliser's position in the narrative world to directly face the character on a shared horizontal plane.

USING FOCALISATION CHOICES TO MANIPULATE AUDIENCE VIEWPOINT | 143

Shifting contact can be used to construct and colour interpersonal relationships through choices of the length and stability of the character's gaze at the focaliser, on a continuum from a prolonged stare to a brief glance, or through intermittent glances over the length of the shot (Jewitt, 2009). Shifting contact can be initiated by camera movement (pan around/across, tilt up/down, zoom in) to capture or focus attention on the focalised subject's direct gaze out to the focaliser, or by moving the focaliser's view away from the subject's direct eye contact. Focalised subjects can turn their eyes/head/body toward the camera to establish direct gaze, or turn away from camera to remove eye contact with the viewer. A combination of camera and subject movement can also be deployed to work in conjunction to create a contact or no contact situation.

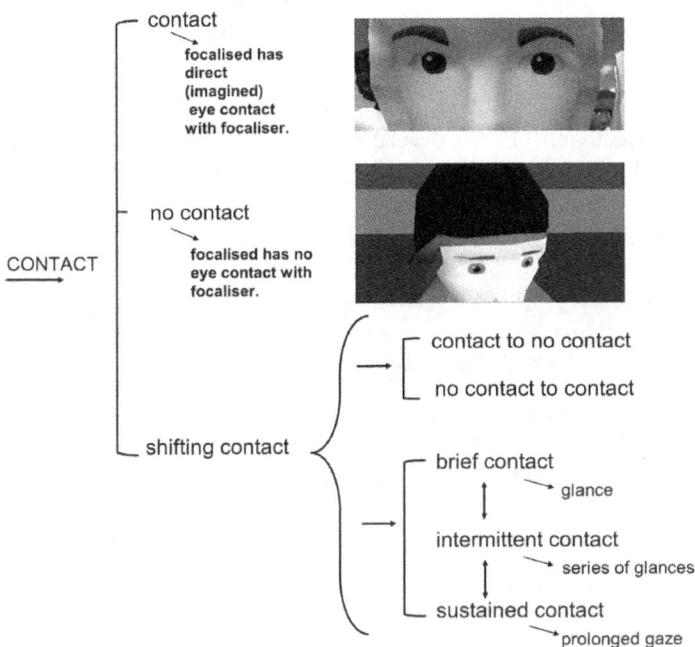

Fig 7.7. The primary oppositions in a Contact system.

ATTITUDE SYSTEM

The focalising system of Attitude in Figure 7.8 accounts for the bodily orientation or angle of depicted characters' positions in relation to each other and to the viewer. Two sets of systems operate within the system of attitude: a horizontal dimension that can be used to manipulate degrees of Involvement between the focaliser and the focalized, and a vertical dimension that can be used to construct hierarchical Power relationships between the participants (Kress & van Leeuwen, 2006).

INVOLVEMENT

The horizontal dimension creates viewer involvement or solidarity where the depicted subject faces the focaliser front on. The opposite effect, when the subject is angled obliquely away from the focaliser, can create the perception of viewer detachment. Kress and van Leeuwen (2006) describe how level of involvement between the focaliser and the focalised subject is realised through the degree of the horizontal angle on a continuum from most involved viewer-subject connection to least involved, with many degrees of meaning in between. When the focalised subject is presented "front on" to the viewer at a close social distance, particularly if in conjunction with direct contact such as in the example in Figure 7.7, it can create a sense of maximum involvement between the worlds of the focaliser and focalised; this, as van Leeuwen (1999) describes, can be quite confronting. The focaliser has nowhere else to look and so is forced into the interaction.

High detachment from focaliser	+ detachment (- involvement)	High involvement with focaliser

Fig 7.8. Degrees of involvement of subject in relation to focaliser through choice of horizontal position.

In contrast, placing the subject at an oblique angle to the focaliser creates a sense of detachment, a feeling of seeing the action on the sidelines. The degree of the horizontal angle in positioning how a character faces or turns away from the focaliser can be used to create an increased sense of detachment between them, but this always depends on the choices made simultaneously in the other focalising systems, in particular the Social Distance implied between the focaliser and the focalised subject.

While Kress and van Leeuwen (2006) argue that within this Attitude system the most detached feeling or lack of relationship is created by a character's back to the focaliser, Unsworth (Chapter 6 in this volume) points out that when social distance is considered as well, a close rear view is actually an important part of creating a strong character/focaliser alignment. A close rear view is in fact almost an "along with character" focaliser position signifying a higher focaliser/focalised character involvement while a more distant back view can signify a strong detachment from or exclusion of the viewer. Student authors Pennie and Beth intuitively used a powerful combination of close social distance and extreme oblique positioning of the characters with their backs to the camera in their final shot to create a compelling sense of shared involvement in this experience.

Camera and character initiated movement can also change these perspectives very quickly. The camera can zoom in or out to increase or decrease the social distance and can pan horizontally to increase or decrease the focaliser's frontal involvement with the subject. The focalised subject can strengthen detachment by turning away from the focaliser (camera) or increase involvement by turning to face the focaliser (camera). Combined camera and subject initiated movement also work together to increase or decrease perceived focaliser involvement with the subject.

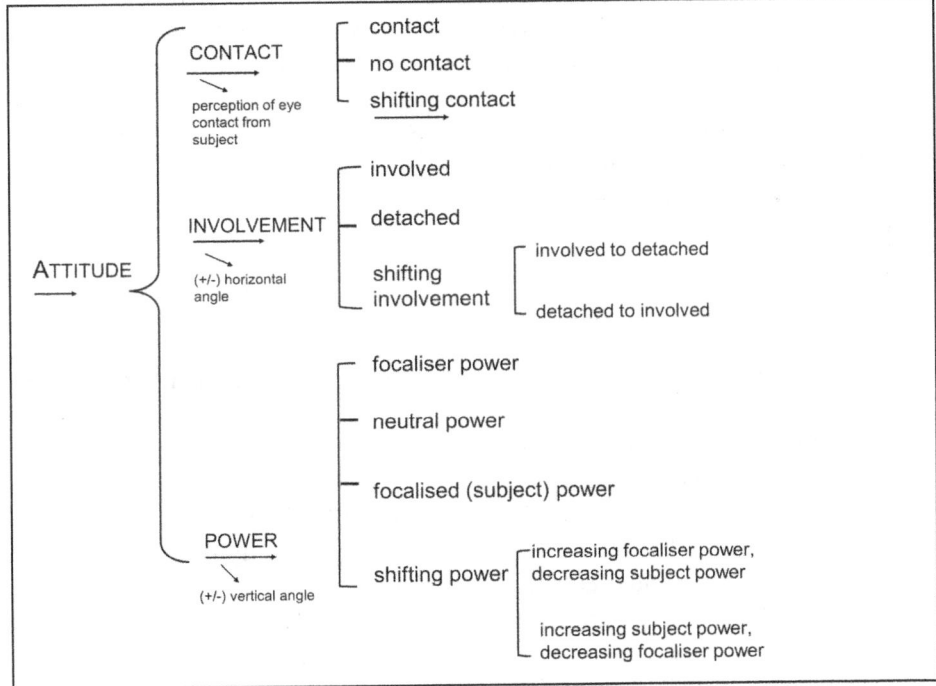

Fig 7.9. The primary oppositions in an Attitude system.

POWER

Realisation of Power in the visual semiotic can be created through the use of vertical angle. The focaliser can be positioned along a power continuum between three meaning options: focaliser power, neutral power, and subject or focalised power (Kress & van Leeuwen, 2006, pp. 140ff, 49). Focaliser power in a relationship can be signified through positioning the focaliser as looking down on the (subordinate) subject. This is realised through the use of a high angle shot, where the camera is above the focalised subject and angled to look down. In reverse, if the focaliser is positioned low and looking up at the focalised subject, this can imply subject power and authority in this relationship. This is realised through the use of a low angle shot, where the camera is placed below the focalised subject and angled to look up.

The degree of implied power imbalance on a spectrum from extreme to insignificant can be realised through variations of these camera angles, the greater the angle, the greater the power imbalance implied between subordination and domination. In the middle is a neutral position whereby all participants in this relationship at this moment are on the same vertical plane, and this is the most common shot angle.

Camera and character movement and combinations of both can dynamically change these perceived relationships. A subject can move from a higher angle perspective to a lower angle in relation to the focaliser by sitting, walking down stairs, or kneeling, for example, with the camera tilting the vertical angle from high to low as it follows. In reverse, a character can stand up to loom over the focaliser or walk up stairs to assume a more dominant position with the camera moving along with the character. The camera can also be tilted to a higher angle or down to a lower one within a shot to change the focaliser's perspective with or without the character moving.

CONCLUSION

The moving image semiotic resources identified and discussed in this chapter are what van Leeuwen (1999) describes as socially accepted rules or codes, conventions, a process of unconscious agreement and enactment within a society (Eggins, 2004), which works as long as the users agree on the meaning (Saussure, Baskin, Meisel, & Saussy, [1916] 2011, p. 110). These conventions are not rigid. For example, a low angle shot does not automatically infer low status in a relationship, and as noted earlier, a turned back does not automatically mean detachment. What is presented here is a pedagogically oriented choice system of semiotic of resources that can be used to guide students in using focalisation to create interpersonal relationships between the text participants—the viewer and the depicted characters within their animation narratives. Such a system for the construction of interpersonal relationships in a moving image text allows us to identify, name (using metalanguage), and therefore make visible the available semiotic design choices available for focalisation. Developing an understanding of the possible semiotic resources within the Focalisation systems of Focaliser, Focalised Subject, and the Focalising systems of Contact, Attitude, and Distance will enable the young author to manipulate potential interpersonal relationships between the viewer and the characters through a growing understanding of the different interpretive possibilities available to support narratorial intention.

The next step is to make this information accessible to students and teachers based on a hypothesis that if students have explicit knowledge of these focalisation choices and how they can be realised using moving image resources, they will draw on these resources in their animations in a purposeful way to enhance the quality of their productions. Already, as seen in the examples discussed, in the early stages of introducing this knowledge of moving image focalisation to middle years students, it is evident that some students have responded in quite innovative ways to this explicit multimodal grammatical design knowledge in composing their narratives. Riley's "Humpty Dumpty" is an important indicator of the value of explicit teaching of multimodal design in supporting students' creative work and proved a useful example for demonstrating the possibilities of varying viewer position in animation narratives. This simple but effective animation is one of many examples collected that demonstrate that students can effectively use this knowledge of focalisation to manipulate viewer perspective and draw on the meaning potential of the semiotic resources available. As Riley said, "When the teacher first mentioned doing first-person things I got a bit interested so I tried to do it." It is hoped that this theoretical work will provide a tool kit of resources to enable others to try to do it, too.

ACKNOWLEDGMENT

The author would like to thank Riley, Pennie and Beth, and Lara for their invaluable contributions to this research and their wonderful teachers for their willing participation in this quest for knowledge.

NOTES

1 Real names are not used.
2 Halliday defines an "act of meaning" as "an instance of meaning formed out of an infinite meaning potential for reflecting on the world and interacting with others in it" (Halliday & Webster, 2009, p. 1).
3 The software is Kahootz, produced by the Australian Children's Television Foundation. Kahootz was provided to every government school in Victoria, Australia, between 2004 and 2011 and used in many schools across Australia. At time of printing, similar currently available software of this type includes Muvizu (http://www.muvizu.com/), Alice (http://www.alice.org), Moviestorm (http://www.moviestorm.co.uk/hub/australia), and Anim8or (http://www.anim8or.com).

4   For further discussion on definitions and terminology see Chatman (1980, 1986), Fludernik (2012), and Jahn (1996).
5   The use of small capital letters such as FOCALISATION indicates an option is also the name of a system in a network.
6   While it is possible for the moving image author to shift focalisers between mediated and unmediated within a shot, it is complex and uncommon. This is not developed in detail as it would only add an unwarranted level of complexity to the process for beginner animation authors.

REFERENCES

Bal, M. (1981). The laughing mice: Or: On focalization. *Poetics Today, 2*(2), 202–210.
Bal, M. (2009). *Narratology: Introduction to the theory of narrative* (C. van Boheemen, Trans., 3rd ed.). Toronto: University of Toronto Press.
Bordwell, D., & Thompson, K. (2010). *Film art: An introduction* (9th ed.). New York: McGraw Hill.
Burn, A. (2013). *The kineikonic mode: Towards a mulitmodal approach to moving image media*. National Centre for Research Methods (NCRM), unpublished.
Burn, A., & Durran, J. (2006). Digital anatomies: Analysis as production in media education. In D. Buckingham & R. Willett (Eds.), *Digital generations children, young people, and new media* (pp. 273–293). Mahwah, NJ: Erlbaum.
Burn, A., & Parker, D. (2001). Making your mark: Digital inscription, animation, and a new visual semiotic. *Education, Communication & Information, 1*(2), 155–179. doi:10.1080/14636310120091913
Burn, A., & Parker, D. (2003). Tiger's big plan: Multimodality and the moving image. In C. Jewitt, & G. Kress (Eds.), *Multimodal literacy* (pp. 56–72). New York: Peter Lang.
Chandler, P. D., O'Brien, A., & Unsworth, L. (2010). Towards a 3D multimodal curriculum for upper primary school. *Australian Educational Computing 25*(1), 34–40.
Chatman, S. (1980). What novels can do that films can't (and vice versa). *Critical Inquiry, 7*(1), 121–140.
Chatman, S. (1986). Characters and narrators: Filter, center, slant, and interest-focus. *Poetics Today, 7*(2), 189–204.
Cope, B., & Kalantzis, M. (2000). Designs for social futures. In B. Cope & M. Kalantzis (Eds.), *Multiliteracies: Literacy learning and the design of social futures* (pp. 182–234). South Yarra: Macmillan.
Eder, J. (2006). Ways of being close to characters. *Film Studies: An International Review, 8*, 68–79.
Eggins, S. (2004). *An introduction to systemic functional linguistics* (2nd ed.). New York: Continuum.
Fludernik, M. (2012). *An introduction to narratology*. New York: Taylor & Francis.
Galloway, A. R. (2006). *Gaming: Essays on the algorithmic culture* (pp. 39–69). Minneapolis: University of Minnesota Press.
Genette, G. ([1972] 1980). *Narrative discourse* (J. Lewin, Trans., 2nd ed.). Oxford, UK: Basil Blackwell.
Hall, E. (1966). *The Hidden Dimension*. Garden City, New York: Doubleday.
Halliday, M. A. K. (1973). *Explorations in the functions of language*. London: Edward Arnold.
Halliday, M. A. K. (1978). *Language as a social semiotic: The social interpretation of language and meaning*. London: Edward Arnold.
Halliday, M. A. K. (2004). *An introduction to functional grammar* (3rd ed.). London: Edward Arnold.
Halliday, M. A. K., & Hasan, R. (1985). *Language, context and text: Aspects of language in a social semiotic perspective*. Waurn Ponds: Deakin University Press.
Halliday, M. A. K., & Webster, J. (2009). *The essential Halliday*. London: Continuum.

Jahn, M. (1996). Windows of focalization: Deconstructing and reconstructing a narratological concept. (rhetoric and poetics). *Style, 30*(2), 241(27).

Jewitt, C. (Ed.). (2009). *The Routledge handbook of multimodal analysis*. London: Routledge.

Jewitt, C., & Kress, G. (2003). *Multimodal literacy*. New York: Peter Lang.

Kress, G. (2010). *Multimodality: A social semiotic approach to contemporary communication*. London: Routledge.

Kress, G., & van Leeuwen, T. (2006). *Reading images: The grammar of visual design* (2nd ed.). London: Routledge.

Kuhn, M. (2009). Film narratology: Who tells? Who shows? Who focalises? Narrative mediation in self-reflexive fiction films. In P. Hühn, W. Schmid, & J. Schönert (Eds.), *Point of view, perspective, and focalization: Modeling mediation in narrative* (pp. 259–277). Berlin: Walter de Gruyter.

Macken-Horarik, M., & Andoniou, M. (2007). Genre and register in multiliteracies. In B. Spolsky & F. M. Hult (Eds.), *The handbook of educational linguistics*. Chichester, UK: John Wiley and Sons.

Martin, J. R. (2011). Systemic functional linguistics. In K. Hyland & B. Paltridge (Eds.), *Continuum companion to discourse analysis* (pp. pp 101–119). London: Continuum.

McGuire, S. (1998). *Visions of modernity*. London: Sage.

Murphet, J. (2005). Point of view. In H. Fulton, R. Huisman, J. Murphet, & A. Dunn (Eds.), *Narrative and media* (pp. 86–95). Cambridge: Cambridge University Press.

Nunning, A. (2001). On the perspective structure of narrative texts: Steps toward a constructivist narratology. In W. van Peer & S. B. Chatman (Eds.), *New perspectives on narrative perspective* (pp. 207–224). Albany: State University of New York Press.

Painter, C., & Martin, J. R. (2011). Intermodal complementarity: Modelling affordances across image and verbiage in children's picture books. In F. Yan (Ed.), *Studies in functional linguistics and discourse analysis* (pp. 132–158). Beijing: Education Press of China.

Painter, C., Martin, J. R., & Unsworth, L. (2013). *Reading visual narratives: Image analysis of children's picture books*: Equinox Publishing Limited.

Saussure, F. D., Baskin, W., Meisel, P., & Saussy, H. ([1916] 2011). *Course in general linguistics* (R. Harris, Trans.). New York: Columbia University Press.

Sheridan, M. P., & Rowsell, J. (2010). *Design literacies*. London: Routledge.

The New London Group. (1996). A pedagogy of multiliteracies: Designing social futures. *Harvard Educational Review, 66*(1), 33.

van Leeuwen, T. (1999). *Speech, music, sound*. Basingstoke: Macmillan.

van Leeuwen, T. (2005a). *Introducing social semiotics*. New York: Routledge.

van Leeuwen, T. (2005b). Moving English: The visual language of film. In S. Goodman & D. Graddol (Eds.), *Redesigning English: New texts, new identities* (pp. 82–103). London: Open University.

van Sijll, J. (2005). *Cinematic storytelling: The 100 most powerful film conventions every filmmaker must know*. Studio City, CA: Michael Wiese Productions.

Verstraten, P. (2009). *Film narratology* (S. van der Lecq, Trans.). Toronto: University of Toronto Press.

WEB RESOURCE

Creating multimodal texts: http://creatingmultimodaltexts.com/
This website is a repository of tools, resources, and examples of student-made multimodal texts designed for use by literacy teachers. The 3-D animations described in this chapter can be viewed in the Animation section.

FURTHER READING

Kress, G., & van Leeuwen, T. (2006). *Reading images: The grammar of visual design* (2nd ed.). London: Routledge.

Murphet, J. (2005). Point of view. In H. Fulton, R. Huisman, J. Murphet, & A. Dunn (Eds.), *Narrative and media* (pp. 86–95). Cambridge: Cambridge University Press.

Thomas, A. (2008). Machinima: Composing 3D multimedia narratives. In L. Unsworth (Ed.), *New literacies and the English curriculum* (pp. 167–185). London: Continuum.

CHAPTER EIGHT

Social Media, Education, and Contentious Literacies

MARTIN WALLER

INTRODUCTION

The aim of this chapter is to explore the following three questions.

1. Can some literacies, such as social media, be classified as contentious because they subvert from traditional notions of literacy?
2. Does social media need to be recognised in the education of children in the twenty-first century?
3. Can a classroom blog, which integrates social media, be used as an effective way to develop new literacies?

The chapter is set within the context of the fact that the world has changed and the ability and speed at which we can access information on a global scale has transformed the way in which we live and learn in the world and led to a proliferating mass of new literacies. It has been argued that young people have spent their entire lives surrounded by these new literacies through the use of digital technologies such as video games, digital music, video cameras, mobile phones, and other tools of the digital age (Prensky, 2001). Many citizens of today's society and economy now manage their lives through online services such as calendars, e-mail, documents, social networks, and ecommerce. As a result, these digital practices are becoming embedded in the everyday rituals of how we live and work in the world (Davies & Merchant, 2009). In addition, these new technologies have been instrumental in developing and facilitating new meaning-making systems to create new text types and channels for communication and expression (New London Group, 1996; Prestridge, 2005). This is a time of rapid technological change in the way that we live and work in the world and it shows no indication that it will slow down. Furthermore, literacy practices are embedded in many of these new meaning making systems and communication channels, which has implications for educators (New London Group, 1996). As Walsh (2008) states:

> If we consider the process of literacy within new mediums of communication it is evident that "reading" can involve the reading of written text, interacting and responding as well as viewing and listening, while "writing" can involve talking, interacting, designing and producing. In fact the traditional ideas of text are blurred, as are the processes of literacy, as many contemporary texts are hybrid texts that may involve a range of processes. (p. 102)

Such assertions have caused intense debate about the true nature of literacy in society and pose significant problems for educators who are trying to address the cultural and linguistic diversity in their classroom against claims and counterclaims of a canon of literature, the importance of grammar and the need to get "back to basics" (Kalantzis & Cope, 2000). This includes using technologies as an "add-on" to replicate existing practices rather than embracing the increasing convergence of media through digital and Internet technologies to ensure that educators address the skills and competencies—the multiple literacies—that are required by the whole range of contemporary media in a systematic and integrated way, rather than in isolation (Buckingham, 2002). Various theories have highlighted the importance of acknowledging and developing real-world social literacy in the classroom. Two such examples are that of *Multiliteracies* (New London Group, 1996) and *New Literacy Studies* (Street, 1984, 1997, 2003).

Multiliteracies also includes a pedagogical framework for approaching teaching and learning focused around designs of meaning and progresses through various stages (Table 8.1). As the New London Group (1996) state:

> Multiliteracies also creates a different kind of pedagogy, one in which language and other modes of meaning are dynamic representational resources, constantly being remade by their users as they work to achieve their various cultural purposes. (p. 4)

Table 8.1. The Pedagogy of Multiliteracies (Kalantzis, Cope, & Fehring, 2002, p. 3)

Multiliteracies Phases	Definition
Situated Practice *Immersion in experience*	Either the various knowledge, interests, and experiences students bring to school or immersion in new experiences that are familiar and make at least half sense when introduced to learners

Overt Instruction *Describing patterns in meaning*	Explicit teaching, for example, uncovering the underlying patterns in meaning and communication
Critical Framing *Locating purpose*	Explaining purposes, that is, what a piece of communication is for. To get what done? For whom? Why?
Transformed Practice *Added meaning*	Applied learning. Real-world meanings, communication in practice, applying understandings to a new context

This view, which presents Multiliteracies as a transformative approach to the teaching of literacy, also acknowledges the fundamental changes that digital technologies have on our social world (Prestridge, 2005) through online participation, networking, and collaboration (Davies & Merchant, 2009). Such a view also links with the social factor of New Literacy Studies (Street, 1984, 1997, 2003) in which literacy educators and students should see themselves as "active participants in social change" (New London Group, 1996, p. 5). The reasoning behind the blogging project outlined in this chapter is founded in the idea that choosing to ignore or reject technology or regard it as somehow ideologically neutral are dangerous options (Ellis, 2001). As Buckingham (2002) suggests:

> Digital technology is increasingly permeating nearly every aspect of children's everyday lives—and particularly their leisure time. In the process, it has become much more than a matter of information technology. On the contrary, new digital media are rapidly becoming the dominant means of entertainment, communication and cultural expression. (p. 7)

It is clear that such technologies are altering the underlying architecture of literacy in society and leading to a proliferating mass of new literacies. As Barton (2007) attests there are many different literacies that can be associated with different domains of life, particularly home, school, and work. If the education system has the responsibility to provide children with the skills and understanding necessary for interpreting the constructed nature of popular culture and the meaning-making system in society then changes need to be made to content, pedagogy, and progression with literacy and digital technologies. Jenkins and colleagues (2006) have developed a set of competencies that they believe highlights effective new media literacy practice in today's society (Table 8.2).

Table 8.2. New Media Literacies Competencies (Jenkins, Purushotma, Clinton, Weigel, & Robinson, 2006, p. 4)

Skill/Competency	Definition
Play	The capacity to experiment with one's surroundings as a form of problem solving
Performance	The ability to adopt alternative identities for the purpose of improvisation and discovery

Simulation	The ability to interpret and construct dynamic models of real-world processes
Appropriation	The ability to meaningfully sample and remix media content
Multitasking	The ability to scan one's environment and shift focus as needed to salient details
Distributed Cognition	The ability to interact meaningfully with tools that expand mental capacities
Collective Intelligence	The ability to pool knowledge and compare notes with others toward a common goal
Judgment	The ability to evaluate the reliability and credibility of different information sources
Transmedia Navigation	The ability to follow the flow of stories and information across multiple modalities
Networking	The ability to search for, synthesize, and disseminate information
Negotiating	The ability to travel across diverse communities, discerning and respecting multiple perspectives, and grasping and following alternative norms

These competencies presented by Jenkins and colleagues (2006) provide a useful lens for ascertaining children's engagement with new literacy practices. The increasing convergence of media and embedding of digital practices into people's lives (Davies & Merchant, 2009) means that we need to be addressing the need for skills and competencies in a systematic and integrated way, rather than being an "add-on tool for learning" (Buckingham, 2002, p. 12).

Within this context of Multiliteracies and New Literacy Studies, I therefore build on my existing work into the use of social networking in the classroom (Waller, 2010, 2011). In this chapter I look at the way new social technologies such as web blogs (blogs) have altered the underlying architecture of how many people communicate and subsequent implications for education. Despite boyd (2007) arguing that some educators have viewed such technologies in a negative way and fail to "let go of pre-existing assumptions about how the world works" (p. 1), I aim to explore ways in which such social technologies can be implemented in classrooms to add value to teaching and learning. This work includes case studies from my own classroom and field data and interviews with the children in my class. This work is framed within the lens of New Literacy Studies (Street, 1984, 1997, 2003) and Multiliteracies (New London Group, 1996) as well as the work of Jenkins and colleagues (2006). The overall aim is to explore whether social technologies can truly promote a view of literacy that is consistent with the New Literacy Studies and Multiliteracies or whether dominant discourses of literacy continue to influence meaning-making even when using digital technologies in a relevant and meaningful way.

BLOGGING AS A NEW LITERACY PRACTICE

A classroom blog is at the centre of this research as blogs are strong examples of literacy as a social practice and multimodal texts (Davies & Merchant, 2009). Blogs are online public writing environments in which postings (individual writing segments often containing hyperlinks to other online sources) are listed in reverse chronological order (Blood, 2002, in Ellison & Wu, 2008). They also link to theories of multimodality as Davies and Merchant (2009) suggest:

> Blogs, as multimodal texts, allow us to represent these activities in text form, in still and moving image, or in audio format—and, of course, some of the most interesting blogs are a judicious combination of these modes. (p. 31)

Furthermore, blogs need to be understood as part of a wider network of texts and the process of publishing makes a difference to the way they mean and the role they play in society (Lankshear & Knobel, 2006). The read/write functionality of blogging, wherein readers are encouraged to comment on blog posts and thus become part of an evolving, public discussion, is a primary reason behind blogging's popularity (Ellison & Wu, 2008). Blog reading in this sense is better understood through the participation in online text production as well as through reading widely across online content (Davies & Merchant, 2009). At the centre of the practice of blogging is always the notion of literacy as a communicative practice, which also links to the competencies outlined by Jenkins and colleagues (2006).

Blogging has been adopted sporadically in classrooms across the globe but there is little empirical evidence regarding the effectiveness of blogs compared to other traditional forms of pupil writing (Ellison & Wu, 2008). However, if blogging is looked at through the lens of developing digital literacies and social literacy it embodies many of the skills evident in both New Literacy Studies and Multiliteracies. As Marsh (2008) states:

> The primary appeal of blogging for teachers and pupils alike may be that it enables writing to occur for authentic purposes for "real" audiences. Readers of blogs can comment on individual posts and this promotes interactivity and writing as a collaborative process. (p. 174)

Blogs in this sense can be classed as Web 2.0 systems (O'Reilly, 2005), which signal increased social interaction through online collaboration, networking, and collaboration (Davies & Merchant, 2009). For many young people online self-expression and media consumption is a deeply engrained and engaging part of their lives (Ellison & Wu, 2008). Blogging is therefore a typical contemporary literacy practice that characterises social networking practices that many children and young people engage in outside of school (Dowdall, 2006; Marsh, 2008). Blogging may not necessarily be an existing literacy practice for young children in this study but it does offer them the opportunity to develop competencies with new literacy practices. In this sense the use of classroom blogs can potentially extend the children's literacy practices to include Web 2.0 systems that have been traditionally ignored in classrooms (Davies & Merchant, 2009). Furthermore pupils may be more invested in their writing if they know they are writing for an audience and their peers (Ellison & Wu, 2008). Blogs are also multimodal texts where written text, still and moving images, or audio content can be used when composing posts as Davies and Merchant (2009) suggest:

> They can learn how to use the affordances of different semiotic modes to make meaning, how to hyperlink their text to others, and get a sense of what online participation is actually like through commenting, and responding to comments, on their own and other people's blogs. (p. 91)

In this sense blogging encapsulates aspects of multimodality (Kress, 2003), New Literacy Studies, and Multiliteracies through the creation of multilayered texts that allow for social participation and co-construction of knowledge. However, as the New London Group (1996) suggests, "strong pedagogy needs to be embedded in the use of educational blogs since blogging does not always necessarily promote social participation, because it is possible to use blogging software without using any hypertextual features" (Davies & Merchant, 2009, p. 89). Blogs can emulate traditional writing environments and features through the written word. However as Prestridge (2005) attests:

> The conventional view does not consider the transformative impact of new technology and would therefore support a notion of "adding-on" or accommodating ICTs. However, theoretically the concept of Multiliteracies has been presented as a transformative approach to the teaching of literacy. Multiliteracies acknowledges the fundamental changes that current technologies have on our social worlds. (p. 9)

Where blogging is used as a means of emulating traditional writing practices its potential as a system for multimodal meaning-making through digital technologies is squandered. The effects of blogging on both attainment and perceptions of literacy have not been well-documented. However it is clear that blogging (like any new technology) will not independently or autonomously increase student learning as Ellison and Wu (2008) cautioned:

> Most important, blogging (like any new technology) is not a panacea and will not independently or autonomously increase student learning. Sound instructional techniques must be developed and practiced in order to achieve increased student learning. (p. 116)

It is important that all educational activities planned by educators should embody sound teaching and pedagogy such as that of Multiliteracies in the sense that children progress through various stages to transform and consolidate their learning and understanding of literacy as a communicative practice. The importance of experience with real texts and practices associated with them is therefore crucial if pupils are to be introduced to a new communicative system such as blogging. Furthermore social participation of students who already use the Internet at home and are becoming critical users of information is central to the blogging platform promoting a view of literacy that is consistent with Multiliteracies and New Literacy Studies. As Buckingham (2002) suggests, young people have a strong sense of their autonomy and authority as learners and they want to contribute rather than simply consume. The use of a classroom blog may be an effective strategy to support such an ethos of contribution within the lens of New Literacy Studies and Multiliteracies.

CONTEXT AND METHODOLOGY

The research presented in this chapter was conducted in a suburban state primary school in the United Kingdom and is focused around a class of Year 2 children (six- and seven-year-olds) whom I teach full-time. The blogging work described was taking place independently from this research project as part of a Year 2 blogging project. This meant that time was set aside in the timetable for the children to be supported in their introduction to the classroom blog as part of their curriculum provisions, which Ellison and Wu (2008) describes as essential. The children were interviewed before and after the blogging project in small discussion groups. As part of this research write-up all names were replaced with pseudonyms and removed from screenshots. The children also adhered to the following rules:

1. Always use appropriate language and grammar in posts and comments.
2. Never write children's first and last names together. Children may only mention first names in blog posts and comments.
3. Children should not upload pictures of themselves, their friends, or their family that would make them identifiable.
4. Everybody should be respectful of people's achievements and efforts when leaving comments.
5. If children are unhappy with anything that is written on the blog they must tell a member of the school staff immediately.

The rules were discussed with the children and they were asked to describe a consequence of not following each of the rules. Such e-safety discussions and precautions should always be built into projects involving children using the Internet. There were also many safety mechanisms built into the actual blogging platform. While the entire Internet population could read the content of the class blog posts, only I could create user accounts and allow people to post information onto it. This meant that the children had a global audience who could read their work and submit comments for approval to offer feedback on work. In addition user roles were set up so that children did not have access to system settings. The pupil user role meant that children could not automatically publish work but instead had to click "Submit for Approval," which sent the blog post to the teacher who could publish it. The process was also the same for comments. Only the administrator account could instantly publish comments onto the blog. If a pupil or external visitor commented on a particular post then I moderated the comment before it was published. This meant that the pupils could engage with the social nature of literacy embedded in the commenting system in a safe yet meaningful manner. Such an approach of social literacy links with the theory of New Literacy Studies (Street, 1984, 1997, 2003) but also promotes the safe use of Web 2.0 systems as typified by Davies and Merchant (2009) who suggest that children need to learn e-safety protocols in a relevant and authentic context.

The children used the blog for approximately three months as part of the curriculum provisions. They were allowed to write about anything that interested them so that they could make reference to their own popular cultures and social worlds. Blog posts and comments were tracked throughout the whole project for analysis of the links between New Literacy Studies and Multiliteracies. Children received training and demonstrations on ways to use the blog and features such as uploading of videos and embedding of multimedia content. This was initially through scheduled lessons where the children were able to explore a range of blogs and then experiment with the technical affordances available. Effective modelling is part of any successful teaching strategy and links specifically with Multiliteracies pedagogy where pupils look at a range of available designs (New London Group, 1996).

ANALYSIS AND FINDINGS

Children who were taking part in the project were interviewed using audio recordings. Once the transcription process was complete the data were analysed using a filtering process of highlighting key themes. Blog post and comment feeds were also tracked throughout the duration of the whole project. This meant that I was able to draw out key themes and examples that promoted a view of literacy that was consistent with New Literacy Studies and Multiliteracies. Blog posts were also analysed in terms of the modes and meaning-making systems employed (Kress, 1997, 2000, 2003) in addition to the competencies with digital technologies that were employed by the children (Jenkins et al., 2006).

All the children in the class used the classroom blog inline with their regular curriculum provisions in school. Dedicated ICT lessons were given over to blogging activities and children were encouraged to use the blog in free-reading and writing sessions. Engagement with the blog varied vastly across the class. Some children did not use the blog at all outside of scheduled class time whereas others were exceptionally enthusiastic and blogged at home regularly. Content varied from highly complex written texts to posts that included images and videos. Many of the children also chose to comment on blog posts by their peers.

The children became aware of the blogging system and the affordances that it offered them in multimodal meaning-making as well as the global nature of online publishing. In this sense the blogging system acted as an extension to their repertoire of communicative practices. The children have not had access to such a platform in the past but their use of the classroom blog allowed them to engage with literacy as a social practice (Gee, 1996; Street, 1984, 1997, 2003). As Eve suggests:

> You can write things on it and everyone in the world can see it. You can put comments on it and we can put pictures on and you can put pictures on and you can put videos on.

This demonstrates that Eve understands the way in which meaning is made through multimodal modes of communication (Kress, 2003) and that meaning should not be constricted to the written word. It also allowed her to use new literacy practices rather than her existing repertoire of practices. As a result she was able to use forms of literacy such as video implicitly and also began to develop an understanding of multimodal conventions. This was evidenced by the fact that I observed the children beginning to recognise how the meaning we make arises from the interdependence of words, images, and other elements in a wider context (Merchant, 2007). For example, Figure 8.1 shows a blog post by one of the children that includes written text, images, and comments:

Fig 8.1. Screenshot of a child's multimodal blog post.

The post in Figure 8.1 was written by a child on a topic of their own interest. They also used the technical affordances of the blog to add additional elements such as images so text creation is seen as an act of design (New London Group, 1996) where audience is addressed in a different way than when speaking to their peers (Davies & Merchant, 2009). They therefore demonstrate the Play competency after they have experimented with image upload as well as the Transmedia competency when they are able to follow and create meaning across multiple modalities (Jenkins et al., 2006). Also, as Kress (2003) states, decisions about whether it is better to use a combination of modes or a single mode are related to audience and purpose. In this example modal choice has been influenced by the writer's view of what the reader or audience will need to help them understand meaning (Bearne & Wolstencroft, 2007). However, even though the child combined the modes effectively, they were unable to articulate this type of literacy during verbal discussions. Their multimodal authoring was clearly based upon existing experience with reading such texts. As Millard (2003) attests:

> Different modes of meaning imprint themselves powerfully on the consciousness in turn, as the emphasis falls on one, then another mode of replication. (p. 3)

The child has experienced a range of multimodal meaning systems and decided to use their knowledge of the print and visual modes to create a new text. They have included an image which they have drawn and uploaded themselves to convey further meaning to the audience. In this sense the blog has opened up new meaning-making systems to the children and as a result they see it as liberating from the constricted nature of "traditional" literacy work that they are accustomed to:

> **Rachel:** You can do anything you want on the blog, but nothing silly and you have to do the work that you get told in your literacy books.

In this sense the blog is seen as facilitating a transformative pedagogy (New London Group, 1996) where literacy is "free from the constraints of books and regimented practices where control is exerted through targets and the timed delivery of key skills" (Millard, 2003, p. 4). This links with the work of Kress (2003) who states that in such contexts:

> In a multimodal environment the realisations of this are aided by the varying affordances of the modes and the facilities of the new media of information and communication. (p. 49)

Literacy is ideological in this context and not autonomous as the children are free to make meaning through the various modes available. Furthermore the blog supports the view of Multiliteracies (New London Group, 1996) where meaning is made using not just digital technologies but also through the act of design where children can use the technical affordances of the blog to shape a multilayered text using the range of meaning-making systems. Web 2.0 standards such as hyperlinks were also used within blog posts such as that in Figure 8.2.

> ## Growing Greener
>
> You can get on the <u>growing greener</u> website there are lots of fun recipes on there. Mr Waller set it up! There are lots of gardening tips on.
>
> This entry was posted on July 23, 2011and is filed under <u>Blog</u>. You can follow any response to this entry through <u>RSS 2.0</u>. You can leave a <u>response</u> or <u>trackback</u> from your own site.

Fig 8.2. A Representation of a blog post with hyperlink.

This demonstrates that the children are able to recognise the conventions of multilayered texts and Web 2.0 systems where information is shared and distributed across multiple sites and fields of information. Hyperlinking is a complex task but this seven-year-old child has demonstrated the technical mastery of the blogging platform to be able to do it effectively. Through such work the children also developed a greater understanding of writing for audience and purpose:

MW:	What does publishing mean?
George:	Err, you just send it to you and you can send it online.
MW:	Who sees it when it goes online?
Adam:	Everybody... it goes on the blog.
MW:	Is that a good or bad thing?
George:	Good.
MW:	Why is it a good thing?
George:	People can make their ideas and send them forward.

Literacy as presented in this extract is not only globalised but also typified with the sharing of information, which links to the new media literacy competencies of Networking and Collective Intelligence (Jenkins et al., 2006). The children see the blog as a means of sending information forward to the rest of the population and as such typifies the social nature of literacy as promoted by New Literacy Studies (Street, 1984) and Multiliteracies (New London Group, 1996) where literacy is presented through social participation. The children clearly see literacy within this lens when using the blog and recognise the effectiveness of such a transmission system. Furthermore the commenting system on the blog allows the children to comment on posts and also receive feedback on their work. As Eve suggests:

Eve:	I put it on the blog and everyone clicked on it and I was really happy because I got lots of comments.
MW:	What were the comments saying?
Eve:	One was saying you put something in that Hello magazine.
MW:	How did that make you feel when people were commenting all over the world?
Eve:	Really happy and excited because I was waiting for more.
MW:	Would that happen if you were doing literacy in a book?
Eve:	No.

The above extract is in relation to a blog post about the Royal Wedding that received an influx of comments from visitors of the site (Figure 8.3).

The Royal Wedding of Will and Kate

The Royal family were so excited about the wedding that they wanted to look the best. The Queen had a blanket on her knees as soon as the driver opened the door the Queen dropped her blanked on the floor. After that Will and Harry arrived at Westminster Abbey. Kate arrived she smiled a lot she was so happy. Then the wedding started William did not want a ring that is what sum boys are like but Kates ring as very pretty. the end

This entry was posted on June 6, 2011, 9:14am and is filed under Blog. You can follow any response to this entry through RSS 2.0. You can leave a response or trackback from your own site.

COMMENTS (5)

#1 on June 6, 2011 – 1:14pm
Great to see you guys back on Twitter. I did not notice the Queen's blanket, so I have learnt something today. Thanks for the story.

#2 on June 6, 2011 – 1:55pm
What a brilliant report of such a great story. Well done all of you, keep up the good work.

#3 on June 6, 2011 – 4:01pm
I love how you reported on small details that even the newspapers and 'Hello Magazine' missed. Well done!

Fig 8.3. A representation of a blog post and comments written by one of the children.

The comments included in Figure 8.3 demonstrate that literacy is not a single essential thing constrained to a literacy lesson but a global discussion. This demonstrates that Eve's literacy practices within the blog link to the Networking competency as she is able to disseminate her work to a global audience and take part in a discussion about it (Jenkins et al., 2006). This links to the work of Marsh (2010) who talks about the use of such discussion within online social networks:

> Reading is, in this example, a social practice that extends beyond the walls of the classroom and enables children to engage in forums in which inter-generational literacy is commonplace. (p. 30)

Furthermore such intergenerational literacy inspires the children to write more for their audience as Eve suggests.

MW: Why does it make you want to do more?
Eve: So we get more comments, if we get more comments it means we can write on the blog more. If people are sending us comments it means they want us to write more and I'm happy with that.

Davies and Merchant (2009) state that one of the traditional challenges for teachers is to create authentic contexts for writing for audience and purpose. The blog as used within this project appears to achieve this along with promoting a view of literacy where knowledge is shared and discussed in a social nature through new media technologies. Incidentally, commenting was seen as one of the primary motivations of using the blog. This links to both New Literacy Studies (Gee, 1996; Street, 1984) and Multiliteracies (New London Group, 1996) as it promotes literacy as a social practice. There were also many examples where children chose to reply to their peer's work and offer feedback on their learning. Such use of the blog can be described as a community of practice (Wenger, 1998) where the children demonstrate a developing variety of communicative practices where mutual engagement is essential and the complimentary processes of participation and reification are interdependent for meaning to be negotiated (Dowdall, 2006).

In addition, blog posts such as that by Eve about the Royal Wedding (Figure 8.3) show that children are able to understand meaning in one mode and then re-create, reshape, and publish their own interpretations of meaning through other channels, thus linking with the new media literacy competency of appropriation and transmedia navigation (Jenkins et al., 2006). Furthermore, Eve was able to demonstrate the competency of simulation as she interpreted and constructed models of real-world processes that she has experienced (Jenkins et al., 2006). In this example Eve has experienced a real-world literacy event (Heath, 1983) of the Royal Wedding that was drawn from her own popular culture, and she then re-configured the modes of image and print to create a new multimodal text. This also links with the concept of transduction (Kress, 2003) and promotes a critical view of literacy where information is analysed, critiqued, and reconfigured for new meaning (Comber, 2001). The blog in this sense allowed Eve to reference popular culture texts that represented her interests and identities, thus blurring her online and offline worlds (Davies, 2006; Marsh, 2007). In addition this also links to the concept of design presented by the New London Group (1996) in "A Pedagogy of Multiliteracies." Table 8.3 highlights the processes of Multiliteracies pedagogy that Eve experienced when creating her blog post.

Table 8.3. Links Between Multiliteracies Pedagogy and Eve's Blogging Process

Multiliteracies Phases	Definition (Kalantzis et al., 2002)	Eve's Process
Situated Practice *Immersion in experience*	Either the various knowledge, interests, and experiences students bring to school or immersion in new experiences that are familiar and make at least half sense when introduced to learners	Eve experienced the Royal Wedding event on national television. She was also exposed to various media coverage of the event through television, the Internet, and print media. She regularly brought Royal Wedding supplements and DVDs into class.
Overt Instruction *Describing patterns in meaning*	Explicit teaching, for example, uncovering the underlying patterns in meaning and communication	Eve experienced Royal Wedding-themed activities in school through various media and activities. She also learned how to use the technical affordances of the blog.
Critical Framing *Locating purpose*	Explaining purposes, that is, what a piece of communication is for. To get what done? For whom? Why?	Eve used her understanding of contemporary media and print texts to design her own blog post about the Royal Wedding. She decided that she wanted to make her work unique so she looked at information that was excluded from other coverage.

| Transformed Practice
Added meaning	Applied learning. Real-world meanings, communication in practice, applying understandings to a new context	Eve applied her understanding of media conventions when designing her own blog post about the Royal Wedding. She communicated real-world events that were of interest to her in a new media. She also included elements such as the Queen's "blanket" that were ignored by news organisations. As such Eve applied her own knowledge of popular culture while using standard conventions of print and online publishing.

Furthermore the fact that the children are engaging with a Web 2.0 system suggests that using the classroom blog promotes a view of literacy consistent with that of Multiliteracies since it allows the children to develop competencies with digital technologies (New London Group, 1996). There were various references to such competencies, which can be drawn from the interview data. For example, George and Adam are able to easily talk about the process of saving and uploading images to the classroom blog:

MW: What other sorts of things have you used?
Adam: Colour Magic to do pictures.
MW: And what do you do with Colour Magic?
Adam: Save it.
George: Yeah you save it.
Adam: And then you type in what it wants to be, go back to the blog and click the little sun.
MW: And what does the sun do?
Adam: Takes you to all your documents and stuff.
MW: Right?
Adam: Takes you to "My Recent Documents" and then you look at the picture you named it. You can't look at the picture you have to look at the name you named it and then click on it to let it load.
MW: And then what do you do?
Adam: Let it go through the blog. Click on Upload.

In this process George and Adam describe a self-taught process of saving an image in a paint package and then uploading it to the classroom blog. It could be argued that these children could be classed as digital natives due to the ease with which they navigate and use the blogging environment (Prensky, 2001). They describe shortcuts such as using the "My Recent Documents," which they have learned through experimentation, and working together in blogging sessions. This links with the work of Multiliteracies theorists such as Luke (2000) who suggests:

> The ability to import, download, drop and drag text and imagery from an inexhaustible global library of information creates new skills, processes and multimodal forms of "textual" production that encourage interdisciplinary creativity and imagination, collaborative authorship, editing, reading and writing, and problem-based learning. (p. 87).

In this sense the children were able to learn digital practices of saving and uploading in an integrated and meaningful way. The relevance of the task in the context of blogging meant that the children would be able to replicate the digital practice in new situations. Furthermore, the discussion extract shows the blog has promoted an ethos of collaboration, discussion, and collective intelligence. The children clearly demonstrated a sophisticated understanding of the processes and conventions of working with Web 2.0 systems even though they are six and seven years old. They also demonstrated many of the new media literacies competencies when using the blog such as play (experimenting with uploading images), multitasking (saving the image and then relocating it), and distributed cognition (interacting meaningfully with tools that expand their understanding) (Jenkins et al., 2006). The children were also able to fit their existing use of technologies at home around the school blog. For example, Rose clearly demonstrates a mastery of other technologies when using the blogging system:

MW:	What other things have you used when you have been blogging to help you? Which other gadgets?
Rose:	iPod?
MW:	iPod?
Rose:	Not an iPod an iPad. We use the iPad in school and I use my iPod Touch at home.
MW:	So do you use your iPod Touch to blog at home?
Rose:	And the computer.
MW:	Right, so how do you get onto the blog on your iPod Touch at home?
Rose:	Err, I go onto Safari or YouTube or something and I go to the top where you can type things in and I type in the blog address and then it just comes up and I log myself in and then I write what I want to.
MW:	Right, on your little iPod Touch? That's quite clever. Who taught you how to do that?
Rose:	No one.

This shows that the blog has allowed them to not only develop their traditional communication skills but also new media competencies and communicative practices such as transmedia navigation and distributed cognition (Jenkins et al., 2006). Such skills are crucial as the range of communication needed in the children's future lives requires them to be able to combine different modes and meaning-making systems as well as being able to communicate with traditional and nontraditional texts that combine these modes and systems (Walsh, 2008, p. 106).

The discussions and blog posts also linked to children's popular culture and home worlds, which have traditionally been ignored in schooling (Buckingham, 2002). For example, the post within Figure 8.3 is based on the Royal Wedding, which was a major event at the time the blog post was written. The blog therefore allowed the children to write about their own interests, priorities, and cultures, which links with the work of Genishi and Dyson (2009) who suggest that such areas are traditionally ignored in schooling. This demonstrates that the use of the classroom blog is consistent with the way in which the children experience literacy and meaning-making in the real world. Below, Amy offers an insight into her home use of digital technologies:

Amy: Because for one thing, my mam only goes on the computer if she wants to go shopping and my sister only ever goes on if she wants to play on a game on Cbeebies and my dad just goes tweeting, not on this blog, another blog.

In this sense the child sees blogging as parallel to the digital literacy practices of her own family in a home setting. This is partly because the blog transcends the home/school boundaries in contrast to traditional schooled literacy practices where there is an "awesome disconnect" (Genishi & Dyson, 2009) between home and school practices. It also links to the work of Jenkins et al. (2006) who suggest that negotiating different spaces both online and offline is an essential competency of being literate in today's society.

A large proportion of the literacy practices on the blog also linked explicitly with the New Media Literacies competencies by Jenkins et al. (2006). These links have been drawn together in Table 8.4.

Table 8.4. New Media Literacies competencies from Jenkins et al. (2006, p. 4) and the links to blogging as a new literacy practice

Skill/Competency	Links to blogging
Play	Experimentation of the affordances of the blogging system such as uploading of images and audio
Performance	Ability to adopt an online identity to produce and consume information through the blog with an audience

Simulation	The ability to interpret and construct dynamic models of real-world processes through blog posts such as the Royal Wedding
Appropriation	The ability to meaningfully sample and remix media content using the affordances of the blogging system such as existing texts that the children wrote about in their blog posts
Multitasking	The ability to scan the blogging environment and shift focus as needed to salient details such as creating of images, researching of information offline/online, and commenting.
Distributed Cognition	The ability to interact meaningfully with tools that expand mental capacities through creation of new multimodal texts
Collective Intelligence	The ability to pool knowledge and compare notes with others toward a common goal through shared blog posts and/or the commenting system
Judgment	The ability to evaluate the reliability and credibility of different information sources when researching topics for blog posts as well as when reading others' texts
Transmedia Navigation	The ability to follow the flow of stories and information across multiple modalities using multilayered representations. Blogging also allows the children to create their own texts across multiple modes.
Networking	The ability to search for, synthesize, and disseminate information through the blogging system and have it be visible to a global audience
Negotiating	The ability to travel across diverse communities of practice and view multiple perspectives through the creation of texts and reader-response through the commenting system

It is clear from analyses of blog posts that the children are engaging with literacy as a social practice linked to New Literacy Studies (Gee, 1996; Street, 1984, 1996, 2003) as well as an act of multimodal design (Kress, 2003; New London Group, 1996) and New Media Literacies (Jenkins et al., 2006). However, during discussions the children articulated a perception of literacy that was focused around the importance of print literacy in contrast to the actual practices that they were demonstrating on the blog. This links to the dissonance between the children's understanding of the word/schooled subject of literacy and what they "do" in the classroom when using the blog. When engaging with literacy practices on the blog they operate within wider definitions of literacy that link to New Literacy Studies and Multiliteracies but when questioned they speak about definitions linked to dominant discourses of "traditional" literacy.

CONCLUSION

In schools, literacy has been treated as an autonomous neutral object to be studied and mastered in unconnected ways compared to how people actually use it in their lives (Hall, 1998). The impact of digital technologies cannot be ignored as they have created many new forms of communication (Buckingham, 2002) and are instrumental to being literate in society (New London Group, 1996). However, access to technological means of transforming literacy learning are often minimal in school and even when they are employed serve to reinstate the privilege of more literary forms (Millard, 2003).

The aim of this research was to provide an authentic context using a classroom blog to promote a view of literacy as a social practice that is consistent with both New Literacy Studies (Gee, 1996; Street, 1984, 1997, 2003) and Multiliteracies (New London Group, 1996). In addition, the aim was to promote multimodal authoring (Kress, 2003) and the new media literacy competencies through the authentic use of digital technologies (Jenkins et al., 2006). The emphasis was on modal choice and selection of appropriate modes, which is crucial to theories of New Literacy Studies and Multiliteracies. As Davies and Merchant (2009) have suggested, blogs do not necessarily promote such a view of literacy linked to Multiliteracies and do not necessarily involve new literacy practices but rather their social and technical affordances present opportunities for such work. This links to Luke (2000) who attests:

> The effects of technologies are never intrinsic to a particular media, but are always mediated by the uses to which technologies are put and the contexts in which they are used. (p. 74)

The emphasis throughout the whole project was on appropriate use of the classroom blog as a way of engaging children in literacy as a social practice and multimodal act of design that linked to the real world. Throughout the project the children continued to believe that literacy was a single essential thing (in their case a literacy lesson focused on reading and writing), which would suggest that their views are more aligned to the autonomous view of literacy presented by Street (1984) as opposed to the ideological model of New Literacy Studies (Street, 2003) and pluralist views presented in "A Pedagogy of Multiliteracies" (New London Group, 1996).

However, the way the children used the blog allowed them to demonstrate competencies linked with those of Jenkins et al. (2006) as well as develop an understanding of multimodality (Kress, 2003) and literacy as a social practice (Gee, 1996; Street, 1984). The children's blog posts referenced many of their own interests and popular cultures (Genishi & Dyson, 2009; Millard, 2003) and demonstrated that literacy was linked to their own interests and home worlds. In addition, they used a range of modes and technical affordances to create multi-layered texts such as images, typography, and hyperlinks when creating their own multimodal texts. They also used their critical reading of other multimodal texts as well as transduction (Kress, 2003) to create their own representations of existing taken-for-granted texts (Comber, 2001). In this sense the blog not only promoted a view of literacy that encapsulated digital technologies and thus linked with Multiliteracies (New London Group, 1996) and New Media Literacies (Jenkins et al., 2006), but also promoted a Critical Literacy approach to pedagogy (Comber, 2001; Comber & Nixon, 2004; Vasquez, 2004).

The commenting system of the blog also meant that the children were able to engage in literacy as a social practice as promoted in the New Literacy Studies (Gee, 1996; Street, 1984). This allowed the children to understand that literacy is a communicative practice that transcends the boundaries of the classroom and allows for powerful writing that derives from the immediacy of publication as well as from social alliances made online (Davies, 2006). In addition, the comments and discussions that took place through the blog were highlighted as a strong motivating factor for the children.

Although the blog did promote the use of multimodal forms of communication there were many posts using traditional forms of writing. However, as Merchant (2007) attests, "digital literacy extends out of print literacy, despite the fact that the process, surfaces and spaces of production and consumption are different" (p. 122). After the project the children still held the view that literacy was a "lesson" rather than a practice and there was a strong dissonance between the multimodal literacy that they actually engaged with on the blog and the way they verbalised their understanding of literacy after using the blog.

It is clear that the use of the classroom blog in this piece of research promoted a view of literacy that was consistent with both New Literacy Studies (Gee, 1996; Street 1984, 1997, 2003) and Multiliteracies (New London Group, 1996) as well as multimodality (Kress, 1997, 2000, 2003) and new media literacy competencies (Jenkins et al., 2006). The children who took part in the project evidently produced a range of multimodal texts and engaged in social practices that demonstrated this. However, the pedagogisation of literacy has taken place so deeply in the education system (Hall, 1998) that the children still verbally prevail to the dominant discourses of literacy in society that are consistent with some policy documents meaning that new and digital literacies become secondary and are seen as contentious. Further research into this area needs to focus on the sustained use of these systems and the fact that they cannot simply change perceptions of literacy instantly, but rather such a development needs to be an incremental process as the boundaries between print and digital forms of literacy become increasingly blurred (Buckingham, 2002). This will mean that official definitions of literacy are further challenged so that systems such as blogs are not seen as contentious literacies and can be used effectively to allow children to develop the skills necessary to become successful participants in today's (and tomorrow's) society.

REFERENCES

Barton, D. (2007). *Literacy: An introduction to the ecology of written language*. Oxford: Blackwell.
Bearne, E., & Wolstencroft, H. (2007). *Visual approaches to teaching writing: Multimodal literacy 5–11*. London: Paul Chapman.
boyd, d. (2007). Social network sites: Public, private or what? *Knowledge Tree, 13*. Retrieved from http://www.danah.org/papers/KnowledgeTree.pdf
Buckingham, D. (2002). New media literacies: Informal learning, digital technologies and education. In D. Buckingham & A. McFarlane (Eds.), *A digitally driven curriculum?* (pp. 7–19). London: IPPR. Retrieved from http://www.ippr.org/uploadedFiles/projects/digital_curriculum.pdf
Comber, B. (2001). Critical literacies and local action: Teacher knowledge and a "new" research agenda. In B. Comber & A. Simpson (Eds.), *Negotiating critical literacies in classrooms* (pp. 271–282). London: Routledge.
Comber, B., & Nixon, H. (2004). Children reread and rewrite their local neighbourhoods: Critical literacies and identify work. In J. Evans (Ed.), *Literacy moves on: Using popular culture, new technologies and critical literacy in the primary classroom* (pp. 97–114). Oxon, England: David Fulton.
Davies, J. (2006). Escaping to the borderlands: An exploration of the Internet as cultural space for teenage wiccan girls. In K. Pahl & J. Rowsell (Eds.), *Travel notes from the new literacy studies: Instances of practice*. Clevedon, England: Multilingual Matters.
Davies, J., & Merchant, G. (2009). *Web 2.0 for schools: Learning and social participation*. New York: Peter Lang.
Dowdall, C. (2006). Dissonance between the digital created worlds of school and home. *Literacy, 40*(3), 153–163. doi:10.1111/j.1467-9345.2006.00421.x
Ellis, V. (2001). Analogue clock/digital display: Continuity and change in debates about literacy technology and English. In A. Loveless & V. Ellis (Eds.), *ICT, pedagogy and the curriculum: Subject to change* (pp. 131–151). Oxon, England: Routledge Falmer.
Ellison, N., & Wu, Y. (2008). Blogging in the classroom: A preliminary exploration of student attitudes and impact on comprehension. *Journal of Educational Multimedia and Hypermedia, 17*(1), 99–122. Retrieved from https://rhhstechcomm.wikispaces.com/file/view/ Blogging.pdf
Gee, J. P. (1996). *Social linguistics and literacies: Ideology in discourses* (2nd ed.). London: Francis Taylor.
Genishi, C., & Dyson, A. H. (2009). *Children, language and literacy*. New York: Teachers College Press.
Hall, N. (1998). Real literacy in a school setting: Five-year-olds take on the world. *The Reading Teacher, 52*(1), 8–17. Retrieved from http://www.jstor.org/stable/20202003
Heath, S. B. (1983). *Ways with words: Language, life, and work in communities and classrooms*. Cambridge: Cambridge University Press.
Jenkins, H., Purushotma, R., Clinton, K., Weigel, M., & Robinson, A. J. (2006). *Confronting the challenges of participatory culture: Media education for the 21st century*. Retrieved from http://www.newmedialiteracies.org/the-literacies.php
Kalantzis, M., & Cope, B. (2000). Multiliteracies: The beginning of an idea. In M. Kalantzis & B. Cope (Eds.), *Multiliteracies: Literacy learning and the design of social futures* (pp. 3–8). London: Routledge.
Kalantzis, M., Cope, B., & Fehring, H. (2002). *PEN: Multiliteracies: Teaching and learning in the new communications environment*. Marrickville, Australia: PETA. Retrieved from http://www.eric.ed.gov/PDFS/ED465170.pdf
Kress, G. (1997). *Before writing: Rethinking the paths into literacy*. London: Routledge.
Kress, G. (2000). Multimodality. In M. Kalantzis & B. Cope (Eds.), *Multiliteracies: Literacy learning and the design of social futures* (pp. 182–202). London: Routledge.

Kress, G. (2003). *Literacy in the new media age.* London: Routledge.
Lankshear, C., & Knobel, M. (2006). *New literacies: Everyday practices and classroom learning* (2nd ed.). Berkshire, England: Open University Press.
Luke, C. (2000). Cyber-schooling and technological change: Multiliteracies for new times. In M. Kalantzis & B. Cope (Eds.), *Multiliteracies: Literacy learning and the design of social futures* (pp. 69–91). London: Routledge.
Marsh, J. (2007). New literacies and old pedagogies: Recontextualizing rules and practices. *International Journal of Inclusive Education, 11*(3), 267–281. doi:10.1080/13603110701237 522
Marsh, J. (2008). "Am I a couch potato?" Blog: Blogging as a critical literacy practice. In K. Cooper & R. E. White (Eds.), *Critical literacies in action: Social perspectives and teaching practices* (pp. 171–184). Rotterdam, The Netherlands: Sense Publishers.
Marsh, J. (2010). The ghosts of reading past, present and future: The materiality of reading in homes and schools. In K. Hall, U. Goswami, C. Harrison, S. Ellis, & J. Soler (Eds.), *Interdisciplinary perspectives on learning to read: Culture, cognition and pedagogy* (pp. 19–31). Oxon, England: Routledge.
Merchant, G. (2007). Writing the future in the digital age. *Literacy, 41*(3), 118–128. doi:10.1111/j.1467-9345.2007.00469.x
Millard, E. (2003). Towards a literacy of fusion: New times, new teaching and learning. *Reading, Literacy and Language, 37*(1), 3–8. doi:10.1111/1467-9345.3701002
New London Group. (1996). A pedagogy of multiliteracies: Designing social futures. *Harvard Educational Review, 66*(1). Retrieved from http://wwwstatic.kern.org/filer/blogWrite44ManilaWebsite/paul/articles/A_Pedagogy_of_Multiliteracies_Designing_Social_Futures.htm
O'Reilly, T. (2005). *What is Web 2.0?* Retrieved from http://oreilly.com/web2/archive/what-is-web-20.html
Prensky, M. (2001). Digital natives, digital immigrants. *On the Horizon, 9*(5), 1–6. Retrieved from http://www.marcprensky.com/writing/Prensky%20-20Digital%20Natives,%20Digital%20Immigrants%20-%20Part1.pdf
Prestridge, S. (2005). Exploring the relationship between multiliteracies and ICT. In *Proceedings of the Pleasure, Passion, Provocation AATE/ALEA National Conference.* Broadbeach, Brisbane, Australia: Gold Coast Convention and Exhibition Centre.
Street, B. (1984). *Literacy in theory and practice.* London: Cambridge University Press.
Street, B. (1997). The implications of the new literacy studies for education. *English in Education, 31*(3), 45–59. doi:10.1111/j.1754-8845.1997.tb00133.x
Street, B. (2003). What's "new" in new literacy studies? Critical approaches to literacy in theory and practice. *Current Issues in Comparative Education, 5*(2), 77–91. Retrieved from http://www.tc.edu/cice/Issues/05.02/52street.pdf
Vasquez, V. (2004). Creating opportunities for critical literacy with young children: Using everyday issues and everyday text. In J. Evans (Ed.), *Literacy moves on: Using popular culture, new technologies and critical literacy in the primary classroom* (pp. 78–96). Oxon, England: David Fulton.
Waller, M. (2010). It's very very fun and ecsting—Using Twitter in the primary classroom. *English Four to Eleven, 39,* 14–16. Retrieved from http://www.le.ac.uk/engassoc/publications/411910.html
Waller, M. (2011). "Everyone in the world can see it"—Developing pupil voice through online social networks. In G. Czerniawsku & W. Kidd (Eds.), *The student voice handbook: Bridging the academic/practitioner divide.* London: Emerald.
Walsh, M. (2008). Worlds have collided and modes have merged: Classroom evidence of changed literacy practices. *Literacy, 42*(2), 101–108. doi:10.1111/j.1741-4369.2008.00495.x
Wenger, E. (1998). *Communities of practice, learning, meaning and identity.* Cambridge: Cambridge University Press.

CHAPTER NINE

Teaching *Inanimate Alice*

ANGELA THOMAS, JENNY WHITE, & ROS LIPPIS

INTRODUCTION

Inanimate Alice (The BradField Company, 2005–2013) is an exemplar of digital fiction and is a "born-digital" text (see Thomas, Chapter 3 this volume), meaning it was conceived of and produced solely in digital form. It has been used successfully in teaching contexts across the world and has inspired students to create their own digital novels. The aims of this chapter include the following:

1. To identify what makes *Inanimate Alice* an excellent focus for study in classroom contexts
2. To share a unit of work based on Inanimate Alice that was conducted by two Australian teachers
3. To share and analyse a student version of an *Inanimate Alice* digital novel

Inanimate Alice (The BradField Company, 2005–2013) is the story of Alice, starting at eight years old, and follows her journey across countries and time as she develops. Alice is home schooled until the age of 14, as she lives in a range of remote locations across the globe due to her father's profession. The novel was developed collaboratively by media producer Ian Harper, writer Kate Pullinger, and digital artist Chris Joseph. It is an example of a digital novel that utilises the multiple affordances of a piece of digital fiction: multimodality, hypertextuality, spatiality (the narrative is episodic as it unfolds over many years in time), and it requires various levels of user interactivity to progress the story. As explained by BradField Company (2005–2011), the novel is both episodic and multimodal,

> ... [e]ach a self-contained story, the chapters become more complex as the narrative unfolds reflecting Alice's age and competency as she develops towards her calling as a game animator and designer.... [It] uses text, images, music, sound effects, puzzles and games to illustrate and enhance the narrative. (para. 3)

What makes *Inanimate Alice* unique is the way in which it has used the affordance of spatiality. Not only has each episode been published some years apart, but each episode jumps approximately two years in the life of its central character Alice. This gap in time, both in *real time* and in *story time*, has opened up a space for multivocality (Bakhtin, 1981) to occur—a space where teachers have encouraged children to fill in the gaps with their own voices, and their own *reversionings* of Alice's story. Hundreds of stories worldwide have appeared online showing children's versions of what happened in those intervening years. Two teachers who have worked with this idea in Tasmania are Jenny and Ros, and below is their story and the pedagogical sequence they used to work with *Inanimate Alice* in their classrooms.

ROS AND JENNY: USING *INANIMATE ALICE* TO TEACH NEW LITERACIES

Our Teaching Rationale

Today's students have grown up in a technology-rich world. Unlike many teachers, they have never known a time without computers. Multitasking with various technologies is a normal feature of their daily life and they are confident and capable of using a range of technologies to enhance their learning. We acknowledge that English curriculums now reflect the need to incorporate digital literacy into the classroom program. All students need to be given the opportunity to create and respond to a range of multimodal texts. Students *think* digitally every day. Usage of smartphones, iPods, and other devices allows them to connect to their digital world with ease and a level of confidence not shared by most adults. To engage today's learners we believe schools need to incorporate technological tools to promote effective instruction for active learning and student engagement. This requires a shift by teachers in rethinking programs, planning, pedagogy and assessment around digital technologies.

With this in mind, we recognised the need to enhance our English program to facilitate the use and creation of multimodal texts, to move toward a more digital learning environment. We felt that this would enhance learning outcomes and experiences for some of our reluctant writers and readers and other generally disengaged students. We strongly believe that if digital resources are integrated into the curriculum, the learning possibilities for students will be huge.

In the Australian curriculum, Information and Communication Technologies (ICT) is a general capability embedded in every learning area. *Inanimate Alice* affords a practical classroom opportunity to meet the ICT competencies of creativity and innovation, critical thinking, problem solving, ethical ICT use, communication, and collaboration within and beyond the classroom.

We believe that teachers no longer need to hold all the knowledge (be the expert) before they begin a new teaching and learning challenge; instead, they can join their students and learn together. It was time for us to release more responsibility for the learning to our students. The line between who is the student, teacher, and learner changes frequently and this blending of roles can benefit all stakeholders.

Why *Inanimate Alice*?

Storytelling is a rich component of any culture and has always been an important tool for the passing on of beliefs and values that define a society. *Inanimate Alice* uses a simple, predictable narrative format that allows students to gain an understanding of the schematic structure of narratives. However, there is an interesting twist to the known format in that the characters are "inanimate" and as such are never shown to the viewer. This affords a fantastic opportunity for work on character development that is not influenced by impressions based on appearance.

As a born digital text, each of the *Inanimate Alice* episodes have been created for a digital world rather than being a text-based story converted to digital media. Alice is like today's learners in that she confidently integrates technology into her daily activities and uses technologies regularly for self-expression. The creators/authors worked within a digital headspace and so *Inanimate Alice* provides a unique example of an interactive piece of digital fiction to present to students. Technology facilitates storytelling, but it should be remembered that the creation of the story is the primary focus, *not* the technology used to create it.

A narrative connects the reader to a situation, but a digital narrative affords greater opportunity for the reader to become part of the situation. As readers read they are engaged in analysing and synthesizing the content in a way that print text doesn't afford. In addition a digital narrative can easily be created to include interactive features that require the reader to take an active role while reading/viewing, as is the case with the *Inanimate Alice* episodes. This not only provides context for the reader but also builds and deepens understanding. Interacting with and producing multimodal texts requires students to engage the higher order thinking skills of analysing, creating, and evaluating. Alice is an impressive example to work with.

Planning Considerations

When Alice first became part of our literacy program we referred to and adapted the teaching resources available on the Alice website. The *Inanimate Alice: Education Portal* offers a range of teaching ideas and resources. We also accessed the extensive planning posted by Margo Edgar and Kate Story's wiki (see below for links to these sites).

Integrating Alice into the broad context of the literacy program means there are opportunities for

- analysing reading practice
- making meaning from text
- recognising features of the narrative structure
- identifying the features that give the story continuity
- character knowledge and character development
- learning to integrate the modes (sound, visual, and text) and analysing their role in making meaning from the text

Essentially there were two components to our program—reading and interpreting each of the *Inanimate Alice* episodes with children, and then inviting the children to create their own reversionings of *Inanimate Alice* as multimodal texts. In creating their own reversionings, we decided to use Microsoft PowerPoint as the medium. While we acknowledge there are a variety of platforms that could be used to create our Alice episodes, Microsoft PowerPoint afforded us a simple, user-friendly platform that enabled students to easily insert such things as hyperlinks, music, images, video, sound effects, and voice-overs. Students were able to use other creative software such as Audacity, Paint, GarageBand, Picasa, and Pivot. This use was often initiated, shared, and managed by the students themselves.

Below is an outline of the pedagogy we implemented to teach *Inanimate Alice*.

Table 9.1. Pedagogical Process: The Teaching Process

Lesson 1: Reading text script of Episode 1	Groups read the text-based script of *Alice*: Episode 1. Students brainstorm questions based around script reading. • What do you know? • What don't you know? • What do you want to know? Teacher facilitates a discussion around the sharing of ideas about this script. Record questions and ideas.
Lesson 2: Initial review of Episode 1	Groups view *Alice*: Episode 1. Students discuss/record and share their impression of this episode. Students complete: "Student Resource 1—The Digitally Literate Classroom: Reading *Inanimate Alice*, Episode 1," one of the resources found in the *Inanimate Alice* education pack, developed by Laccetti (2007).

Lesson 3: Reading analysis	Students analyse the ways in which they read and made meaning from Episode 1. Teacher records and displays responses around the classroom.
Lesson 4: How we read print and digital texts	Teacher leads a discussion/brainstorm to compare how we read print and how we read digital text, using the table developed by Walsh (2007) as follows: Table 9.2. Differences between reading of print-based and multi-modal texts (from Walsh, 2007, p. 35) | Reading print-based texts	Reading multimodal texts
Words: The words 'tell' including the discourse, register, vocabulary, linguistic patterns, grammar, chapters, paragraph and sentence structure.	**Visual images**: The images 'show' including layout, size, shape, colour, line, angle, position, perspective., screen, frames, icons, links, hyperlinks.
Use of senses: visual some tactile.	**Use of senses**: visual, tactile, hearing, kinaesthetic
Interpersonal meaning: developed through verbal 'voice' - through use of dialogue, 1st, 2nd, 3rd person narrator.	**Interpersonal meaning**: developed through visual 'voice': positioning, angle, perspective – 'offers' and 'demands'.
Verbal style: including tone, intonation, humour, irony, sarcasm, word play, developed in the use of 'words'. Typographical arrangement, formatting, layout, font, punctuation.	**Visual style**: choice of medium, graphics, animation, frames, menu board, hypertext links.
Verbal imagery: including description, images, symbolism, metaphor, simile, alliteration [poetic devices with words, sound patterns].	**Visual imagery**: use of colour, motifs, icons, repetition.
Reading pathway: mostly linear and sequential. **Reader mostly follows.**	**Reading pathway**: use of vectors – non-sequential, non-linear. **Reader has more choice and opportunity to interact.** | Consider these questions with respect to Episode 1 of *Inanimate Alice*: • Is this a good story to read? Why or why not? • What are the features that make it engaging for the reader/viewer? • Write three questions you would like to ask the author and creators of this episode?
Lesson 5: Devices used by writers and readers	Students revisit the questions they recorded in Lesson 1 after reading the script. Ask students questions such as: • Have your questions been answered? • How did you get that information? Teacher discusses devices used by writers and readers to convey meaning, for example, music, sound effects, graphics, text formatting, etc. Discuss how devices are used to convey meaning—in movies, picture books, music videos, advertisements, promotional literature. *Examples of devices used by authors, illustrators, and digital creators* • flashbacks • foreshadowing • inclusion of details

	• omission of details • personalisation • print size and print selection • symbolism • understatement • artistic style • colour • composition and page design • medium • size of images • transitions types • volume • tone • setting the mood	
Lesson 6: Features of a narrative text type	Teacher reviews structures/features of narrative text types Students view *Alice*: Episode 2. Students identify, list, and recognise the features of a narrative text type.	
Lesson 7: Structures of printed and digital narratives	Whole class or groups create display charts to compare structures/features of printed and digital narrative text types. Display in classroom for quick reference. The chart below was compiled by 2011 students:	
	Print text • No pictures made it harder to understand • You had to imagine China • Is words on a page and a mental view • Has less description than a digital text • In print text you have to use mental images • Seemed like there were things missing but digital text left just as many questions • Gives lots of room to imagine • Tells the story in writing • Read and hear (if read aloud) • Just writing and you have to picture the illustrations in your head • Can give you misunderstandings • Just a script with really no description • Is easier to understand	Digital text • Digital text is words, sounds, and pictures and it's easier to understand • It has more description because you see the pictures • Digital text is like a movie with words but it has an explanation of ideas • You could imagine the story by listening to the sounds and looking at the pictures • It's harder to read and it confused me instead of letting me imagine • Digital text is like watching a movie but more confusing • Just didn't seem long enough

	• Leaves more questions • Is not describing everything and leaving the reader wondering	• The photos helped answer questions • Digital text already has the pictures so you don't have a chance to imagine • Tells a story with pictures and sounds • The pictures made it easier to understand • Blurred images made it harder to understand • Digital text gave more of an idea of things • We could see what things looked and sounded like • You have more to take in with digital text
Lesson 8: Multimodal devices	Groups list devices used to write/create multimodal texts. Refer back to *Alice*: Episodes 1 and 2.	
Lesson 9: Character analysis	Teacher introduces character analysis techniques. Students draw Alice. Explain using labels. Students make a list of things Alice would do and things she wouldn't do. Support this with examples from the episodes. Consider questions: • How did Alice's character change across the episodes? • How did her circumstances affect her character? Students' thoughts about Alice: • Alice loves to draw and play on her baxi. • Ming and John put too much responsibility on Alice. • Alice is mature for her age. • Alice is independent because she doesn't rely on anybody. • Alice is mature because she can make the right decisions by herself. • Alice is responsible because she can take care of herself. • Alice is creative because she makes an imaginary friend in Brad. • She is adventurous. • Alice is not social because she has never been around other kids as they were always travelling. • She is a problem solver. • I reckon if Alice went to school she would be a pretty awesome friend because she does lots of cool stuff that I like.	

	Alice wouldn't:
	• Straighten her hair
	• Wear makeup
	• Fuss about what she is wearing
	• Wouldn't want the latest fashion because she doesn't socialise with other girls/boys
	• Be influenced by peer pressure
Lesson 10: Common elements	View *Alice*: Episode 3. Students identify and list common elements and their purposes found in all *Alice* episodes, for example, music, games, maps, baxi.
Lesson 11: Technology	Teacher leads discussion about how the episodes were made. Students brainstorm list of technical elements, for example, transitions, audio volume, hyperlinks, split screens, moving images. Teacher demonstrates some technical skills when using Microsoft PowerPoint, Audacity, Picasa. Examples of technical skills taught: hyperlinking, slide animation and transition, manipulating images, videos and music, adding voice.
Lesson 12: Storyboarding	Students begin to plan their own episode of *Alice*. Groups storyboard their own narrative plan incorporating the common elements identified in Lesson 10. Storyboarding offers a way of organising the creating of the narrative. It also allows writers to incorporate their ideas about the digital perspective of the story, for example, the inclusion of a range of modes such as lighting, camera shots, sound effects, etc. Storyboarding helps students to make the vitally important connection between text, images, and sounds, which leads the learner into a more multimodal and interactive world. By selecting and adding images, video, sound effects, voice-overs, etc. the students gain a deeper understanding of the "what, why, and how" of engaging their audience. *Storyboard Evaluation* (prior to creating episode) Consider these questions: • Does your episode have all the elements of a narrative? • Are all your ideas possible? • Will your group be able to finish the task within the time frame? • Will your story be interesting and entertaining for others to read? • Would you want to read your story? • Will it make sense to other readers? • Does your story plan include interesting interactive elements? • What devices have you as authors used to influence the reader? • What photos, animations, movie clips, music, hyperlinks do you need and how will you source them?

Lesson 13: Creation	Students create their own *Alice*: Episode 2.5 (2.5 limits students to an appropriate and familiar age level for the character of Alice). Considerations: <ul><li>Students work in pairs or small groups to develop a collaborative story.</li><li>The teacher needs to allow groups to explore and create various multimodal elements.</li><li>The teacher needs to offer regular feedback without changing the planned narrative.</li><li>The teacher offers support with any technical problems.</li><li>Students need to be continually reflecting as a writer and a reader on their own progress and adjusting their forward planning. We asked out students to maintain a learning journal for their work on *Alice*, in which they keep a record of their progress and their plans for future action to complete the work.</li><li>Students should be referring back to the original Alice episodes as needed, so as to scaffold their understandings.</li><li>Peer assessment and feedback should be facilitated regularly from the reader's point of view.</li><li>Students problem-solve for each other. (We used a class wiki to facilitate this.)</li></ul>
	One student's *Alice* Learning Journal entries *Journal Entry 1:* *Today our group had an Alice meeting. We looked at our original planning and then used the assessment rubric to evaluate our work so far.* *We decided we need to:* <ul><li>*Add our "next page" hyperlinks*</li><li>*Add a little bit more movie*</li><li>*Touch up our ideas*</li><li>*Check punctuation*</li><li>*Add more interactive elements*</li><li>*Change font size*</li><li>*Check all sound and music*</li></ul> *Journal Entry 2:* *Today we had an Alice meeting. To finish our project we need to:* <ul><li>*Fix up some sound*</li><li>*Polish our story*</li></ul>
	Technical aspects we need to sort out are: <ul><li>*Insert a good scream*</li><li>*Timing of sounds*</li></ul>

	We will seek help from: • Writing on the class blog *Asking questions to people that have come across the same difficulties and who have fixed them already*
Lesson 14: Reflection	Reviewing of episodes Groups use a rubric to assess the episode considering the writing and creating phases. Culminating self-assessment consideration: • As a narrative writer how have you improved? • Explain what you have learnt about the craft of reading and writing? • If you were to do this again what would you change?

Examples of student feedback

Does multimodal literacy have a place in your world? Explain why/why not?

- I think that it will because it is a good way to learn and it is more interesting than print text.
- I think that is has a big place in my world because it is a great way to learn and it is challenging, interesting and exciting. Multimodal text is great but I wouldn't completely chuck print text down the drain!
- Yes, it does because it helps us learn more computer skills and with the programs we used it was fun and challenging.
- I think multimodal literacy is more exciting and fun so it has a big place in my world because it has music and videos that make it better to watch than read print text.
- I think multimodal literacy is better than just normal literacy. Technology is becoming a big part of this world so we should use it in our learning.
- Multimodal literacy I think is more exciting for children our age because after a while print text gets boring!
- I think it does have a place in our world because our technology is growing and is being used more. This is also great fun and you learn more when you are having fun.

Outline any changes you would make if you ever made another episode. Please explain…

- We would change/add more music because in our game the music we had did not fit with it. To add music we would add more the make it flow better.
- We would add more music. We would change the scene. We would add a game to set the scene. We would bold the writing so the viewer would see it clearly.
- We would put in more music and transition effects and more interesting pictures to help show the story.
- We would have put more of Alice's thoughts into the episode.
- We should have done more interactive slides.
- We would have more sounds and a game on the baxi, put background on the slides and made it a little bit longer.

List the negatives for your group that were felt/experienced while making your *Alice* episode.

- The amount of time we were given wasn't very long so we couldn't put as many sounds in.
- ……… always hogged the computer.

- We had a compressing error.
- Audacity was not transferring to Alice.
- …… always did the hyperlink and sounds.
- Saving, because we lost all our slides as they did not save properly.
- Had trouble inserting sounds because we didn't know they had to be saved as a wav. file.
- Time was an issue for us because we had to put lots of sounds and pictures in.
- We had to slash and burn some of our work.
- Hyperlinks didn't want to work some of the times.
- We had to work on our own sometimes because we both weren't there all the time.
- We had different ideas to the other person so we had to do lots of work arounds.
- Group members were not always focused.
- We had some problems with sound and our hyperlinks didn't always work.

What skills did you need to create your story?

- You need good PowerPoint skills, like hyperlinking, inserting media and sounds.
- You need a lot of patience and team work.
- You need to know your way around PowerPoint.
- You need to have creative thinking.
- You need common sense!
- You need to know but also learn computer skills. It's like Writer's Workshop but the story is more detailed on the computer.
- You need to hyperlink. You need to use sounds.
- You need good computer skills to create a multimodal story!
- You need to have a creative mind and story.
- You need to know how to use PowerPoint and hyperlink. You need good skills on the computer.
- You need to listen to what your partner thinks. You need to be on task!

Reflect on the whole *Alice* experience—record some of your thoughts and opinions.

- I think *Alice* is full of computer skills.
- It was an interesting experience. We used lots of skills to make an interesting episode.
- I think that *Inanimate Alice* was good because we learnt how to use different software programs, e.g., Audacity, PowerPoint and Paint to create our one episode.
- I think that *Inanimate Alice* was good because it uses good/fun programs so that you can learn different things.
- We think it is a great experience to film and to take our own photos, then to use them in our *Inanimate Alice*.
- We think it helped us with computer and literacy skills.
- We got better computer skills using *Alice* and we learnt more new programs.
- I think *Inanimate Alice* is a really good part of our literacy learning. It is fun and you learn a lot at the same time.
- I think *Inanimate Alice* was a great experience because it was different to other literacy activities.

- I think *Inanimate Alice* was a good project to learn more about computer skills and literacy because we had to tell a story on a computer.
- We learnt to use PowerPoint better.

List the positives for your group that were felt/experienced while making your *Alice* episode.
- We learnt how to hyperlink to different slides.
- We learnt how to use PowerPoint, hyperlink and to use the audio and how to fix it up.
- We learnt how to hyperlink.
- We got to use different programs and learnt more about PowerPoint.
- You can share your ideas to improve your episode.
- I found that being with a friend helped me work better! If I had of worked with someone I didn't know I would of got distracted!
- You got to know the person you were working with.
- Partners make it easier because you have two brains which means more thinking.
- We learnt more computer skills and have more about PowerPoint.
- Having partners means having more thoughts in the storyline.
- We learnt to put sounds in the right place and to work with others.
- We learnt to work as a team. We learnt how to use many different programs in one!
- We learnt to experience the way that PowerPoint goes together.

List the learning involved for your group while creating your new episode of *Alice*.
- Inserting sound files, images and videos.
- Learning to hyperlink pages, trim sounds and insert them and matching sound to play over an amount of slides.
- We learnt how to insert media such as audio sound files and animations.
- We learnt how to insert sounds and then hide them from the slide.
- We learnt how to hyperlink and how to add sounds.
- We learnt how to hyperlink slides, input sounds, input pictures and music.
- I learnt that you can place more than one type of computer file into PowerPoint, e.g., Pivot, clip art, videos, Audacity.
- I never knew that you could use Audacity.
- I learnt that you can use hyperlinks! I didn't know there were such things!
- We learnt how to use PowerPoint, hyperlinks, import sounds and Pivot files as well as how to use Audacity.

How could we improve this learning experience for you and your group?
- Give us more time so we could add more depth into the storyline.
- I think it would be better if we could see Alice and the other characters.
- Have more time to get involved in the storyline and so we could put more sound and images in.
- I think it would be better if the structure was not always the same.
- They could have taught us more advanced skills to improve the story.
- I think it would be better if we knew more about how to input sounds better.
- It would be better if we got more time, to have make it perfect.
  - We think we could use more time to improve and add items and media to our Alice episode.

STUDENT REVERSIONING OF *INANIMATE ALICE*

Emily and Susan created their own chapter 2.5 of Alice's story. In preparation for working on it, they created storyboards to map out their version and formed a list of elements that would be required for each part of the story. This included a list of images, movie clips, audio, and sound effects that would be used. They wanted to set Alice's story in Australia and, using the same storyline in the online episodes of Alice becoming lost or afraid, decide that she will become lost in the Australian bush. When the class went on a camping trip to the bush, Emily and Susan took a digital camera and shot several of the film sequences and images there to later be used in the story.

Their story commences with a screen of information similar to the other episodes.

Episode 2.5
Our story has interactive hyperlinks that you will need to click on to get to the next slide. Each link is either two arrows with a line underneath, a word or a picture with a red box around it.
Our story takes approximately 3 minutes to view.

These words are also in the style of other episodes: white text on a black screen. It is immediately recognisable as an episode because of the style.

Similarly, screen two is white text on a black background, reading:

My name is Alice.
I am 12 years old.

A hyperlink is available at the bottom of the screen. On the next screen are the words:

My Mum (Ming) and I have just driven four kilometres to find a nice place to sit.

Accompanying the words is a short film clip of passing countryside, apparently taken from within the car window. The sound of wheels on the road and wind in the air underscores the clip. The clip is set to loop and play continuously, while a hypertext link appears at the bottom of the screen after some seconds, ready for the user to click when ready. This resembles the moving film clips in episode 1 of *Inanimate Alice*.

The next part of the story is constructed of a composite of five PowerPoint slides, which run seamlessly together as though on a single screen. The words that begin this section are:

Ming paints and I take photos with my Baxi player.

The five slides are used to build up a painting and add in progressively more photographs to demonstrate the action taking place over time. The final slide includes a hypertext link for the user to take back control in the reading. This sequence is shown in Figure 9.1.

Fig 9.1. Sequence of Slides to Support One Line in the Story.

This matches what we know of Ming and Alice from Episode 1, where we learn that Ming paints. The layering of photographs is also a technique used in episode to show what Alice is doing over time. This sequence is also accompanied by music that is a gentle piano melody, symbolising the relaxing time mother and daughter are sharing together. The music marks the emotional state of the narrative at this time—tranquil, the calm before the storm.

The next screen reads:

My Dad (John) is at base camp working.

A map of Australia accompanies this and on it is a red dot marking out a spot in Western Australia to indicate where Dad is working. A variety of narrative images (such as the photographs and paintings) and conceptual images (such as maps) are deployed across all episodes and are effective in providing the reader with technical information and context to support the narrative.

The next screen reads:

My house

It is accompanied by three images: the map of Australia from the previous screen, an exterior photograph of a house, and a black and white house plan. Throughout the episodes online readers are introduced to the changing locations in which

Alice and her family reside—the sense of place is an important aspect of the narrative, since it changes with each episode. It is consistently referenced by Alice sharing her perspective about these places, and this is echoed by students Emily and Susan.

Next we read:

We're travelling back to base camp now.

A second film clip of passing bushland accompanies this text, as well as a hypertext link. When the hyperlink is clicked, a sequence of three slides flash past—the first is a shot of the road taken from the driver's point of view. In the middle of the road ahead of the car is an animal, and the slide is accompanied by the screeching of tires. There is no hyperlink on this page; rather, the reader is forced to listen to the full audio track of the screech before the slide is automatically moved to the next shot, which is a slide of total blackness. No hypertext or potential for reader navigation is available on this slide, either. The slide is progressed automatically after several seconds, to a slide with a black background and the white text:

ALICE!

This is followed by a similar slide with the text:

I'm stuck
go find help.

Alice then uses her baxi to try and call for help, but there is no phone reception out in the bush. This is represented through a series of slides that requires the user to interact with the baxi as if they were Alice, and successive attempts at interaction yield the image in Figure 9.2. This results in Alice opening the image of Brad for solace (a recurring theme throughout all episodes of *Inanimate Alice*).

Fig 9.2. Reading and Interacting with the Story from Alice's Point of View.

The story progresses to show Alice gaining courage and walking forward. The motion of walking forward is captured in a series of three video clips which Emily and Susan captured while on school camp in the bush. The camera angle starts by being pointed down at their feet walking along the grassy path, but by the following slide the reader sees shots of the forest becoming darker and darker, symbolising time passing, and the text included is:

I've been walking for hours and its starting to get dark.

This is accompanied by low-pitched haunting music, and is then followed by the image in Figure 9.3.

Fig 9.3. Alice Grows Tired.

This image is cleverly framed by overlaying black onto the forest scene, with the shape of eyes looking out at it, and the forest is depicted as blurry. This suggests Alice's tiredness is affecting her vision and gives a strong visual congruence with the words "so tired." The haunting music continues in a loop, almost hypnotically.

The following slide is black but has sound effects of a car driving along the road. Readers are then given the option to help Alice run to find the road and flag down the car, and this includes a mini "game" where readers can click on one of three options to try to find the road. Susan and Emily have included the game element in their story as this is also a common interactive feature with all other *Inanimate Alice* episodes.

After successfully playing this game (which includes snakes and rivers blocking the path), readers are taken to the final sequence of slides that show that Alice's father John is the driver of the car. The sound effect of a door shutting is heard (indicating John has hopped out of the car) and the final two slides are simple black slides with one word on each:

John!
Alice!

And then the closing credits roll. This is a really effective ending, requiring readers to fill in the gaps and imagine a reunion between Alice and her father, and the resolution to the story.

CONCLUSION

This chapter has explored the work of two teachers and the pedagogy implemented in their classroom to encourage students to read, interpret, and create their own digital fiction. The digital novel *Inanimate Alice* is an exemplar of digital fiction that allows both interactivity and multivocality with its unique episodic structure that has created large gaps of story time between episodes, a perfect space in which teachers such as Jenny and Ros have found a place for their students' creative reversionings of *Inanimate Alice*. Using a known text structure, format, characters, and plot devices is an ideal way to scaffold students' understandings about digital fiction and new semiotic meaning-making resources. One interesting aspect of the students' responses above was that even though Jenny and Ros had expressed concern about the amount of time they spent on the unit of work, many students voiced the opinion that they would have loved more time. The students' enthusiasm and dedication to this unit allowed the creation of innovative and imaginative multimodal narratives, which used many of the affordances of the best exemplars of digital fiction. That this is possible for students who are 11 and 12 years of age is a result of both excellent exemplars of digital fiction suitable for children, such as *Inanimate Alice*, and excellent pedagogical practice, such as demonstrated by Ros and Jenny.

REFERENCES

Bakhtin, M. M. (1981). *The dialogic imagination: Four essays* (Michael Holquist, ed. and trans.). Austin: University of Texas Press.

Laccetti, J. (2007). Inanimate Alice *education pack*. Retrieved from http://inanimatealice.com/education.html

The BradField Company Ltd. (2005–2013). *Inanimate Alice*. Retrieved from http://inanimatealice.com

Walsh, M. (2007). Reading visual and multimodal texts: How is "reading" different? *Australian Journal of Language and Literacy, 29*(1), 24–37.

FURTHER READING

Ohler, J. (2006). The world of digital storytelling. *Educational Leadership, 63*(4), 44–47.

Stewart, G. (2010). The paratexts of *Inanimate Alice*: Thresholds, genre expectations and status. *Convergence: The International Journal of Research into New Media Technologies, 16*, 57–74.

Thomas, S., Joseph, C., Lacetti, J., Mason, B., Mills, S., Perril, S., & Pullinger, K. (2007). Transliteracy: Crossing divides. *First Monday, 12*(12). Retrieved from http://journals.uic.edu/ojs/index.php/fm/article/view/2060/1908

WEB RESOURCES

Alice and Friends wiki: http://aliceandfriends.wikispaces.com/
Inanimate Alice Education Portal: http://www.inanimatealice.com/teach.html
Inanimate Alice Education Services Australia: http://www.inanimatealice.edu.au/
The Space—The Arts: http://thespace.org/

CHAPTER TEN

Empowering Older Adolescents as Authors

Multiliteracies, Metalanguage, and Multimodal Versions of Literary Narratives

JULIE BAIN & LEN UNSWORTH

INTRODUCTION

This chapter shares three vignettes from the first author's experience as a senior secondary school teacher of English in a small regional centre in a rural area in the state of New South Wales (NSW) in Australia. In sharing experiences of teaching older adolescents in this rural area, we will seek to respond to three questions:

1. How can adolescents alienated from the English curriculum be re-engaged with the study of literature through the deployment of ubiquitous computer applications such as Microsoft Excel and PowerPoint and Apple's GarageBand in literary analysis and response?
2. How can adolescents with low self-esteem as writers be enthused to create texts through exploration of multimodal narratives, visual art, and alternative representation modes?
3. How can teachers develop students' understanding and use of a metalanguage of multimodality as a resource for text interpretation and composition?

As students in New South Wales complete their last two years of senior high school education they prepare for a final examination (the Higher School Certificate (HSC)) that will determine a score on which their eligibility for admission to Australian universities will be based. The HSC English examination requires students to be able to analyse and interpret both historical and contemporary literary texts and to be able to write effective interpretive responses to such texts. Despite their 12 years of schooling, many students in their senior school years in communities like this one are not strongly engaged or confident in interpreting literature and also lack confidence as writers. The vignettes shared here indicate the potential for a multimodal reconceptualization of literary and literacy pedagogy to enhance the engagement of these students with literature and to build their confidence as effective interpreters and authors of different forms of narratives.

The first vignette introduces Michael as an initially disengaged student in the English classroom. But with encouragement to explore the adaptation of "infographic" software to literary analysis and to construct a multimodal presentation of his literary response, Michael becomes a confident participant in innovative orientations to literary discussion. The second vignette connects multimodal resources in teaching with students taking up positive positions as writers who adopt styles from different literary eras to demonstrate their ability and skill as successful students of English. The third vignette indicates the positive impact of introducing secondary school students to the basic concepts of a grammar of visual design (Kress & van Leeuwen, 2001/2006). The introduction of explicit teaching of this visual grammar and its metalanguage provided the students with what they saw as tractable tools for investigating and discussing the construction of meaning in multimodal texts, which they evidence through their analysis and interpretation of a popular film trailer.

Reflecting on these experiences, the chapter concludes with recommendations for infusing the teaching of literature in senior high school with digital multimodal versions of literary narratives, multiple forms of analysis, presentation software, the use of ubiquitous digital tools such as Microsoft PowerPoint and Inspiration, and, most significantly, the explicit introduction of a metalanguage of multimodality as a shared basis for discussing the meaning-making resources of images in multimodal texts.

IMPETUS AND INSPIRATION: MULTILITERACIES, TRANSFORMATIVE TEACHING AND LEARNING

The overall aim of this unit of work involved two related objectives. The first was for students to use the language of literary analysis to demonstrate their understanding about how texts from different literary eras have been constructed. The importance of this rests partly in the notion that the way students write is influenced by what they read, and to be successful writers they need to read widely. The second objective was for the students to appropriate ubiquitous digital technologies to demonstrate different ways of communicating their interpretive response to texts using modes of their choice.

In senior secondary school English in New South Wales, there is a widespread belief that written language is the most important mode of expression in the English curriculum, but a concern for Julie is that many of her students don't position themselves as successful writers in subject English. The intention, therefore, is to show students that they can succeed and exceed their own expected levels of achievement while linking to the school's teaching and learning program which voices the rationale of the NSW Syllabus, which states: "The study of English enables students to recognise and use a diversity of approaches and texts to meet the growing array of literacy demands, including higher-order social, aesthetic and cultural literacy." While this statement includes three aims, the primary focus for this chapter is demonstrating the ways multiliteracies pedagogy (Cope & Kalantziz, 2000; Unsworth, 2001) can realize both aesthetic and cultural literate practices in a matriculation level English classroom while improving students' understanding and literary appreciation of a range of texts.

Distinctive literary narratives such as iconic texts from authors like Mary Shelley and Fyodor Dostoevsky were crucial to this unit of work. It was important for the students to learn that narrative encompasses a broad range of genres and styles. This unit aimed also to encourage active reading. Active reading meant not just reading the text completely but undertaking activities such as re-presenting the narrative in various forms for students to demonstrate how the selected texts make meaning. In response to the reading the students could choose visual texts, film texts, and spoken texts to demonstrate their understanding of the language and meanings of the literary narratives. The outcomes for the unit included demonstrating understanding of the relationships among texts, describing and analyzing the ways that language forms and features influence reader response, and engaging with the detail of textual construction and reflecting on students' learning.

The final prescribed text list included the following short stories:

"Viii, a story" from *The Art of Walking Upright* (Colquhoun, 2010)
The Mortal Immortal (Shelley, 1833)
The Tell-Tale Heart (Poe, 1843)
The Honest Thief (Dostoevsky, 1846/1949)
The Last Lesson (Daudet, 1945)
Australian narrative *Leaving* (Solomon, 2010)

Each text was chosen to demonstrate particular ways in which narratives are constructed. Glenn Colquhoun's "Viii, a story" is a narrative poem where the persona's voice in the poem uses first-person narration to relay a story. It is rich with metaphor and likens narrative to timelessness as well as a "simple conversation" between writer and audience. *The Mortal Immortal* reflects a Gothic sensibility, told from a first-person perspective, which connects a desire for infinite life and the paradoxical wish to grow old with one's lover. Poe's *Tell-Tale Heart* was chosen for a couple of reasons, one of which may appear trivial. However, the popular iconic television text *The Simpsons*, which many students are familiar with, provided a populist hook to link to a contemporary text, while simultaneously affording opportunities to explore the concept of appropriation and intertextuality, two concepts important for senior school studies of English. Dostoevsky's *The Honest Thief* was chosen because of the complexity of its narrative and the ways characters' voices within the story further the plot. The final selected text, *Leaving*, by Trevor Solomon was written in 2010 but constructs a scene from the Australian goldfields in the 1850s.

The aim of the unit was also to demonstrate that the conventions of literature can be identified across different styles and genres of texts. Students were required to choose from a variety of modes to map the structure of the world of the narrative within a text selected from the above list. They were also required to compare this text with another of their choosing. They could choose a speaking task supported by visual images to explain the structure of their choice of the selected texts. They could role-play characters from within the text to demonstrate the orientation, climax, or conclusion of their chosen narrative. They could also make films to construct reviews that used images, graphs, and diagrams to demonstrate how elements within the texts were constructed, or they could choose to use auditory texts to support a visual presentation.

Active reading affords students the opportunity to change their place in the world of reading. One student (Michael—not his real name) decided he would graph the conflict within the narrative of two texts. But we should explain a little about Michael, the English student, before explaining the work he undertook in this unit.

Michael has, through his school career, been a reluctant reader who by his own admission says that English is just made of "stuff and nonsense" that requires no particular analysis, just "a lot of raving on." He "gets" mathematics and science subjects because there is a closer connection between fact and analysis. In the English class, he was often disengaged from discussions until, in class, Julie demonstrated how to use the visual thesaurus, an online tool (http://www.visualthesaurus.com/), and he would frequently search alternative words to make occasional responses to questions and discussions in class. Because of his disengagement in English, Michael had a propensity for disrupting other students' learning through social conversations. At times he would become argumentative, which also caused distractions from the topics at hand.

When it came to writing Michael often argued he could respond sufficiently in a couple of sentences to essay questions so he loudly pondered why he should write extended responses. The 1999 English syllabus mandated by the New South Wales state government states that "proficiency in English enables students to take their place as confident articulate communicators, critical and imaginative thinkers and active participants in society" (NSW Board of Studies, 1999, p. 6), and a key wish in working with Michael was for him not only to develop his confidence in analysis of texts for the study of English as well as increasing his ability to write extended responses, but more importantly for him to position himself successfully as an English student.

The task of mapping the structure of a narrative, visually, appealed to the way Michael approached investigation and learning. The concrete task of mapping the elements of a literary narrative included key points that afforded Michael the opportunity to identify, describe, explain, analyse, and synthesise his information in such a way that students in the class elicited conversation with Michael and a buzz of understanding erupted in response to his presentation. More important, however, is that Michael has since changed his approach to English and has shifted from being a reticent and reluctant English student to one who embraces the challenge of analyzing English texts. He has developed relationships with literary texts! How did this magic happen?

Michael appropriated several ubiquitous digital technologies and software including Microsoft's Excel and PowerPoint and graphed, using evidence from his selected text, the ways conflict moved the plot of *Leaving*, "to show both sophisticated reading and authoring skills" (Kimber & Wyatt-Smith, 2010). He further supported this visual analysis with a voiceover that he'd constructed using Apple's GarageBand. Michael demonstrated his understanding of rising and falling action, exposition, orientation, and climax and confidently fielded questions about his work that connected analysis with judicious evidence from the selected texts.

Initially, Julie posited the question to Michael about whether one could use Microsoft Excel to map a narrative in something like a graph. Michael was quite taken with this idea and tried to figure out how the x and y axes of a graph for a narrative might be approached. Julie indicated that she felt mathematically challenged in much the same way Michael felt challenged by English. An important moment was shared reflecting on how mismatching skills and knowledge to those that seem needed in negotiating particular concepts provokes feelings of learning frustration. It was this moment of shared frustration that cemented a productive teaching and learning relationship between teacher and student.

First, Michael approached two texts informally. He did rough drawings graphing narrative elements of *Leaving* from the prescribed text list and *Undertow* (Tan, 2008). *Undertow* is a narrative that starts with the preposterous scenario of a dugong being found on a suburban front lawn. A dugong is a rare sea mammal similar to a manatee. They have small flippers and are sometimes called sea cows. These large grey mammals live their lives grazing on sea grass along the coasts of northern and western Australia. They have a tail like a whale, a face like a walrus, and are large and slow moving. These animals only break the surface of the sea to breathe. Shaun Tan's (2008) narrative is ostensibly about a boy struggling with the notion that he is invisible to his family and the image of the dugong arguably represents aspects of being alienated and disenfranchised from the boy's suburban life.

While Michael thought he could graph the structure of a narrative, he resorted to initially drawing the graph identifying exposition, climax, and elements of the resolution (Figure 10.1).

'Undertow' (Shaun Tan) narrative structure

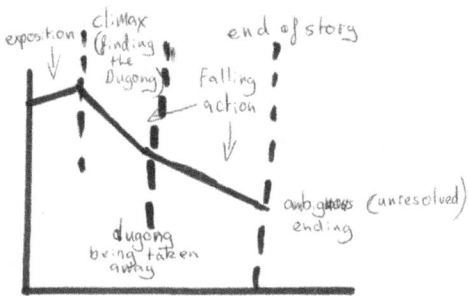

Fig 10.1. Michael's drawing of the narrative structure in *Undertow* (Tan, 2008).

This drawing was rudimentary. However, the content demonstrated Michael's ability to visualize the way structure can be developed within a text. These sketches also gave Michael a way into recognizing that English analysis had some concrete aspects about which he could reflect, which linked directly to the outcome that required reflection about a student's learning.

Michael was then shown some infographics to demonstrate how information might be disseminated visually. Infographics are texts that combine visual representations of information utilizing image, graphical information such as tables and charts and data arranged in various forms. These examples seemed to provide Michael with an "aha" moment.

Michael was also required to present his findings about narrative structure of one of the prescribed texts and a comparison text to his classmates. His reluctance, generally, to participate in classroom activities coupled with his classmates' particular expectation that Michael wasn't a successful English student was a major hurdle to overcome for this student. There was a palpable tension when he stood up in front of his class to share his presentation. Because Michael's previous presentations had been glib and unsubstantial, his peers assumed there would be more of the same in this presentation.

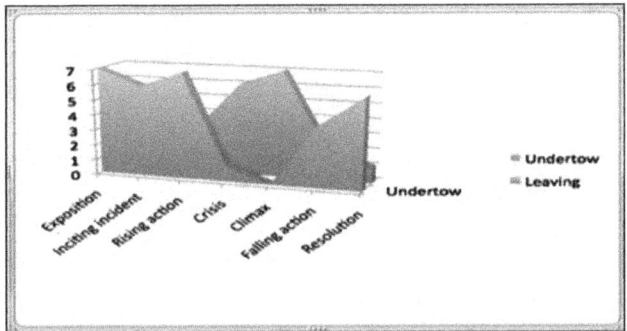

Fig 10.2. Michael's assignment presentation visual comparing the narrative structure of *Undertow* (Tan, 2008) and *Leaving* (Solomon, 2010).

Interestingly Michael's peers' attitudes changed when they saw that Michael had constructed a multimodal presentation (Figure 10.2). He had constructed a voiceover to accompany his visual presentation. His voiceover was well timed with the content of his presentation and rather than racing through the work he'd done because of the inevitable onset of nerves, his measured digitally recorded tone and deliberate pacing significantly improved the confidence of the delivery of the content of his work.

Michael is usually reluctant to use quotes from literary texts to support his opinion. This may be partly due to the fact that he has been unsure about the purpose of accessing these quotes. The simple exercise of graphing the narrative afforded Michael the opportunity to recognize where pertinent quotes could be located within the short stories for this exercise. He used numerous but judicious references from his prescribed and chosen texts to demonstrate how the different areas of narrative were realized through language within the literary texts. He connected these excerpts with the different narrative elements that included orientation, rising action, conflict, climax, and falling action. Michael identified how the characters in the text demonstrated their disinterest in the boy by identifying the quote focused on the dugong and how "the neighbours were far more concerned with attending to the stranded animal using buckets, hoses and wet blankets" (Tan, 2008, p. 37) while "nobody saw the small boy clutching an encyclopedia of marine zoology" (Tan, 2008, p. 38).

What was gratifying in this shift in Michael's perspective rested partly in his changing attitude to English and this was enhanced as his classmates recognized the change in his approach and the value of his contribution to the class dynamic. Rather than wasting class time he'd demonstrated that he could form opinions and support them with his written, spoken, and re-presented work. After his formal presentation to the class, he fielded questions about his choices in making graphs in an English class. He also defended his position saying that while English was supposed to be the study of literature, his appropriation (and he used that word!) of digital media in deconstructing the literature helped him to feel more comfortable in approaching his work. He also explained that by using GarageBand to record the narration that supported the visual elements of his presentation he didn't feel nervous presenting in front of the class. This reflective statement was received with a positive murmur from the majority of the class, who find that presenting to peers is a confounding and challenging activity.

The students were surprised by how the use of PowerPoint was supported by Michael's well-edited voiceover. Occasionally Michael paused the voiceover and added his opinion, offered examples, and included explanations he'd gleaned from the two texts he was analyzing. A few of his classmates whispered to each other about how impressed they were with his confident delivery, how surprised they were that he'd successfully used quotes from the short story, and how intelligent Michael's responses appeared. There was no sense of derision in the whispering. Michael had the attention of the class and the students took notes and at the end of the presentation asked questions that demonstrated that they had not only listened to his presentation, but also queried him appropriately on his assertions about the structure of each of his texts. Astoundingly, instead of rushing back to his table, Michael answered the questions and referred back to his presentation as well as pulling more details from his chosen texts.

This was the first time Michael's credibility was recognized by his peers as a successful student of English, but more importantly Michael himself recognized this change in perception. He swelled with pride after the questions ceased and on returning to his table was patted on the back and congratulated by those students in the class who position themselves as capable English students. While the change in Michael's attitude to approaching work has been consolidated during the last couple of terms, his use of the visual thesaurus has also meant that he searches alternative words in his writing, which has also further enhanced his achievement in English.

By provoking Michael's assumptions about his ability to understand how he can develop his own critical and multiliteracy skills to enrich his experience of school English, this approach to teaching enabled him to prove he could succeed in the complex terrain of secondary senior English. These magical moments can be attributed to multiliteracies education that expresses the interrelationship of modes of meaning by weaving linguistic, visual, auditory, gestural, or spatial modes (Kress, 2000; New London Group 1996) and also by extending "communication, representation [of meaning] and interaction as something more than language" (Jewitt, 2009, p. 1).

USING MULTIMODAL RESOURCES AND DIGITAL TECHNOLOGIES FOR WRITING STIMULI

Nearly every year Julie is assigned a preliminary matriculation (Higher School Certificate) group in Advanced and Extension 1 English. She begins the course with a question: "Who here (within the class) considers themselves to be a writer?" Almost without exception there is just one student who considers himself or herself a writer. This is after almost 13 years of education where writing is fundamental to every Key Learning Area across the secondary school curriculum. A concern for educators should be in balancing reading and writing because literacy education rarely evenly balances reading and writing activities (Hammond, 1996, p. 208).

A pedagogical approach to writing that also models writing as an act of creativity across all genres while referring to specific literary eras informs students about ways into writing for particular purposes and allows students to re-envision themselves as independent writers. Students' writing is influenced by what and how they read. Therefore, until they've read a diverse range of texts they cannot emulate different styles of writing. Where, you might ask, does multiliteracies education fit within the nexus between reading and writing? Multiliteracies education is fundamental to re-visioning how students see themselves, as students, as social human beings, and as contributors to society because "education is one of the key sources of social equity" (Cope & Kalantzis, 2009, p. 168).

Teaching writing serves several functions including showing students that they *can* write for whatever purpose that is presented to them. Furthermore, multimodal resources provide students with ways into texts that are accessible socially, culturally, and personally as well as ways of identifying how literature has, over time, contributed to society and human expression. The aim therefore is to show that students can succeed and reposition themselves as successful writers. In 1996, the New London Group talked about design and representation and recontextualising texts to make new meanings. The focus within this unit is to address this kind of design in teaching. In terms of teaching practice the concept of multiliteracies education provides students with resources that support their learning in many different modes but, more than this, recontextualises a design of learning where both teachers and learners can "conceive meaning-making as a form of design or active and dynamic transformation of the social world" (Cope & Kalantzis, 2009, p. 166).

If we give students texts that they can read for academic purposes as well as for enjoyment, to improve their reading experience regardless of their starting point, they can develop relationships with texts that transform the meaning of how they see themselves and then they can transform the text into a redesigned form. In this context the term *redesign* is not just about appropriating texts that are considered excellent literary texts, such as those written by the Brontës, Thomas Hardy, or

Shakespeare. This redesign is transformative (Jewitt, 2008). It emerges within the context of developing resources to enrich student literacy and empower students as social beings. The conscious use of a range of modes supported by multiliteracies provides students with tools for making and remaking meaning, which subsequently supports both creativity and critical thinking for the creation and analysis of texts. The notion of transformative education supports Jewitt's (2008) assertion about knowledge and how it is represented and the crucial aspect of knowledge construction, making the form of representation integral to meaning and learning more generally.

This unit of classroom work begins with writing fiction. We have so many kinds of narrative available to us in digitised forms, including YouTube, audio books, and sound bites. If we continue with the archaic practice of giving students a novel to study in isolation we are removing so much multimodal digital context that enriches the experience of reading (Mackey, 1994, 1999, 2001, 2002, 2003). The first move in exploring different forms of multimodal narrative was to revisit visual grammar (Kress & van Leeuwen 2001/2006) and then other modes that contribute to meaning, including spatial, gestural, aural, as well as discussing language and meaning in terms of literariness. The modes don't exist in isolation and some of the metalanguages describing meaning-making affordances can apply across modes. Understanding the ways that different modes and the interaction of modes contribute to meaning provides a basis for textual precision in discussing multimodal literary narratives. This demonstrates to students that there is a precision in learning in English that can affect and influence how students learn, how teachers teach, and this enriches both teachers' and students' experience of the subject.

The first multimodal text explored with the class was the opening sequence of David Lean's (1946) adaptation of Charles Dickens's *Great Expectations*. It is available on YouTube (http://www.youtube.com/watch?v=eXyo68s-f1E). In this movie segment the voiceover is delivered in clipped English dialect in the way the opening page is read, and it matches Dickens's novel word for word. The discussion with the students first focused on the way the auditory mode influenced their perception of the relationship shown in the text and how a sense of space was constructed. The students also produced their own oral reading of the opening:

> ... my infant tongue could make of both names nothing longer or more explicit than Pip. So, I called myself Pip, and came to be called Pip.
>
> As I never saw my father or my mother, and never saw any likeness of either of them (for their days were long before the days of photographs), my first fancies regarding what they were like, were unreasonably derived from their tombstones.
>
> ... I am indebted for a belief I religiously entertained that they had all been born on their backs with their hands in their trousers-pockets, and had never taken them out in this state of existence.
>
> Ours was the marsh country...

...the dark flat wilderness beyond the churchyard, intersected with dykes and mounds and gates, with scattered cattle feeding on it, was the marshes; and that the low leaden line beyond, was the river; and that the distant savage lair from which the wind was rushing, was the sea; and that the small bundle of shivers growing afraid of it all and beginning to cry, was Pip.

He gave me a most tremendous dip and roll, so that the church jumped over its own weather-cock. (Dickens, 1996, p. 1)

Close examination of the above excerpts enabled discussion of the ways characters can be constructed through language and, in particular, how Philip Pirrip's character was constructed through the voice of a child, a child who couldn't even pronounce his full name. Further discussion ensued about Pip's position in the family. A couple of students talked about the image of a whole family lying, fully clad, as if resting, in their graves. The apparent pragmatic approach to death and the ways the description "they had all been born on their backs with their hands in their trousers-pockets, and had never taken them out in this state of existence" (Dickens, 1996, p. 1), seemed to capture Pip's world with wry humour was also discussed.

After close reading of the opening page of *Great Expectations* the discussion turned to the different ways students saw the excerpts and whether the YouTube clip matched or mismatched with their imaginings of Dickens's young Philip Pirrip. Opportunities to explore the different ways modes are used in print and digitized texts open up areas of debate and conjecture about the texts. The clip was in black and white and none of the students imagined Dickens's landscape devoid of colour. The discussion led to consideration of the filmic adaptation of texts and how filmmakers edit out elements of printed texts, constructing interpretive possibilities that are different from the book version.

Further to watching the black-and-white version of the 1946 *Great Expectations* clip, and to build on the interpretive challenges of negotiating visual representations of relations, the classroom work progressed to looking at images of sculptures by Ron Mueck. The visual impacts of Mueck's works are interesting because they are hyper-realistic but also many of his sculptures are exaggerated in size. These works stimulated talk about the difference between the flatness of images on screen to the possibility of three-dimensional figures. Close examination was given to Mask II (2001–2002) and *Boy* (2000), a fibreglass, resin, and silicone sculpture of a five-metre-tall boy who is folded in a crouch. Finally, the class looked at *Big Baby II* (1997), a polyester resin, fibreglass, silicone, and synthetic hair model of a (huge) baby. Some time was spent looking closely at the baby's toes and toenails and discussing different ways such details added to the development of a depiction of character.

After discussing the statues and how the students felt about the size and detail within them, the students then undertook a writing exercise. Their in-class task was to create a written depiction of a character in a time-limited three minutes. One interesting aspect of this exercise was that the students, without exception, chose to write their character using pen and paper rather than using Microsoft Word or Apple's equivalent, Pages, even though computers were available for each of them. While this and other exercises are introductory exercises, the aim was to give students experiences that would assist them to develop skill sets that would allow their writing to be both adaptable and adaptive. The following are two students' responses to the three-minute character sketch writing task:

> Dead centre of the room he sat, huddled into a ball. Tiny thin arms wrapped around equally tiny knees. His eyes shone through the unbearable darkness of the room, like two white lights in a world of misery. But here, it was the lights that held the misery. You could almost hear them screaming out, desperate for love and acceptance. Desperate to be a part of the world, to be welcomed into other's lives. But instead, these eyes were trapped. Trapped in this dark, caliginous room. Trapped in this helpless, undernourished body. But most of all, trapped in his insane, out of control mind. (Alex)

> In the lonely misty street where the city hides its ugly side, the charcoal black walls slightly coloured with fading graffiti masterpieces are drawn over with lines and scribbles. Decay. Alley cats scamper along the road disappearing into the black. Lying in the street an old man with broken glassy eyes tells you a story without a word. His greasy long white hair sprouts from the side of his cap. His weathered cardboard blanket crinkles as he lays on the dirty ground. Life isn't worth living anymore. (Kit)

The students then read their work to their peers and discussed whether or not the characters were believable and accessible, what opened possibilities for development of that character, and what inhibited those possibilities. This sharing became a fundamental part of the writing class and built trust within the group. A safe place had been created where criticism and praise were shared. Students enjoyed the exercise, and this facilitated the next move to an exercise focusing on how perspective might build on their initial composing.

The introductory discussion for this task involved different ways space might be used and the metalanguage that describes the meaning-making resources of the various ways that space could be dealt with. Questions such as the following were explored:

- Does the space provide a story about place or time?
- Is the space interior, exterior, or psychological?
- Does the space evoke a mood that is expansive or restrictive?
- Within the space, are characters (or participants) active or reactive, inhibited, or demonstrative?

- Is the space shadowed or light filled?
- Can any particular feelings be attributed to people within the space? This question is significant particularly because we are undertaking the exercises within a school classroom (Westby, 2009).

The perspective exercise built upon our understanding of character in various ways. It included physically moving into certain spaces and subsequently, from whichever perspective the students had taken, describing in writing exactly what they saw and sometimes what they felt.

One student was folded under a chair, another lay on her back on the floor, while one of the other students stood on his chair facing away from his peer. The physicality of this exercise tapped into the spatial mode and facilitated discussion of concepts such as proximity, spacing, layout, interpersonal distance, territoriality, architecture/building, physical scapes, and both symbolic and realistic shapes. All the students were within a few metres of the others and the aim of the exercise was to demonstrate the ways perspective altered perception. The intervention of using space assisted students in constructing both spatial and emotional contexts for their writing. At this point the students were referred back to the way perspective was captured in the *Great Expectations* excerpt where Pip's perspective is radically altered as he's grabbed by the antagonist Abel Magwitch who holds Pip by the ankle and Pip experiences "a most tremendous dip and roll, so that the church jumped over its own weather-cock." The perspective exercise is nonthreatening, the students write exactly what they see, and follow-up discussion shows that each viewpoint is valid and as important as all the other perspectives shared by the students. This building of trust and faith in their own view further builds on the trust being established in the class.

This is two days into the unit. The next step explored another view of perspective while simultaneously introducing works from literary modernism.

Efficiency in using resources is imperative for the crammed English curriculum. New media, such as digital and audio texts, along with print media and film, help students develop literary understanding in various ways. The ways modes interact and the meanings that are constructed within and between modes affords students opportunities to view, hear, and experience texts simultaneously. Multiple modes articulate meaning in experiential and rich ways and digital forms of texts provide students openings into literate worlds both during class time and outside of the classroom. For the introduction into modernism this class listened to the following opening segment of an audio version of William Faulkner's *The Sound and the Fury*, narrated by Grover Gardner.

> Through the fence, between the curling flower spaces, I could see them hitting. They were coming toward where the flag was and I went along the fence. Luster was hunting in the grass by the flower tree. They took the flag out, and they were hitting. Then they put the flag

> back and they went to the table, and he hit and the other hit. Then they went on, and I went along the fence. Luster came away from the flower tree and we went along the fence and they stopped and we stopped and I looked through the fence while Luster was hunting in the grass.

The aspect of modernism addressed was their attempts to find new ways of expressing narrative experience, with less emphasis on character and more about the concepts and imagination. The students were asked what they thought the sequence is about. The characters in the novel's orientation are doing something, in this case, playing golf, but there is no reference in this excerpt about what exactly it is that they are doing. The discussion with the students was then about the possibility of writing something without referring directly to the characters or the action that the characters are undertaking. This was one of the most exhilarating moments in the class because there was a palpable excitement and the students wanted to write. Some preliminary writing about things in the classroom was begun but the lesson finished and the students agreed that they would write at home, bringing their writing to class for the next lesson. The exercise they were to undertake was:

> WRITE about something without referring directly to it by name—create essential qualities.

The next lesson began by viewing a YouTube clip that captured some stream-of-consciousness writing taken from *Ulysses* by James Joyce (2002). However, work on this clip was suspended because the students insisted that they wanted to share their writing from the previous lesson. The excitement stemmed from the students' drive to write, to explore new ways of expression. The following are two samples of student writing:

> Sample 1: An iota of black lay in the middle, panning in every direction at beautiful surroundings. A delicious, chocolate brown mixed with splashes of yellow, black and red swirled around like a cup of tea until the round, thick, black brim held it back from overflowing out into the perfect white expanse that followed. But with each stir, came a deeper, more beautiful swell of magnificent colour. And with each stir, the chocolate brown beauty came dangerously closer and closer to the edge, until it spilled and leaked out beyond the thick, black brim and into the white, forbidden land.

> Sample 2: The curved moon stretches across the arched horizon. A sea of wrinkled waves fan out interminably, deeper to the bones that creak and crack like an old cutter. Later it smoothes. The shiny surface still crinkly. The whooshing sound wipes across the surface. No need for a conch shell to hear the ocean.

As a collaborative task the class tried to determine what the writing meant, what the writing was actually about. The students studied their peers' writing closely and it was delightful watching the interaction between the students about what the focus of their writing was on. Students tried to justify what meaning they'd made of their peers' work using examples from the texts and the colours and feelings they ascribed therein.

It was a moment of gratification for the writers when they revealed the focus of their writing. Sample one was one girl's dog's eye while the second sample was a hand.

The final exercise in the study of literary eras is an exploration of postmodern texts, which explore notions of fragmentation, paradox, playfulness, and bricolage. With texts ranging from Jonathan Safran Foer's (2005) postmodern novel *Extremely Loud and Incredibly Close* to the trailer for Ruhermann and Tan's (2010) animated film *The Lost Thing*, the class analysed and discussed the ways voice, character, and relationships were developed through visual modes, auditory modes, spatial, gestural modes, and modes of language in each of the texts and then used ubiquitous technologies such as PowerPoint and Microsoft Word to construct texts that typified postmodern literature. Excitingly, the students' capacity and drive that overflowed from these discussions and analysis allowed the students the same sort of critical eye as they created their own postmodern texts.

If students' "sense of themselves...as literate is circumscribed by the restricted range of opportunities available to display their knowledge and to engage in meaningful participation in the classroom" (Vasudevan & Campano, 2009, p. 447), broadening the range of opportunities to display their knowledge using multiple modes is a teaching imperative.

The highlight of working through both the literature and the technologies in this program of learning experiences was developing pedagogies of collegiality (Mills, 2010) between teacher and student. The success of the work relies not only on the pedagogic techniques that enabled students to reposition themselves as authors across a range of texts but is also facilitated through the texts that are available in different forms and through different media, including digital media.

USING MULTIPLE MODES FOR ANALYZING FILM TRAILERS

This final vignette outlines learning experiences involving students using a "grammar of visual design" (Kress & van Leeuwen, 2001/2006) to analyze still images from a film trailer to appreciate the manner in which the portrayal of images contributed to the construction of the nature of the relationships among the main characters. The movie *Samson and Delilah* (Scarlett Pictures, 2009) follows two young indigenous teenagers who live in a remote Aboriginal community in the Central Australian desert. They leave their community and discover the harshness of life outside of the world they have known. The film explores their vulnerability as marginalized youth and their growing love for each other. The Australian released trailer of *Samson and Delilah* can be found at https://www.youtube.com/watch?v=N69RgtW6S8o.

The grammar of visual design (Kress & van Leeuwen, 2001/2006) derives from the systemic functional linguistic notion that language simultaneously constructs three kinds of meaning in every spoken or written text: ideational meaning, the participants, processes and circumstances in the material world, including imagined worlds; interpersonal meaning, the ways in which language is used to exchange information and goods and services among participants and constructs relationships of power, solidarity, intimacy/remoteness as well as personal evaluations of phenomena in the material or imagined worlds; and textual meaning, the ways in which language coheres to form whole texts (Halliday & Matthiessen, 2004; Martin, 1992). Kress and van Leeuwen (2001/2006) referred to these types of meanings as representational, interactive, and compositional. Just as grammatical descriptions of language provide a metalanguage that indicates how particular linguistic forms construct the three kinds of meanings, Kress and van Leeuwen identified the meaning-making aspects of images that constructed such meanings. For example, with respect to representational meaning, "vectors" or action lines indicated by the angle of depiction of characters' limbs can indicate running, or catching or throwing and so on; for interactive meaning, images where the gaze of the represented participant is directed at the viewer involve the viewer in a kind of pseudo-interpersonal engagement with the character, where as if the represented participants' gaze is directed elsewhere, the viewer is positioned as more of a detached observer of what is depicted; compositional meanings in images are influenced by factors such as the borders or framing of images and by what is the largest or most colourful component conveying salience. A detailed account of this grammar of visual design is provided by Kress and van Leeuwen (2001/2006) and others have provided richly illustrated accounts of its application to picture books, illustrated literary narratives (Lewis, 2001; Unsworth, 2001), and school curriculum texts (de Silva Joyce & Gaudin, 2007). The basic concepts of the grammar of visual design were introduced to the students in a series of workshop lessons that included teacher demonstration of image analyses and extensive exploration and analyses of different kinds of images by students supported by detailed learning scaffolds, which can be found at http://www.webquestdirect.com.au/webquest.asp?id=650&page=4923. Key questions used to analyse visual texts can include the following:

1. What is the purpose of the text?
2. What is the *salient* image?
3. How are the *vectors* within the image used to *frame* the subject of the text?

4. Who are the represented participants and what sort of relationships are developed in the text, through the gaze, social distance, and interactions?

The film trailer learning task begins for the students by listening to the soundtrack only of the trailer, so that without images the soundscape dominates students' consciousness. Then the film trailer is played without sound, just running through the moving image. The students then watch the trailer in full. Finally, students access still footage snapped from the film trailer. A number of still images from the film trailer where the characters Samson and Delilah are represented are captured and stored on the school computer network. The task for the students is to identify the visual means through which the interactions between the characters establish their relationship.

Throughout the film trailer several aspects of the characters' relationship are captured, including interest, hostility, friendship, and intimacy. The students were required to construct an analysis of the images to highlight the ways conflict is built by identifying the deployment of the resources of a grammar of visual design such as types of gaze, eye line vectors, and spatial relationships among characters within the frames. After analyzing several still images, the students posit, through discussion, their opinion about the resolution of the narrative.

Microsoft PowerPoint was used to undertake and display the analysis of the still images. The images are imported into the PowerPoint slides and then the analysis is supported by the editing tools available in the PowerPoint tool kit. Using the shape tool on the menu students select circles to identify the represented participants, the salient image. They select lines and arrows to identify vectors and squares from the toolbox to frame the gaze of the represented participants within the image. To demonstrate the way to use PowerPoint for analysis two images are chosen from the opening of the trailer. The Australian trailer for the film opens with a wide angled view of the Australian landscape at sunrise. The camera cuts to an image of a lone boy sitting atop rocks. The audience shares the boy's perspective as he looks down upon the road running through a small, isolated town. He's holding a small metal can. The camera pans around to the front of the protagonist whose gaze is not directed outward to the viewer and is hence is an offer in terms of the Kress and van Leeuwen grammar of visual design—an image not requiring a pseudo-interpersonal engagement from the viewer. The two opening images from the trailer annotated using PowerPoint are shown in Figure 10.3.

The mind-mapping software Inspiration was used to enable the students to sequence their analysis so that their three separate analyses of representational, compositional, and interactive meanings could be presented in a format that was easy to read. The students inserted their analyzed images, in either chronological sequence or as images representing emotional or character development, in an Inspiration document.

Identifying the meanings constructed by the images consolidated the students' understanding and use of the metalanguage of the grammar of visual design (Kress & van Leeuwen, 2001/2006), but the diversity of responses that mapped the emotional journey of the characters was the interesting part of the student work. While some students kept within the chronology of the viewing of the film trailer, others looked for different connections. Some students tracked the images from peace to violence, another chose entrapment to freedom, and yet another chose to identify how love developed within the frames. Because there were only half a dozen images in the folder for the students to analyse, the diversity of their responses was both thought provoking and inspiring. This diversity demonstrated several different perspectives on the meanings privileged in the film trailer.

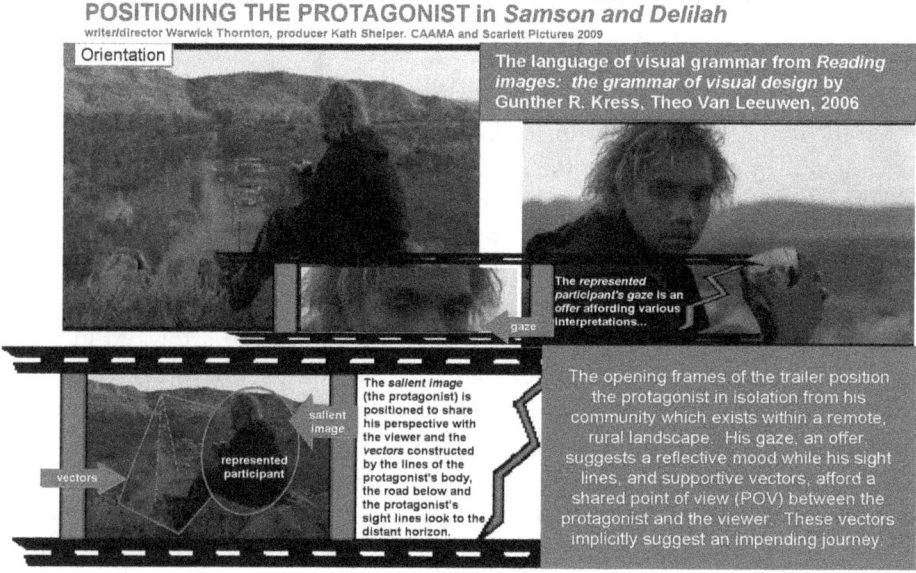

Fig 10.3. Annotated still images from the opening 3scene of *Samson and Delilah*.

CONCLUSION

The interpretation of literature and the expression of this through writing as the widely regarded pinnacle of achievement in the NSW senior secondary school English curriculum remained a central determinant of the work undertaken in this rural high school classroom. The significant change was that these students began to see that engaging with and achieving success in negotiating literary interpretation and response was not only possible but also an enjoyable and engaging endeavor. This turnaround occurred through enthusiastic teaching marshaling three dimensions of pedagogic practice: The first was making use of the readily accessible, freely available Web-based multimodal versions of established literary narratives, principally from http://www.youtube.com. The second was the appropriation of well-known software such as Microsoft Excel and PowerPoint and other software such as Inspiration to the analysis and presentation of various forms of multimodal text analysis. The third was the incorporation of exploration of different modes of meaning-making and the explicit teaching of a grammar of visual design as resources for text-analytic approaches to literary interpretation. This orientation to senior secondary school English teaching sees the affordances of the digital multimodal communication landscape as facilitative of developing literary appreciation—celebrating the partnership of literature and the digital world (Dresang, 1999).

REFERENCES

Colquhoun, G. (2010). *The art of walking upright*. New Zealand: Steele Roberts.
Cope, B., & Kalantzis, M. (Eds.). (2000). *Multiliteracies: Literacy learning and the design of social futures*. Melbourne: Macmillan.
Daudet, A. (1945). *Bedside book of famous French stories* (M. McIntyre Trans.). New York: Random House.
de Silva Joyce, H., & Gaudin, J. (2007). *Interpreting the visual: A resource book for teachers*. Sydney: Phoenix.
Dickens, C. (1996). *Great expectations*. London: Penguin Classics.
Dostoevsky, F. (1949). *Short stories by Fyodor Dostoevski: The world's popular classics*. New York: Crest Publishing House.
Dresang, E. (1999). *Radical change: Books for youth in a digital age*. New York: Wilson.
Faulkner, W. (2005). *The sound and the fury*. New York: Random House.
Halliday, M. A. K., & Matthiessen, C. (2004). *An introduction to functional grammar*. London: Arnold.
Hammond, J. (1996). Reading—Knowledge about language and genre theory. In G. Bull & M. Anstey (Eds.), *The literacy lexicon*. Sydney, Australia: Prentice Hall.
Jewitt, C. (2008). Multimodality and literacy in school classrooms. *Review of Research in Education, 32*(1), 241–267.
Jewitt, C. (Ed.). (2009). *The Routledge handbook of multimodal analysis*. London: Routledge.
Joyce, J. (2002). *Ulysses*. New York: Random House.
Kimber, K., & Wyatt-Smith, C. (2010). Secondary students' online use and creation of knowledge: Refocusing priorities for quality assessment and learning. *Australasian Journal of Educational Technology, 26*(5), 607–625.
Kress, G. (2000). Multimodality. In B. Cope & M. Kalantzis (Eds.), *Multiliteracies: Literacy learning and the design of social futures* (pp. 182–202). Melbourne: Macmillan.
Kress, G., & van Leeuwen, T. (2001/2006). *Reading images: A grammar of visual design*. London: Routledge.
Lean, D. (1946). *Great expectations* [Video]. Retrieved from http://www.criterion.com/films/566-great-expectations

Lewis, D. (2001). *Reading contemporary picturebooks*. London: RoutledgeFalmer.
New London Group. (1996). A pedagogy of multiliteracies: Designing social futures. *Harvard Educational Review, 66*(1), 66–92.
NSW Board of Studies. (1999). *Stage 6 English syllabus*. Sydney: Author.
Mackey, M. (1994). The new basics: Learning to read in a multimedia world. *English in Education, 28*(1), 9–19.
Mackey, M. (1999). *The changing powers of readers in a time of new technology. Unleash the power! Knowledge—Technology—Diversity*. Paper presented at the Third International Forum on Research in School Librarianship, Birmingham.
Mackey, M. (2001). The survival of engaged reading in the Internet age: New media, old media, and the book. *Children's Literature in Education, 32*(3), 167–189.
Mackey, M. (2002). *Literacies across media: Playing the text*. London: RoutledgeFalmer.
Mackey, M. (2003). Researching new forms of literacy. *Reading Research Quarterly, 38*(10), 356–385.
Martin, J. R. (1992). *English text: System and structure*. Amsterdam: Benjamins.
Mills, K. (2010). A review of the "digital turn" in the new literacy studies. *Review of Educational Research 80*(2), 246–271.
Mueck, R. (1997). *Big Baby II*. Retrieved from http://www.youtube.com/watch?v=4CmqOIRpPYc
Mueck, R. (2000). *Boy*. Retrieved from http://www.tumblr.com/tagged/ron-mueck?before=1332259842
Mueck, R. (2002). *Mask II*. Retrieved from http://www.brooklynmuseum.org/exhibitions/ron_mueck/mask_ii.php
Poe, E. A. (1843/2008). The tell-tale heart. In C. Berkin & S. C. Imbarrato (Eds.), *Encyclopedia of American literature* (rev. ed.). New York: Facts on File.
Ruhermann, A., & Tan, S. (Writers). (2010). *The lost thing* [Short film]. Australia: Madman Entertainment.
Safran Foer, J. (2005). *Extremely loud and incredibly close*. London: Penguin Books.
Scarlett Pictures. (2009). *Samson and Delilah trailer*. Retrieved from https://www.youtube.com/watch?v=N69RgtW6S8o
Shelley, M. (1833). *The mortal immortal*. Retrieved from http://www.rc.umd.edu/editions/mws/immortal/mortal.html
Solomon, T. (2010) *Leaving*. Retrieved from http://auslit.net/2010/ 09/17/leaving-by-trevor-solomon/
Tan, S. (2008) *Tales from outer suburbia*. Sydney: Allen & Unwin.
Unsworth, L. (2001). *Teaching multiliteracies across the curriculum: Changing contexts of text and image in classroom practice*. Buckingham, UK: Open University Press.
Vasudevan, L., & Campano, G. (2009). The social production of adolescent risk and the promise of adolescent literacies. *Review of Research in Education, 33*(1), 310–353.
Westby, C. (2009). Assessment of cognitive and language abilities through play. *Language, Speech, and Hearing Services in Schools, 11*(3), 154–168.

FURTHER READING

Cope, B., & Kalantzis, M. (2009). Multiliteracies: New literacies, new learning. *Pedagogies: An International Journal, 4*(3), 164–195.
Grenville, K. (2010). *The writing book: A practical guide for fiction writers*. Crows Nest, NSW: Allen & Unwin.

Macken-Horarik, M., & Morgan, W. (2011). Towards a metalanguage adequate to linguistic achievement in post-structuralism and English: Reflections on voicing in the writing of secondary students. *Linguistics and Education, 22*(2), 133–149.

WEB RESOURCES

Bain, J. *Multimodal tools—Analysis, process, meaning:* http://prezi.co m/kx0glikc7t0d/multimodal-tools/

Bain, J. *Representations of Belonging:* http://www.webquestdirect.com.au/webquest.asp?id=650

Bain, J. *Stories for teaching and learning: Realism, modernism, postmodernism:* http://prezi.com/wakgkzihot3b/realism-modern ism-postmode rnism/

McGraw, K. *Creative writing:* http://kellimcgraw.com/tag/creativ ewriting/

CHAPTER ELEVEN

Augmented Reality in the English Classroom

WINYU CHINTHAMMIT & ANGELA THOMAS

INTRODUCTION

This chapter will address the following three key questions:

1. What is Augmented Reality and how has it been used for educational contexts?
2. How has Augmented Reality been used for storytelling?
3. How can teachers use the affordances of Augmented Reality for children's multimodal storytelling?

As we outline the answers to these questions, we will demonstrate the potential for teachers—even with limited technical expertise—to be able to introduce Augmented Reality storytelling in their classrooms immediately.

WHAT IS AUGMENTED REALITY?

The interface between humans and computers has increasingly become an important research topic in computer science. As we are becoming dependent on computers, the way in which we interact or interface with them will directly influence the productivity of our work. Over the past few decades, new fields of research into this human/computer interaction have emerged to describe the different kinds of interface paradigms that are possible, such as Virtual Reality and Augmented Reality. Milgram et al. introduced the Reality-Virtuality continuum (Milgram & Colquhorn, 1999; Milgram & Kishino, 1994) to outline the framework of these emerging fields. Figure 11.1 illustrates this continuum.

At each end of the continuum are the absolutes: reality and virtual reality. The far left is reality without any computer interface and on the far right is a *virtual* environment where the entire environment is constructed using computer graphics. Between these two environments exist two kinds of "mixed reality" where both the real and virtual coexist. While there are many forms of virtual environments such as driving simulators, flight simulations, immersive virtual worlds such as Second Life, and computer games, the development of mixed reality environments is relatively new. One particular mixed reality environment is the focus of this chapter: Augmented Reality (AR).

According to Alexander (2011), there have been a number of popularist terms used to describe Augmented Reality: a *magic window, mixed reality, reading the environment, annotating the world, laminating the physical,* and a *looking glass* into an invisible world. However, technically AR is defined as an interactive system that is capable of overlaying and co-locating computer-generated images or content (which can be described as virtual objects) in the real world.

Azuma (1997), one of the pioneers in the field, defined AR as a system that has three characteristics: (1) it combines the real and the virtual world; (2) it involves real-time interaction; and (3) it registers in three-dimensional (3D) space. The virtual objects are anything that is generated by a computer, such as digital text, digital images, 3D models, or 3D animation.

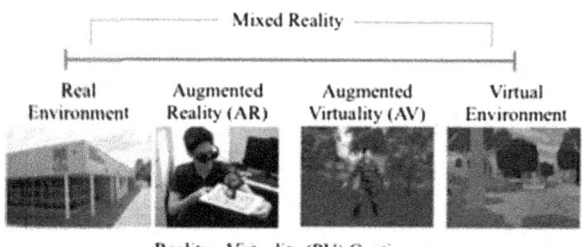

Fig 11.1. Reality-Virtuality Continuum (from Milgram & Colquhorn, 1999; Milgram & Kishino, 1994).

Azuma's first characteristic emphasizes the concept "augmented," meaning the real world is augmented or enhanced in some form using a virtual object. Furthermore, *both* real and augmentation (virtual) are required to appear in the field of view. For example, a computer-generated online game is not considered AR due to the lack of the real-world component, as everything is virtual. The second characteristic of AR is the capability to be interacted with in real time. That is, the AR system will have to be capable of adjusting the virtual augmentation in real time with respect to the changing position of the user's viewpoint. This also explains the last characteristic of AR, the registration in 3D. The registration is what makes virtual contents (e.g., 3D models of houses) coexist virtually with real-world objects in the real world. For example, an architect might walk into a house and with an augmented reality application be able to show where renovations might occur and what they look like. As the architect moves through the house with the application, the augmented reality images will change according to the architect's changing position and location. Augmented reality generally consists of four components as explained by Chinthammit (2007):

1. **Display.** A user will view the visual information through a display device. The device could be as simple as a computer screen, a mobile phone, or a tablet such as an iPad. Or it might be a more sophisticated device such as specialized glasses or a Head Mounted Display, which is worn on the head.
2. **Movement.** Tracking the capture of a user's viewpoint is the first trick that makes the AR interface work. The user's viewpoint is tracked to determine where the user is looking in the real world. There are a number of tracking technologies to track the user's movement, mainly depending on whether the operating environment is outdoor or indoor. Outdoors, most common tracking options use the Global Positioning System (GPS) and digital compasses, which are built into most smartphones.

Fig 11.2. The MagicBook in action.[1]

Indoors, a common option is video tracking, which uses a video frame captured from a video camera or a webcam to calculate the movement of the camera with respect to the real world. The video tracking is based on computer vision algorithms, which simply attempt to recognize *features* in the captured scene. The features are what differentiate the type of video tracking. There are three kinds of features: (1) marker-based, (2) model-based, and (3) natural. The marker-based and model-based features are fundamentally the same as they are prebuilt features that are contained within a physical object that is needed to be placed in the environment. The only difference is in their appearances. The physical object of the marker-based feature tracking is literally a physical marker (i.e., symbol inside black square). The physical object of the model-based feature tracking, on the other hand, can be flexible and not restricted to a marker shape. It can be almost anything that exists in the environment such as a movie poster, book cover, or even your teacup. The last kind is a natural feature which, unlike the previous two, is not a prebuilt feature. The natural feature already exists in the environment such as corners of computer keyboards or outlines of your wall calendar.

Fig 11.3. Outdoor tracking in action.[2]

3. **Computing.** Same as all other computerized systems, the computing unit is the core of AR systems. The ranges of its responsibilities vary from basic control functions such as acquiring data from a tracking unit to advanced computational algorithms such as data optimization.
4. **Graphic rendering.** The 3D models of virtual objects need to be rendered from the current user's viewpoint. This is what makes the registration of virtual objects in the real world look realistic.

Augmented Reality typically works by starting with a user and his or her device moving in the real world. The movement is then tracked or captured and sent to the computing unit, which determines how the AR system should react and respond to the user's current location, and, finally, the action will be translated by the graphic rendering back to the display device for the user to see.

MOBILE AUGMENTED REALITY

Traditionally, Augmented Reality applications were developed to run on powerful desktop or laptop computing platforms rather than a mobile phone or tablet, simply because the former had more computing capabilities and the latter did not have adequate computing capabilities to run an AR application.

However, recent rapid growth of the smartphone technologies (e.g., Apple iPhone, iPad, Android) has changed the Augmented Reality landscape. The smartphone represents a new concept of having information anywhere at any time and this has opened up a new generation of applications. For example, Foursquare (https://foursquare.com/) is a location-based social network mobile application that allows social network friends to share information associated with specific locations such as where they are currently and what they like/dislike about a particular restaurant on 42nd Avenue. If some of your Foursquare friends have left reviews of the restaurants in a particular location, you can look at Foursquare and see those reviews and any other interesting comments they may have made to help you select your restaurant for the evening.

Even though computing capabilities of mobiles are still not as powerful as the ones in desktops and laptops, a powerful mobile can now be considered as another option to run AR applications. An AR application that is operating on a mobile platform is commonly referred to as "mobile AR". For example, a popular mobile AR application is Layar (http://www.layar.com/browser/), in which the digital information is being registered to real-world objects. With a rear camera, a smartphone's display is used as a viewing portal or browser for users to look through to the real world. The background video is the live capture of the real world while AR overlays information into the real world as if it exists. Unlike Foursquare where the restaurant comments are displayed as a pin drop at the location on a 2D map similar to Google map (http://maps.google.com.au/), the Layar will instead display/overlay the restaurant comments at the location where the restaurant is in the real world as if it were a physical extension of the restaurant. With smartphone technologies expected to continue to advance rapidly in the future, it will have a massive impact on the field of AR. More innovative AR applications will be invented and made available on the mobile.

HOW HAS AR BEEN USED FOR EDUCATIONAL PURPOSES?

AR technologies offer the capability to overlay digital content onto the real world and, as such, offer great advantages in many practical applications, such as medicine, manufacturing, television, and science.

In an operating room, for example, a doctor might want to be able to see an X-ray (or an MRI, a CT, or ultrasound) of a patient overlaid onto the actual patient during surgery (Bajura, Fuchs, Ohbuchi, Carolina, & Hill, 1992; Bichlmeier, Heining, Feuerstein, & Navab, 2009; State, Livingston, Hirota, Garrett, Whitton, & Fuchs, 1996). In effect, this would allow the doctor to have X-ray vision to see through the patient's skin. This increases the effectiveness in a workspace for the doctor by eliminating the process of moving back and forth between viewing imaging on the screen next to the operating table and viewing the physical corresponding area on the patient's body.

AR has also found success in television broadcasting. In automobile racing events (e.g., NASCAR), the name of a driver is overlaid on the moving racing car in which the driver is driving. Television audiences are easily able to see who the driver is of the car they are looking at.

With its ability to display visual content in 3D, AR has great potential as a guiding maintenance system. A non-expert user can learn end-user maintenance tasks for a printer through a head-mounted display (Feiner, MacIntyre, & Seligmann, 1993). A driver can view where the engine parts are located in the engine compartment and what they are for—simply by looking at the parts, virtual annotation will appear (Platonov, Heibel, Meier, & Grollmann, 2006).

While there are some successes in other disciplines, AR has not yet made much progress in education. So far, the current AR applications for education purposes are primarily focused on learning basic knowledge and training skill sets.

AR was demonstrated as a successful means for teaching basic chemistry (Fjeld & Voegtli, 2002). Users would bring two physical markers representing two chemistry elements close together to trigger the action of composition of a molecular model. For example, a marker representing hydrogen and a marker representing oxygen could be merged together to elicit the augmented object of a water molecule. Additionally, users could select an element from a booklet in which each page was designed with a distinct marker to represent a corresponding element. By flipping through the booklet using a computer webcam or camera, users could learn the molecular composition of different elements. There are two underlying advantages to attaching Augmented Reality content to a print-based text such as the chemistry booklet: (1) typical 2D content such as an image in a textbook can be brought to life in 3D; and (2) the content can be modified to fit other teaching materials simply by replacing the old virtual content with the new.

AR has also been demonstrated in training new skills. Kumagai, Yamashita, Morikawa, Yokoyama, and Taku (2008) implemented AR in distance education system for teaching manual skills in endoscopic sinus surgery. The trainer and the trainee were at two different locations. The system enabled them to exchange their viewpoints so that the trainer would see how the trainee performed the procedures in terms of placement of tools. On the other hand, the trainer would try to imitate the trainer's movement. Their study demonstrated the potential of AR technologies in distance education.

What we have described so far are typical desktop-based AR applications. However, the benefit of mobile AR is that it enables us to look into the location-based applications where the AR components can be accessible while being at a specific location, using the GPS tracking affordances. This unique aspect of mobile AR gave birth to the term "AR narrative," which is the focus of the remainder of the chapter.

AUGMENTED REALITY STORYTELLING

As outlined above, Augmented Reality can be co-located with reality in a number of ways: through using a defined marker, a model, objects in the natural environment, or a GPS tracking system. This section will explore new and emerging developments in each of these forms, which have reading, storytelling, and creating stories as their main aim. These are ZooBurst, the MagicBook, and locative storytelling applications. In particular we will explore locative storytelling in depth, as this holds the most potential now for the non-expert and uses applications that are freely available for use on most mobile phones.

ZOOBURST

ZooBurst is a simple 3D animated pop-up book creation tool designed by Craig Kapp of NYU. ZooBurst stories can be created in a Web browser but also may be experienced using an Augmented Reality marker. In Craig's words,

> ZooBurst is a digital storytelling tool that lets anyone easily create his or her own 3D pop-up books. Using ZooBurst, storytellers of any age can create their own rich worlds in which their stories can come to life.... Once constructed, books can be inspected from any angle from within a 3D space, and rotating around a book is as easy as dragging and dropping a mouse. In addition, authors can choose to make items "clickable," allowing readers to learn more about individual characters within a story. Each character can have its own "chat bubble" that pops up when that character is clicked. In addition, authors can also record their own voices using the ZooBurst audio recorder to have their characters really "speak" when clicked!
>
> ...Readers who have a webcam installed on their computer can also experience any ZooBurst book in Augmented Reality. Once a book has been loaded, readers can click on the "Webcam Mode" button at the top of the screen. This button will turn on their webcam and allow them to see themselves as though they were looking in a mirror. From here, visitors can hold up a special symbol to the webcam to watch as the book "flies" out of the paper and into the room around them! In addition, Augmented Reality mode also allows readers the ability to interact with a book using simple gestures. For example, simply waving your hand in front of a book will allow you to turn its pages back and forth. (Kapp, 2011)

This is a free tool for all of the basic facilities, and a relatively inexpensive outlay of $30 per year will unlock additional features and capabilities. It comes with a manual but is quite intuitive to use and suitable for very young children. Content is customizable, meaning that although it comes with an existing library, children are able to upload their own images, sounds, and drawings. The book and reading the book is located within a 3D space; however, the actual images are mostly limited to 2D pop-up images, so the experience is more a blend between 2D and 3D.

ZooBurst could be used by teachers as a simple introduction to both multimodal authoring and Augmented Reality. The interface is simple—click and drag and adjust are the main requirements, so technology skills need only be minimal for simple stories, but it allows more sophisticated technology use for children (with its in-built sound effects and audio recording function) or those who learn to make their own animated images (such as with tools like gickr or gifninja). Another lovely feature is the social one of being able to leave written or audio comments on a friend's creations. This could be invaluable for providing peer feedback and creating a sense of community within a class.

In terms of narrative capabilities, the ZooBurst platform is a blend of traditional and new forms of narrative. Clearly using the traditional metaphor of a book, it can be read from beginning to end in a linear fashion. However, each double-page spread has objects spread out over the 3D space and can be clicked or understood in a nonlinear fashion. The option of a narration for each double-page spread is a means for tying together the meaning coherently, and the "pieces" of narrative, whether they be sound effects, voiceover dialogue, or text pieces, make each double page much more exploratory and affect the reader by requiring the reader to make cognitive sense of those pieces. In Chapter 5 of this volume, a list of affordances of digital storytelling were explained. ZooBurst uses all of these affordances and as such offers teachers an easy way into exploring digital multimodal authoring.

That ZooBurst stories can be activated using AR is an added bonus, but at this stage the AR capability doesn't really enhance the narrative potential. That is, there is no explicit "added value" to the literacy or literary experience by using the AR. However, there is an excellent option to capture the real environment behind the digital story with a photograph with one click. This opens up new opportunities for storytelling that could in fact make use of the AR capability. For example, the children could become a character within a new meta-story told via these images.

THE MAGICBOOK

The MagicBook was designed in the New Zealand HIT Lab (Human Interaction with Technology Laboratory) and is not a freely available tool now. However, it is worth discussing here as in the future it may become more widely accessible. Essentially the MagicBook is a graphic novel or picture book that has multimedia content tagged to each page, so that when the novel is viewed through a camera the multimedia content is activated. A paper page in the novel might, for example, have an image of people at a cinema on it and when viewed with a camera the reader is able to see animations of those people and the actual movie they are watching. The novel or picture book can be read normally without the AR content, but the AR content is said to add value to the narrative, making it more complex, enriched, or adding additional layers to it (see Figure 11.2 above).

At this stage, several studies of the MagicBook by HITLab NZ researchers (Dünser & Hornecker, 2007a, 2007b; Grasset, Dünser, Seichter & Billinghurst, 2007; Hornecker & Dünser, 2007) have focused on user experience with the technology and enjoyment and motivation of the reading experience, rather than exploring the potential of the experience as a literacy or literary one. It should be noted that the designers of the MagicBook were clearly focusing on developing prototypes that use innovative and leading technologies to enhance and transform everyday experience and are more proof of concept at this stage than a genuine literary experience. However, as children's authors and writers are exposed to and embrace such concepts, the range of creative and exciting possibilities to enhance narrative through multimodality via the AR capabilities remains to be seen.

LOCATIVE STORYTELLING

Locative storytelling is a new genre of storytelling using the GPS system of mobile devices to annotate different locations with a segment of a story using an Augmented Reality applications such as Layar or Wikitude. Readers then need to walk through those locations with their mobile device to discover the segments and piece them together to construct a meaningful story. These applications (Layar, Wikitude) allow the mobile device's GPS system to pinpoint each location, and to tag the location to the segment of story to be uncovered. Locative storytelling might be as simple as an audio or digital tour of a museum. Tasmania's Museum of New and Old Art (MONA) offers users a custom designed iPod called an O that uses text and images to explain and critique what a visitor views, as well as recording each particular museum experience and emailing it back to the user to relive at a later date.

There has been a proliferation of education walking tours applications for mobile phones over the past two or three years, particularly in the UK. The application "Shakespeare's London" allows you to walk around London with your phone displaying a map that has on it overlaid information about the special venues of Shakespeare's time. Similarly, the "Literary London" application plots places on a map to identify the haunts and venues associated with a range of famous authors, such as Charles Dickens and Graham Greene.

The notion of locative storytelling garnered considerable attention online in 2008, due in large part to Charles Cumming's (2008) digital narrative *The 21 Steps* (Figure 11.4), inspired by John Buchan's classic novel *The Thirty-Nine Steps*, which was commissioned by Penguin's digital publishing arm. The story was told through Google's information bubbles and took the reader from the streets of London to Edinburgh, Scotland, with plenty of mini-cliffhangers along the way, and was described as *an adrenaline-fuelled adventure* (Carless, 2008) and *a fast-paced, finely tuned thriller* (Black, 2008).

Fig 11.4. Charles Cumming's (2008) digital narrative *The 21 Steps*.

This story is available online using a simple Web browser, but similar stories also allow a user to wander through the location and pick it up with a mobile device.

As a new genre of storytelling, locative stories push narrative and narrative construction in new ways. The most significant of these is the emphasis on the role of the locations within the story and the movement and action between locations. In *21 Steps*, the movement is described as frenetic and in an interview by games blogger Simon Carless at Gamasutra, the digital publisher at Penguin, Jeremy Ettinghausen, commented:

> What the Google Maps story does is force us to think about the reader experience. While they might not realize it, authors simply don't have to think about this when it comes to books, since they already implicitly know the "design" of books—it's words on page, divided up into chapters, and you can flick back and forth pages to look at the "story history," and bookmark pages to keep your place.

> The design of books is so great that it hasn't changed for hundreds of years, and so we just don't think about it anymore.
>
> When we had the idea for a story based around Google Maps, we knew that it had to incorporate a lot of movement—otherwise what's the point of having a map? So one early idea was a travelogue—a little like Around The World in 80 Days. Another was a thriller, like The 39 Steps. We ended up taking the latter option, due to its frenetic pace, and we asked Charles Cumming, an acclaimed British spy thriller author, to write a story for us.
>
> To begin with, we simply told Charles to "bake movement in" to the story. However, from early on, it became clear that this was rather trickier than any of us had thought; it wasn't enough to have the protagonist walking and driving and flying around the place, they had to do it all the time.
>
> Early drafts of the story saw the protagonist having a very tense discussion for a couple of chapters—riveting stuff—but it was all in one room. Luckily we had a great relationship with Charles and we worked together to incorporate more movement, or references to other locations, in every chapter. (Carless, 2008, para. 19–23)

The significance of using location and making location a central aspect of storytelling affected the narrative of *21 Steps* not only in the ways described by Ettinghausen above, but by focusing on place, movement, and action it did not allow a deep exploration of character psychology, as articulated by the author in an interview with Black (2008) as follows:

> It was limiting only in the sense that I couldn't explore character in any great depth or get into the more psychological or emotional sides of the story. Plot was everything. Suspense was everything. It was all about pace and movement. But that in itself was quite exciting. Once I understood the parameters of what Penguin were trying to achieve, I had a lot of fun with it. (para. 6)

While this limitation of lack of emotion described by Cumming applied to his action thriller location based fiction, other kinds of location based storytelling add a more personal, intimate element to the storytelling whereby stories are biographical stories about communities and their experiences with place. One example is Feral Arts' *PlaceStories*, which encourages communities (particularly rural communities) to create stories and locate them on a map, with the aim of building stronger, more creative communities through developing sustainable storytelling networks (Feral Arts, 2012). These stories can be uploaded via mobile or desktop computer and interact with Twitter and other social media. Although not fictional, the potential for the same kind of emotional depth as developed within PlaceStories is possible, depending on the genre of the story being located to a space.

Although both the *21 Steps* and *PlaceStories* use maps and location as a narrative device and structure, they don't necessarily use Augmented Reality and the mobile device to its fullest potential. Alexander (2011) outlines several biographical locative storytelling projects, such as one centred in Los Angeles called *34 North 118 West*, and another based in Canada called *[murmur]*. In both examples, readers traverse through a range of spaces such as city blocks and their movement triggers their mobile device to display text, sounds, audio, or video that recounts short historical narratives about the people who once lived and worked in those places. These and other examples outlined by Alexander (2011) certainly use both Augmented Reality and the mobile platform well, though the stories were biographical in nature. Fictional locative storytelling experiences that utilise Augmented Reality to its fullest extent are rarer, except for the more commercial games and locative experiences such as *Haunted London* and *The Westwood Experience*.

Haunted London was a project created by students from the University of the Arts London (2009) and is a locative, interactive storytelling experience based on walking through a haunted trail of London and using a blend of real and fictional content. Using a mobile application, participants work in pairs to unlock the hidden fictional narrative within the trail. According to Profumo (2011) of the Behance LCC blog, a description of the application is as follows:

> Our app is a story/narrative that's embedded with a haunted trail in London. As the user walks the trail, at specific locations they are required to perform certain tasks unlocking the next part of the trail and narrative as they go along.
>
> This experience has been designed as a two-user experience to satisfy the safety concerns that individual users may incur. But to make the experience truly immersive, we have ensured that both users have individual experiences, which are collaborative and sequential.
>
> Using Bluetooth the app will synchronize both devices and start the app when they both arrive at the designated start location. The app will then direct them to location one.
>
> Once they reach a location, based on GPS tags the app will start a narration of the story and history behind the location. This process follows for two more locations. As the users leave location three the actual experience of the app kicks in, with our ghost Emma haunting the user's iPhones. Emma soon begins leading the users to the next locations. At each of the locations she directs each of them to accomplish a task that together unlock Emma's hidden story.
>
> Emma is out to get vengeance and needs a medium to move around, which in this case is the user's iPhone. (para. 3–7)

As yet, this application is not available on iTunes. Next, *The Westwood Experience* is one of the more recent immersive AR storytelling experiences developed and researched by Allen, Tsai, Hinman, and Azuma (2010). The researchers created a location based narrative using mixed reality effects, that is, a combination of fiction overlaid on real world that used Augmented Reality and real artefacts found across a range of locations. The narrative was told through following a map to locate the points of interest of the story, which were linked together through an audio narration, video clips, and other AR effects. The unique feature distinguishing *The Westwood Experience* from previous forms of locative storytelling was the strong driving narrative voice of the character, which was broken up into discrete chunks with respect to the different physical locations traversed throughout the story. Users experienced narrative through a combination of viewing and interacting with images, videos, and other mixed reality effects on the screen of the mobile device (a Nokia 900) and listening to narration via headphones.

The experience took place on Westwood Blvd., Glendon Ave., and a room rented from the Westwood Brewery in Los Angeles, California. For safety concerns, all interaction and narration only took place while the participants were at stationary locations. It began in the historic Crest theatre in Westwood where the honorary "mayor" of Westwood (which was actually a real person, a paid actor during the days the experience ran) started off the tour by introducing himself to the audience (participants) and followed it with an introduction of the tour. Each participant was given a mobile device and headphones. Before they set out, the mayor wrote a map on a piece of paper containing streets, intersections, and street labels to show the tour routine. Participants were invited to take a picture of the handwritten map with their mobile device. This was where the first mixed reality effect occurred. The physical map, when viewed on the device, was suddenly annotated by the correct names of streets (based on a computer recognition algorithm). Also, there was an animation of a moving cursor showing the tour route on the image of the map. Participants could also bring up this annotated/animated map at any time to help with navigation. They were ready to go on a walking tour. To navigate to the next stop point of the story, the participants were shown an image of something located at the next location such as building signs and other unique street marks.

Their first stop was across the street from a building, which is now a Peet's Coffee and Tea restaurant. The participants were asked to take a picture of the restaurant. Another mixed reality effect was used to (1) recognize the building and the position and orientation of the capturing camera; and (2) create a static AR effect by digitally replacing the Peet's logo with a virtual Ralph's sign and other items (e.g., car) to transform the building appearance back in time to the year 1949 where the building was once Ralph's store. The Peet's effect was designed to reinforce a specific point in narration that described the Ralph's store.

The next stop was the Yamato restaurant in a historic building. This location at the centre of Westwood offered views in all directions. The authors recognized the uniqueness of this location by building a panoramic illustration of what the view would look like in 1949. Users can turn around (while holding the phone as if they were to take a picture of the scene) to view the illustration aligned with the real world. A gyroscope sensor was used to measure the orientation of the mobile phone (i.e., user's viewpoint). The changing orientation then altered the viewpoint on the panoramic image while the user is turning, in effect creating an illusion as if the virtual scene existed in the real world. Participants found this effect to be immersive as they could look in any direction and compare the past (on the screen) and present (real world—outside of the screen) buildings.

The user experience to this point was a simple location-based story that connected past and present objects together. However, *The Westwood Experience* was designed to engage audiences even more with a surprise love story. The narrative was turned to focus on a young sailor in 1949 named Pete who would later become the mayor. The narrative described Pete meeting a young beautiful lady for the first time in a diner across the street (where the participants are located at this point in the narrative). The meeting was told through a movie clip displaying an illustration of the diner with audio commentary.

The narrative followed the couple from the diner to a room that was a rehearsal studio in 1949 where the couple had become close. The experience here was different from previous ones by not involving the use of the mobile device but instead relying on a combination of the actual physical rehearsal studio set and spatial audio to deliver the experience. While the physical setup helped transport participants back in time, the spatial audio was used to tell the couple's intimate conversation through audio specifically generated from different locations at a particular time. In effect, the participants would feel they were in the middle of the couple's conversation, hearing their voices as Pete was moving himself from one corner of the room to another.

For the finale, users were guided to a cemetery where the identity of the lady was revealed as the climax of the experience. They were standing in front of Marilyn Monroe's crypt. The narrative was tied to the unique location to great effect.

A PEDAGOGY FOR LOCATIVE STORYTELLING

The concept of locative storytelling using GPS and other affordances of the smartphone is an exemplary model of what is possible with locative storytelling production. In a primary or secondary school setting, the technical complexities and production quality of a locative storytelling experience such as *Haunted London* or *The Westwood Experience* are unrealistic. However, the creation of rich stories using images, videos, and text as well as GPS to make them locative experiences is possible through applications such as wikitude.me.

Wikitude.me and Junaio are both examples of mobile applications that allow users to register and add in their own content in the form of points of interest, which can be text or links to images, videos, and URLs. This is limited in terms of an immersive narrative experience but it is a good starting point until such time as more intuitive locative storytelling creation applications suitable for young people are developed. In Table 11.1 we have explored an approach that might be possible in the classroom, using wikitude.me or other similar AR applications. There are endless possibilities, limited only by the imagination.

Table 11.1. An Approach to AR Storytelling in the Classroom

Lesson 1: Understanding narrative and place	The first step is to find a local place that has some historical or fictional future significance. Place is central to locative storytelling, whether based on the real or imaginary, or somewhere in between. The class should brainstorm what they know about their local history, or about the buildings, and either research online or engage in a preliminary data-gathering excursion to compile interesting facts about the chosen place. Creative license may be taken with the facts, since this is fiction! However, this information gathering process may also involve interviewing real people, note taking, and map making.
Lesson 2: Selecting a literary genre	Next, the class should decide on the literary genre. Two genres that seem to be apposite for locative storytelling: • Science fiction (such as time travel stories where students use AR to go back and forth in time, and the AR is used to show the transformed location) • Mystery (a mystery that requires searching around a place for clues, where AR is used to provide specialized forensic information, snatches of private conversations, secret documents or artefacts of the suspects)
Lesson 3: The narrative imperative: friction	All narratives have a complication or problem—a source of friction. Brainstorm with the class what the central challenge in their story will be: will it be a missing person, a murder to solve, a quest to save mankind?
Lesson 4: The characters	Who will be the main character to suffer the burdens of the challenge, to face the friction, to solve the problem? Answer: it could be *whoever reads your story*! One of the engaging features of locative storytelling is that it's easy to position the reader into the role of the central character, particularly if the genre is a mystery. What will be important is to decide on the minor characters of the story—the friends, enemies, family members, neighbours, and so on who will help to provide the narrative pieces to be constructed together by the reader. This is interactive fiction at its best—children in the class could take on the roles of all the minor characters to create their piece of the story, recording themselves role-playing a scene on video,

		creating an artifact that was significant to the central character, having hushed conversations with each other about the problem, etc., and then tagging this information to a geographical location that will only be found by the reader if following the narrative closely. The class should decide on the name and details of the main character that the reader must pretend to be as they traverse through the narrative—Detective Matthews, Miss Fiona, Doctor Roberts—and this way the reader is immersed into the story as the character.
Lesson 5: Storyboarding		The class should develop a storyboard of events linked to a range of relevant locations on a map. There may be a narrative that links each separate link that is triggered once again by being at a particular location. This task would best be done over several days, with the storyboard positioned on a large whiteboard, and groups adding to it over time. The class could reflect several times on the narrative structure, the narrative logic, and the narrative complexity to ensure that the experience of reading the story and becoming a character in the story will be rich, challenging, and rewarding.
Lesson 6: Creating the narrative pieces		The class should be divided into pairs or groups to create their assigned piece of media: a video of themselves role-playing, a text segment, the narration, audio, images, directions, the map, relevant artefacts.
Lesson 7: Co-locating narrative pieces to a GPS coordinate using the relevant AR app		At this point the AR app can be introduced. Some trial and error will need to be planned for, and tweaking and refining of the narrative may need to occur to make it work seamlessly and fluidly. Each group should upload content to the app at the correct location, test it out, and ensure it works. This might need to be managed one group at a time with teacher assistance.
Lesson 8: Trialing/Refining the experience		Groups can then take turns "reading" the entire narrative experience and preparing critique and feedback for the class to consider and refine.
Lesson 9: Releasing the experience to other classes		Once the entire class is fully confident in the narrative and the experience, groups can be selected to take "buddies" from other classes to participate in the experience, sharing it with all interested people, including parents, as a celebration of their work.

The lessons above are open ended to allow for a multitude of possibilities. At present, the authors of this chapter are involved in a research project that trials this pedagogy with groups of children, and expect to have future publications that report on this research. However, any teachers trialing this with their own class are welcome to contact the authors with their own reflections and stories about its effectiveness.

CONCLUSION

This chapter has reported on a new narrative trend—Augmented Reality storytelling. While the technology is young, the potential is enormous, particularly with the GPS tracking-based Augmented Reality applications that open up possibilities for locative storytelling. The potential is yet untapped for educational purposes; rather, it has tended to be used more for marketing purposes that are sometimes more gimmick than substance. However, in this chapter we have mentioned the emerging research of the use of AR for medical and other scientific purposes, and clearly the technology is also beginning to be used for educational purposes. English teachers are in a perfect position to use the affordances of AR to teach about new forms of narrative that are experienced through its connection to space and time, multimodal, game-like, and understood not by turning a page, but through walking, collaborating, problem solving, and piecing bits of information together to make a coherent whole.

GLOSSARY

Mixed Reality: An environment where both real and virtual content coexist
Augmented Reality: A subclass of Mixed Reality in which virtual content is overlaid in the real environment
Tracking: One of the critical system functionalities in an AR system; an ability to measure the changing relative position between the AR system and the real world

NOTES

1. An example of a form of indoor tracking that uses a model based marker (the graphic novel pages) and a computer camera detects this marker and displays the augmented version on screen. Note that the four film-strip cells on the 2D book are augmented by converting it into a movie on the AR screen version.
2. The real world is transformed through the screen of the mobile device by using Augmented Reality to track the GPS location and add appropriate location-sensitive annotations.

REFERENCES

Alexander, B. (2011). *The new digital storytelling: Creating narratives with new media*. Santa Barbara, CA: Praeger.
Allen, R., Tsai, Y.-ta, Hinman, R., & Azuma, R. (2010). The westwood experience : Connecting story to locations via mixed reality. In *Proceedings of the International Symposium on Mixed and Augmented Reality* (pp. 39–46). Seoul, Korea: IEEE.

Azuma, R. T. (1997). A survey of Augmented Reality. *Presence: Teleoperators and Virtual Environments*, 6(4), 355–385.
Bajura, M., Fuchs, H., Ohbuchi, R., Carolina, N., & Hill, C. (1992). Merging virtual objects with the real world: Seeing ultrasound imagery within the patient. *Computer Graphics*, 26(2), 203–210.
Bichlmeier, C., Heining, S. M., Feuerstein, M., & Navab, N. (2009). The virtual mirror: A new interaction paradigm for Augmented Reality environments. *IEEE Transactions on Medical Imaging*, 28(9), 1498–1510.
Black, D. (2008). *Charles Cumming: The 21 steps*. Retrieved from http://www.coolhunting.com/culture/charles-cumming.php
Carless, S. (2008). *Q&A: Perplex city creators craft "we tell stories."* Retrieved from http://www.gamasutra.com/php-bin/news_index.php?story=17901
Chinthammit, W. (2007). *A hybrid inertial-laser scanning head tracking system for cockpit applications.* (Published PhD thesis). University of Washington.
Cumming, C. (2008). *The 21 steps* [Digital narrative]. Retrieved from http://www.wetellstories.co.uk/stories/week1/
Dünser, D., & Hornecker, E. (2007a). An observational study of children interacting with an augmented story book. In *Proceedings of the 2nd International Conference of E-Learning and Games* (pp. 305–315). Hong Kong: CUHK.
Dünser, D., & Hornecker, E. (2007b). Lessons from an AR Book Study. In *Proceedings of the 1st International Conference on Tangible and Embedded Interaction*. Baton Rouge, LA.
Feiner, S., MacIntyre, B., & Seligmann, D. (1993, July). Knowledge-based Augmented Reality. *Communications of ACM* 36(7), 52–62.
Feral Arts. (2012). *PlaceStories.* Retrieved from http://ps3beta.com/
Fjeld, M., & Voegtli, B. (2002). Augmented chemistry: An interactive educational workbench. In *Proceedings of the IEEE and ACM International Symposium on Mixed and Augmented Reality* (pp. 259–260). Darmstadt, Germany: IEEE.
Grasset, R., Dünser, A., Seichter, H., & Billinghurst, M. (2007). The mixed reality book: A new multimedia reading experience. In *Proceedings of the Conference on human factors in computing systems interactivity* (pp. 1953–1958). New York: ACM.
Hornecker, E., & Dünser, D. (2007). Supporting early literacy with augmented books: Experiences with an exploratory study. In *Proceedings of the German Society of Informatics Annual Conference*. GI-Jahrestagung: Bonner Köllen Verlag.
Kapp, C. (2011). *About ZooBurst*. Retrieved from http://www.zooburst.com/zb_about.php
Kumagai, T., Yamashita, J., Morikawa, O., Yokoyama, K., & Taku, F. (2008). Distance education system for teaching manual skills in endoscopic paranasal sinus surgery using "hypermirror" telecommunication interface. In *Proceedings of the Virtual Reality Conference* (pp. 233–236). Nevada: IEEE.
Milgram, P., & Colquhoun, H. (1999). A taxonomy of real and virtual world display integration. In Y. Ohta & H. Tamura (Eds.), *Mixed reality—Merging real and virtual worlds* (pp. 1–16). Tokyo: Springer Verlag.
Milgram, P., & Kishino, F. (1994). A taxonomy of mixed reality virtual displays. *IEICE Transactions on Information and Systems*, 77(12), 1321–1329.
Platonov, J., Heibel, H., Meier, P., & Grollmann, B. (2006). A mobile markerless AR system for maintenance and repair. In *Proceedings of the 5th IEEE and ACM International Symposium on Mixed and Augmented Reality* (pp. 105–108). New York: IEEE and ACM.

Profumo, S. (2011). *Haunted London locative iPhone application.* Retrieved from http://www.behance. net/gallery/Haunted-London-Locative-iPhone-Application/2215168

State, A., Livingston, M. A., Hirota, G., Garrett, W. F., Whitton, M. C., & Fuchs, H. (1996). Technologies for Augmented-Reality systems: Realizing ultrasound-guided needle biopsies. In *Proceedings of the ACM SIGGRAPH Conference* (pp. 439–446). New York: ACM.

University of the Arts London. (2009). *Haunted London.* Retrieved from http://maimm.arts.ac.uk/ degree_show/1011/hauntedlondon.html

FURTHER READING

Alexander, B. (2011). *The new digital storytelling: Creating narratives with new media.* Santa Barbara, CA: Praeger.

Azuma, R. T. (1997). A survey of augmented reality. *Presence: Teleoperators and Virtual Environments,* 6(4), 355–385.

Grasset, R., Dünser, A., Seichter, H., & Billinghurst, M. (2007). The mixed reality book: A new multimedia reading experience. In *Proceedings of the Conference on human factors in computing systems interactivity* (pp. 1953–1958). New York: ACM.

WEB RESOURCES

Kapp (Zoobust): http://www.zooburst.com/
Layar: http://www.layar.com/browser/
Wikitude: Wikitude.me
Junaio (by Metaio): http://www.junaio.com/
Foursquare: https://foursquare.com/

CHAPTER TWELVE

Virtual Macbeth

Using Virtual Worlds to Explore Literary Texts

ANGELA THOMAS, KERREEN ELY-HARPER, &
KATE RICHARDS

Over the past decade, there seems to have been a widespread shift from children in the role of mere consumers and receivers of digital texts into a new type of child, one who has become an innovative producer of multimedia digital texts. In addition to children consuming and participating within the cultural communities associated with digital texts, the most recent research has demonstrated how children are playing, experimenting, and manipulating the affordances of digital texts for their own pleasures and purposes. Children are creating and managing their own online communities (Thomas, 2004; Unsworth, Thomas, Simpson, & Asha, 2005); participating in online fan fiction communities (Black, 2004; Lankshear & Knobel, 2004; Thomas, 2005); creating role-playing Web forums (Thomas, 2005, 2007); creating, writing for, and editing their own zines (Web magazines) (Lankshear & Knobel, 2005); and publishing their own multimedia weblogs, including photoblogs and podcasts (Lankshear & Knobel, 2006). Furthermore, many children spend hours helping each other to learn the discursive and social practices around virtual communities, willingly volunteering their time and efforts to help their friends become insiders of the communities. Through this, they are developing values, citizenship, and ethics through their participation in the communities in which such texts are produced (Lankshear & Knobel, 2006; Thomas, 2007).

Notwithstanding these emergent phenomena, it is quite clear that children are simply not receiving the schooled apprenticeships into the "digisphere" (Lankshear & Knobel, 2005) that are necessary for their social futures. They are forced to either become proficient in the social practices of digital literacies outside of school contexts, or they are isolated from such opportunities. Studies of young people's use of digital media at home and at school (Chandler-Olcott & Mahar, 2003; Hinchman, Alvermann, Boyd, Brozo, & Vacca, 2004) have emphasized that the digital divide exists "not in terms of access but in the gap between ICT practices at home and school" and that this disjunction has significant implications for school success (Sunderland-Smith, Snyder, & Angus, 2003, p. 5). In addition, studies involving teenagers in a range of countries including the United States (Thorne, 2003), Japan (Ito, 2003), and Canada (Parks, Huot, Hamers, & H.-Lemonnierr, 2003) have pointed to tensions between the pedagogy associated with school learning and the cultural practices and values integral to young people's identities.

The research reported in this chapter will address the following three key questions:

1. What affordances of virtual worlds can be leveraged for educational purposes?
2. How can a virtual world be used in the English classroom?
3. What pedagogical framework could be used by secondary English teachers to explore Virtual Macbeth, an island in Second Life?

BACKGROUND

The Virtual Macbeth project was a collaboration undertaken by the three authors of this chapter, and was funded jointly by the Australian Council for the Arts and the New Media Consortium. The aim of this project was to leverage the affordances of virtual worlds and maximize these for the greatest educational potential. Our intention was to develop a global community of learners who could collaborate in responding to Shakespeare's play and jointly produce new versions, excerpts, or ideas about the play through role-playing, writing, and multimedia production (such as machinima). This included involving learners in using the virtual space to create three-dimensional objects of the more esoteric or metaphorical qualities of the play. It also involved immersing students into the story world by bringing that world to life and surrounding them with the language of Shakespeare through text, spoken dialogue, imagery, and sound effects. The effect of entering a literary space within a virtual world environment is similar to learners walking into a film set or participating in a literary theme park adventure—it is immediately immersive and enables learners to feel and experience the mood and atmosphere of a text. The Second Life space was also developed to provide opportunities for learners to create their own content—to change and add to the world through their participation in interactive experiences.

Virtual Macbeth was designed using a range of intersecting theories from new media literacies (Buckingham, 2007; Gee, 2003; Jenkins, 2006), drama (Neelands, 2000), digital culture (Ito et al., 2009; Silver, 2000), gaming (Taylor, 2009), multiliteracies (Cope & Kalantzis, 2009a, 2009b; New London Group, 1997), identity (Butler, 1999), communities of practice (Wenger, 1998), and play (Galarneau, 2007). Each element of the design was deliberate and carefully planned to allow the maximum level of interactivity, participation, and critical reflection about the play.

Second Life (http://secondlife.com) consists of thousands of individual "islands" that can be purchased and customized to create unique spaces for socializing, exploring, and learning. Islands can be public or private, and access is controlled by the owner of the island. We bought an island in Second Life, called Macbeth, and spent several months in collaboration with the New Media Consortium designing the space and creating an environment to enable exploration of elements of the play. The main design feature on the island is a giant rock/mountain. This rock is in the shape of a head—Macbeth's head. Essentially students take a walk through Macbeth's headspace, which is a metaphorical walk simulating his emotional and psychological journey throughout the trajectory of the play. Visitors do not enter the island and watch the drama unfold, they actually explore the internal world of the story from Macbeth's point of view. Dispersed throughout the giant head, note cards are activated to pose questions, encouraging students to both view and participate fully in the experience. In effect, the learner becomes Macbeth experiencing his descent into madness. The head is lying on its side as (a) it symbolises the beheading of Macbeth and (b) it symbolises the rise and fall of enlightenment and consciousness.

The walk through Macbeth's head is divided into five central spaces or scenes that each reflects a psychological state—ego, temptation, descent into madness, bloodlust, and confusion. A sixth space at the end of the experience offers a moment for meta-level reflection and denouement. Metaphors are reflected both in the content of the space and in the architecture and flow of the experience. Literary techniques such as foreshadowing, drama techniques such as the participant hearing the voices inside Macbeth's head, and digital culture techniques such as playing off the notion of "the uncanny valley" were all employed to heighten the experience and to provide teaching moments for students from a wide cross-discipline perspective. Students are asked to add to the content to the associated wiki (http://virtualmacbeth.wikispaces.com) to make use of the kinds of Web 2.0 social networking practices that are common to online communities.

PEDAGOGICAL FRAMEWORK

The following framework offers a way to explore the virtual world with students. It is suggested that working with students in Virtual Macbeth should be part of a larger unit of work on *Macbeth*, and that students have engaged with aspects of the play prior to the virtual world experience. It is also advisable that students spend time making avatars (their online character) and learning how to move about inside Second Life prior to study. This exploration stage is essential for successful and straightforward engagement with the different areas of the Second Life island. If computers are limited it may be helpful for students to work together in pairs or small groups and share an avatar. The teacher may also like to make a class set of avatars and have them all set up an on the island in "the arrival grove" (the entrance to the island) ready to go.

Table 12.1. Using Virtual Macbeth in the Classroom

Sequence of spaces to explore	Teaching notes, prompts, and ideas
1. Orientation: the arrival grove	Students arrive at "the arrival grove," the entrance to the island. The arrival grove acts as a kind of prologue to the experience to come. Students will have landed on the heath, inside a circular shaped grove of fragmented ruins that form a series of "doorways" leading away from it. Low mist surrounds the grove and is found across the heath in several places. Lines of text from the play are spoken and emitted into the grove to immediately immerse students in the richness, beauty, and wonder of the text. Words from these lines will also be emitted as written text that floats up and around the heath. Lines of text include: • Fair is foul and foul is fair, hover through the fog and filthy air • Unsex me here, make thick my blood • O horror, horror, horror! • By the pricking of my thumbs, Something wicked this way comes.
	 Fig 12.1. Virtual Macbeth—arrival grove.

	Questions to consider: • What do you feel as soon as you are inside this space? • What do you notice first? What do you think the imagery is designed to conjure in your imaginations? • What lines from *Macbeth* can you hear? • Why do you think these lines were chosen for the arrival grove? • What other sounds can you hear as you walk around the arrival grove? • What words or phrases do you see floating through the air?
2. Macbeth's head	 Fig 12.2. Virtual Macbeth—Macbeth's head. The largest building is a giant head, the head of Macbeth. The head is elevated on a cliff—the back of the cliff will have a dramatic, rocky shoreline, raging seas, and stormy weather. The head is literally a head lying on its side, as if fallen there from a beheading. It is distorted and its surface area broken, from the fall as it were. It is a metaphor for the visitors' exploration of Macbeth's motivations, his consciousness and his unconscious. The head has an organic feel to it, it is covered with rocky extrusions, plant life—it's a ruin where visitors can scramble and explore the nooks and crannies, the weird animals living there, and take in the weird visual perspective. The head is lying on its side as (a) it symbolises the beheading of Macbeth and (b) it symbolises the rise and fall of enlightenment and consciousness.

3. The Throne Room	
	Fig 12.3. Virtual Macbeth—throne room.
	This space symbolises Macbeth's ego, the prophecies that speak to his ego. This tall narrow space reminds us of an old medieval hall. There are "German expressionist" extremes, weird physics, and architectural intrigues at its edges. Some of the structure protrudes outside the surface of the head, it is Escheresque, an eyrie from which you can see quite far—raising the question, Did the head break around the structure or did it rise up through the fallen head? Architecture and nature meld.
	This space contains five key features: a gallery, a sound installation, symbols of the ego, a throne, and the text from the letter that Macbeth writes to Lady Macbeth after seeing the witches (Act 1, Scene 5).
	Covering the walls of the Throne room are paintings of Macbeth in multiple adaptations of the play.
	Apparitions haunt the space and play sound files when activated by visitors' proximity to the whole or parts thereof (sound installation). These sound files will contain all of the "golden opinions" expressed about Macbeth at the starting point of the play.
	Questions to consider:
	• What is the emotional journey Macbeth takes throughout the play?
	• Scene 1 is the room that reflects Macbeth's "Call to Ego." How is this reflected in the architecture of the space?
	• Who are the apparitions and where do their lines come from?
	• Can you differentiate the two kinds of calls to ego experienced by Macbeth as indicated in the sound installation?
	• The sound installation is called "Golden Opinions." This comes from a line in the text. Locate the line and find out the context (see below for relevant lines).
	• Click the spilled wine. What happens? What literary device does this signify?

	• In what ways are Macbeth and many of the other characters in the play deceived by poor judgment and self-deception? • Sit on the throne and take a photo of yourself to add to the gallery. • What do the gallery images suggest?
	• Discuss the nature of power and authority, leadership, notions of governance, control and influence over others. Do you consider yourself more of a leader or are you more of a follower? • When have you been in a leadership role? What were your responsibilities? How would you rate your success as a leader out of 10? • What are the most important qualities a leader should have? • How does the design of the Throne Room lead you to consider issues of leadership and identity? Student activities: a. Add another object to signify Macbeth's Kingship in the Throne Room. b. Research the source images in the portrait gallery. Discuss the different interpretations of *Macbeth* in theatre and film. c. Create a Macbeth portrait in your own image. What will be your design theme and style approach? How will you interpret the character of Macbeth? For example, as the misunderstood hero, the hen pecked husband, or the evil tyrant? d. Rehearse and present the banquet scene (Act 3, Scene 4) in the Throne Room. e. What if Macbeth were to emerge victorious in his final battle against Macduff? Rewrite/perform the ending of the play with Macbeth retaining the throne.
	Relevant text excerpts from *Macbeth*: MACBETH: We will proceed no further in this business. He hath honoured me of late, and I have bought Golden opinions from all sorts of people, Which would be worn now in their newest gloss Not cast aside so soon. Act 1, Scene 7 Lines 31–33 FIRST WITCH: All hail, Macbeth! hail to thee, Thane of Glamis! SECOND WITCH: All hail, Macbeth! hail to thee, Thane of Cawdor! THIRD WITCH: All hail Macbeth, that shalt be king hereafter Act 1, Scene 3 Lines 46–48

	KING DUNCAN: O Valiant Cousin, Worthy Gentleman Act 1, Scene 2 Line 24 KING DUNCAN: What he hath lost, noble Macbeth hath won. Act 1, Scene 2 Line 66 CAPTAIN: For brave Macbeth—well he deserves that name— Act 1, Scene 2 Line 16 ROSS: And for an earnest of a greater honour, He bade me, from him, call thee Thane of Cawdor In which addition, hail, most worthy thane, For it is thine.
4. The Wunderkammer inside the Throne Room	A curio cabinet ("wunderkammer") signifies Lady Macbeth's influence in the play and inside Macbeth's head. The cabinet holds symbolic objects that represent the influences on Lady Macbeth. 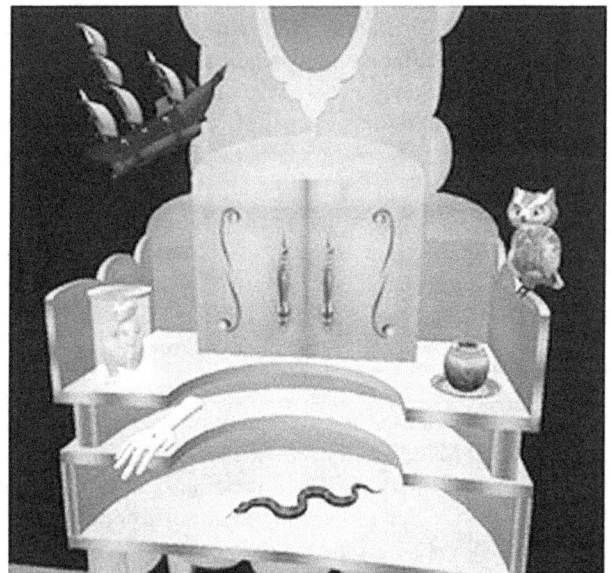 Fig 12.4. Virtual Macbeth—wunderkammer. Questions to consider: • Why is this representation of Lady Macbeth inside Macbeth's mind? • Touch the objects and listen to the soundscape. What do you notice? What can you hear? • What associations do you have to the objects, and the sounds—feelings, thoughts, images, memories?

	• When touching the foetus in a jar, a sound of children laughing is heard. What effect does this have on you and why? (The teacher may prompt students about intermodal divergence, as the meanings of the visual are contradictory to the meanings of the sound, constructing a moment of interpersonal discomfort.) Student activities: • Research original text and find specific quotes that relate to the objects represented in the wunderkammer. • Add or replace one of the objects. • Create a wunderkammer for another character in the play. Make a wunderkammer that represents your life – what objects would you put in the cabinet?
5. Crossroads of conflict	Here an apparition prompts the visitor with an obtuse choice, to follow one of two paths (right or wrong). The right path leads out of the head and off to the "What If?" island, where visitors will imagine what the resulting consequences of taking the moral path would have been (more on space 3 detailed below). This crossroads is the entire crux of the play, as Macbeth chooses the path of temptation. For this reason, the path of good or the corridor of enlightenment is not as easily seen, is darkened, and shadowy. It might not even be noticed on the first exploration of the head.
6. The Path of Temptation	This path initially appears attractive, with flowers or shrubs lining it, but these become grasping hands coming out of the earth, which is dank and riddled with snakes. The change from beautiful garden to the bloody hands and snakes growing foreshadows the horrors to come, and symbolises the change of Macbeth's internal state of mind. Lines of text slithering along the path floor are phrases urging Macbeth on to worse deeds, based on Lady Macbeth's speech in Act 1, Scene 7.  Fig 12.5. Virtual Macbeth—path of temptation.

Questions to consider:
- Discuss the nature of temptation and morality.
- What do the hands signify?
- Why does the text move left to right and right to left, and low level on the ground?
- How do the characters in *Macbeth* influence and affect change in each other?
- What does Lady Macbeth want from Macbeth? What tactics does she use to convince her husband that murder is the only course of action? What is she prepared to do to achieve her want?
- What does Macbeth want from Lady Macbeth? How does he respond to her tauntings?
- Before she arrives Macbeth is by himself and debates whether or not to kill Duncan (Act 1, Scene 7, lines 1–27). What arguments does he present against killing Duncan?

Student Activities

a. Read the scene between Lady Macbeth and Macbeth this space represents. Write your own enticements from Lady Macbeth to Macbeth.
b. Design your own temptation space based on your own experience when faced with making a difficult moral choice.
c. Write an alternative temptation scene for another character/s from the play. For example, the witches enticing Macbeth, Macbeth enticing the murderers.
d. Make a machinima based on the theme of temptation.

Relevant text excerpt from Macbeth:
LADY MACBETH: Was the hope drunk
Wherein you dressed yourself? Hath it slept since?
And wakes it now to look so green and pale
At what it did so freely? From this time,
Such I account thy love. Art thou afeard
To be the same in thine own act and valour,
As thou esteem'st the ornament of life,
And live a coward in thine own esteem,
Letting I dare not wait upon I would,
Like the poor cat i'th' adage?

MACBETH: Prithee, peace.
I dare do all that may become a man;
Who dares do more is none.
LADY MACBETH: What beast was't then
That made you break this enterprise to me?

VIRTUAL MACBETH | 243

	When you durst do it, then you were a man. And to be more that what you were, you would Be so much more the man. Nor time, nor place Did then adhere, and yet you would make both. They have made themselves and that their fitness now Does unmake you. I have given suck and know How tender 'tis to love the babe that milks me: I would, while it was smiling in my face, Have plucked my nipple from his boneless gums And dashed the brains out, had I so sworn As you have done to this. Act 1, Scene 7 Lines 35–59
7. Raven ride	At the end of the path the visitor's journey becomes a ride and continues round the back of the head. The visitor rides a raven and is "drawn" ahead by a flying dagger along a steep and scary flight path round the back of the head and to the front again to the Chamber of Blood. (This relates to Act 2, Scene 1 from the play, where Macbeth sees a vision of a dagger that entrances him and leads him to Duncan's chamber and to committing his first murder.) During the ride we can hear the sounds of a heart beating heavily. This symbolises Macbeth's downfall.

Fig 12.6. Virtual Macbeth—raven ride.

Questions to consider:
- What can you see in the raven's nest?
- What do these objects signify?
- What sounds can you hear?
- Sit on the raven.
- What enables a human being to kill another human being?

	• Macbeth orders the murders of Banquo's son Fleance, Lady Macduff and her children. What causes Macbeth to commit such heinous crimes against women and children? • What kind of a society condones the murder of innocent people? • Why does Shakespeare draw an analogy between Lady Macduff's plight and the "poor birds"?
	Student Activities: a. Research and find recent examples of serious crimes against humanity. Discuss the moral and ethical issues that surround the murder of innocent people in a society, for example, in times of war. b. Role-play/record a chat box conversation between Lady Macduff and Macduff. He explains why he cannot come just yet. What is her attitude to his decision to put fighting Macbeth first over returning to his family? c. Find more examples of Shakespeare's use of animal metaphors throughout the play. Discuss their meaning and significance. d. Make a machinima on the theme of separation. Relevant text excerpts from Macbeth: MACBETH: Is this a dagger which I see before me? The handle toward my hand? Act 2, Scene 1 Lines 33–34 LADY MACDUFF: How will you live? CHILD: As birds do, mother. LADY MACDUFF: What, with worms and flies? CHILD: With what I get I mean, and so do they. LADY MACDUFF: Poor bird, thou'dst never fear the net, nor lime, The pitfall, nor the gin. CHILD: Why should I, mother? Poor birds they are not set for. LADY MACDUFF: Whither should I fly? I have done no harm. Act 4, Scene 2 Lines 31–71
8. The Chamber of Blood	The Chamber of Blood is a womb like, crystalline space. There are no right angles, the sides are sloping, and visitors feel like they have gravity against them. It's Macbeth's Heart of Darkness. Red light seems to pool, the sides are dripping blood and text. Behind the walls we can dimly see animated excerpts of modern twentieth-century warfare and catastrophe—these images are "cut back" behind the blood walls. It's blood lust. Agency is taken away here, and the visitor is forced to engage in a ritualistic and mechanical killing.

This symbolises Macbeth's lack of emotional control as he attempts to kill anybody who he deems a threat to his power.

Fig 12.7. Virtual Macbeth—chamber of blood.

Questions to consider:

- What can you see?
- What can you hear?
- How do you feel when you enter the chamber?
- How does it feel to lose control of your avatar?
- What is the play of *Macbeth* about?

- Discuss: the nature of control, agency, power. What is it like not to be able to control your avatar? When have you ever felt you were not in control of a situation? What happened?
- Discuss themes of bloodlust. What is bloodlust? Name other leaders in history who might also be described as bloodthirsty.
- Discuss the nature of media surrounding crime. What other crimes and atrocities have gained notoriety through the media?
- Imagine you are explaining what *Macbeth* is about to an eight-year-old child. Is there a lesson or moral to your tale?

Student Activities:

a. Research the text and select scene/s that are being represented here.
b. Who could the ghost figures be? Why do they keep reappearing?
c. Discuss the design elements—colour palette, spatial design and movement, use of repetition, soundscape, juxtaposition of 3D animation, and real life documentary footage.
d. What do you think the desired effect of this space might be on the user?

	Relevant text excerpt from *Macbeth*: FIRST WITCH: Show! SECOND WITCH: Show! THIRD WITCH: Show! ALL WITCHES: Show his eyes and grieve his heart Come like shadows, so depart Act 4, Scene 1 Lines 106–110
9. The Maze	The maze is comprised of a series of columns/trees—in fact, it's as if the columns are transmogrifying into trees or vice versa. The purpose for this is that at the end of the play, the forest comes to the castle, so it is Birnam Woods meets Dunsinane Castle. The unusual tree/column used to assemble the maze shows this convergence at the very end of the play, at the point of greatest confusion by Macbeth. As Macbeth realises he was tricked by the Witches' prophecies he wanders aimlessly and crazily about the maze, looking for a way out. It's a chilly space—wintery and monochrome. The Maze spreads into available cavities in the head. This is Macbeth's confusion.  Fig 12.8. Virtual Macbeth—the maze. Questions to consider: • What do you see? • What do you hear? • How does the maze signify Macbeth's journey? • Discuss: the nature of loss, futility, confusion, disorientation.
	• Have you ever been lost? What happened? How did you feel at the time? • Research and find the source quotes written on the walls as graffiti.

	Student Activities: a. Discuss the design of the maze—use of symbol and metaphor, colour palette (and how the colour palette realizes particular interpersonal meanings of ambience), soundscape, and graffiti font. b. Leave your own trace. If you could leave a message, what would you write? c. Select a scene from the play to perform in the maze. d. Repeat the scene in a different space on the island. Compare and contrast your experiences of the effect that the space has on the scene, with specific reference to mood, use of space, and avatar action. Relevant text excerpt from *Macbeth*: MACBETH: Tomorrow, and tomorrow, and tomorrow Creeps in this petty pace from day to day To the last syllable of recorded time; And all our yesterdays have lighted fools The way to dusty death. Out, out brief candle, Life's but a walking shadow, a poor player That struts and frets his hour upon the stage And then is heard no more. It is a tale Told by an idiot, full of sound and fury Signifying nothing. Act 5, Scene 5
10. Cube of Nothingness	In this weird "nothing" space, visitors' avatars are beheaded. This space is a moment of reflection wherein Macbeth is faced with his existential crisis. A window offers the only exit, spewing the avatar out of the mouth and back onto the heath below.  Fig 12.9. Virtual Macbeth—cube of nothingness.
"What if" Copse	The "What if?" copse is a rocky seaside outcrop. This space is designed for the visitors to contemplate the play's moral and ethical dilemmas. Scattered symbolic objects represent the meta themes of the island.

	 Fig 12.10. Virtual Macbeth—what if copse.
	Questions to consider/activities for students for each object: • The bust of Shakespeare reflects the influence of Shakespeare on the English language. Find some resources online that would support the kinds of discussion we might have with students about this. • The statue of Macbeth represents an alternate ending of the play. What would have happened had Macbeth been a hero and celebrated and memorialised in a statue? The statue also speaks to the theme of adaptation, which was introduced inside the Throne Room of the Head. What adaptations of *Macbeth* do you know of? List some links to the IMDB showing some of these. • The theatre masks (comedy/tragedy) reflect the nature of drama. What are some of the elements of drama and how do they work (i.e., crisis, denouement)? Find a resource online that might help students explore this. • The scales represent justice, truth, and morality. Some scholars claim that Macbeth's character was amoral. Can you locate some references to support this? The document wallet with maps and a family tree represents the historical source material Shakespeare is said to have used in creating Macbeth. What do we know about the real Macbeth and the real Lady Macbeth? Locate some resources online that might describe these.
Studio Spaces	There are three studio spaces on the island where students can explore elements of the play, rehearse, and engage in dramatic experiences that probe the themes of the play, and make their own virtual objects relevant to the play. Activities might include the following (some of these have been adapted from Ackroyd, Neelands, Supple, & Trowsdale, 1998):

1. *The Horrid Image*
Read Text Excerpt 1
Contemplate the following questions:

- What are the "two truths" to which Macbeth refers?
- What is "the imperial theme"?
- Why does he refer to it as "the swelling act"?
- What shows Macbeth's uncertainty about the news he has received?
- What do you imagine the "horrid image" to be; what is the picture Macbeth sees?
- Make the horrid image that Macbeth sees as a freeze-frame with your avatars. One person should be Duncan, the other Macbeth. Experiment with the gestures and poses to position your avatar into place. Find a prop in your inventory that might add to the sense of horror. Avatars can look cartoonish and funny, so your challenge is to really subvert the natural Second Life default imagery and find a way to convey horror.

2. *Fair and Noble Hostess*
Locate two key speeches relating to Lady Macbeth: Act 1, Scene 5 (where Lady Macbeth comes to the conclusion that Duncan must be murdered), and Act 1, Scene 6 (where Duncan calls Lady Macbeth a "fair and noble hostess"). These two scenes reflect the outer appearance of Lady Macbeth (fair and noble) and her inward intentions (she is to become a murderer). Consider the process that Lady Macbeth works through to psych herself up to become a murderer.

- Create a sequence of avatars (one for each person in your group) to reflect Lady Macbeth's transformation from her outwardly appearance of a "fair and noble hostess" to her full representation of her character change to becoming a murderer. How can you reflect these changes in her avatar? What positions or poses or gestures can you find to reflect such subtleties?

3. *Remember the Porter*
Read Text Excerpt 2
Some actors who play the porter ad-lib jokes about contemporary events; others exploit the sexual references to full effect; others tell new knock-knock jokes. In nineteenth-century German productions, the Porter was a sober figure who sang a joyful and innocent song to welcome the sunrise. How would the Porter in your own adaptation behave? Experiment with the current porter to see what lines or jokes he offers you (in the throne room).

- Choose one person from your group and transform their avatar to look like the Porter you all agree you'd like to see in your own adaptation. Write a joke (it can be knock-knock but doesn't have to be) that could be inserted into this excerpt to reflect the Second Life culture (or your experiences with it so far).

4. *Bloody Instructions*
Read Text Excerpt 3
Here Lady Macbeth's preparation involves her giving her husband a sequence of bloody instructions of how they will carry out the murder. Compare this to Macbeth's speech from Act 1, Scene 7. What do you notice about the linguistic themes of each sentence (the first word group)? What is the key difference between their speeches and how each one of them is contemplating murder?

- There are five stages to Lady Macbeth's plan. Make five placards and on each one you need to upload a key image to represent that particular stage. Find the images from flickr on a Google image search. Place the placards in a line so that as we walk down the line we can see a representative image of the stage and understand Lady Macbeth's instructions clearly.

Text Excerpt 1:
(Act 1, Scene 3)
MACBETH
Speak, if you can: what are you?
First Witch
All hail, Macbeth! hail to thee, thane of Glamis!
Second Witch
All hail, Macbeth, hail to thee, thane of Cawdor!
Third Witch
All hail, Macbeth, thou shalt be king hereafter!
MACBETH
[Aside] Two truths are told,
As happy prologues to the swelling act
Of the imperial theme.—I thank you, gentlemen.
Aside
Cannot be ill, cannot be good: if ill,
Why hath it given me earnest of success,
Commencing in a truth? I am thane of Cawdor:
If good, why do I yield to that suggestion
Whose horrid image doth unfix my hair
And make my seated heart knock at my ribs,
Against the use of nature? Present fears

Are less than horrible imaginings:
My thought, whose murder yet is but fantastical,
Shakes so my single state of man that function
Is smother'd in surmise, and nothing is
But what is not.

Text Excerpt 2:
(Act 2, Scene 3)
Knocking within. Enter a Porter.
Porter
Here's a knocking indeed! If a
man were porter of hell-gate, he should have old turning the key.
Knocking within
Knock, knock, knock! Who's there, i' the name of
Beelzebub? Here's a farmer, that hanged
himself on the expectation of plenty: come in
time; have napkins enow about you; here you'll sweat for't.
Knocking within
Knock, knock! Who's there, in the other devil's name? Faith, here's
an equivocator, that could
swear in both the scales against either scale;
who committed treason enough for God's sake,
yet could not equivocate to heaven: O, come in, equivocator.
Knocking within
Knock, knock, knock! Who's there? Faith, here's an
English tailor come hither, for stealing out of a French hose: come in,
  tailor; here you may roast your goose.
Knocking within
Knock, knock; never at quiet! What are you? But
this place is too cold for hell. I'll devil-porter it no further: I had
  thought to have let in some of all professions that go the primrose
  way to the everlasting bonfire.
Knocking within
Anon, anon! I pray you, remember the porter.
Opens the gate

Text Excerpt 4:
(Act 1, Scene 7)
MACBETH
We will proceed no further in this business:
He hath honour'd me of late; and I have bought
Golden opinions from all sorts of people,
Which would be worn now in their newest gloss,
Not cast aside so soon.

> LADY MACBETH
> Was the hope drunk
> Wherein you dress'd yourself? hath it slept since?
> And wakes it now, to look so green and pale
> At what it did so freely? From this time
> Such I account thy love. Art thou afeard
> To be the same in thine own act and valour
> As thou art in desire? Wouldst thou have that
> Which thou esteem'st the ornament of life,
> And live a coward in thine own esteem,
> Letting 'I dare not' wait upon 'I would,'
> Like the poor cat i' the adage?
> MACBETH
> Prithee, peace:
> I dare do all that may become a man;
> Who dares do more is none.
> LADY MACBETH
> What beast was't, then,
> That made you break this enterprise to me?
> When you durst do it, then you were a man;
> And, to be more than what you were, you would
> Be so much more the man. Nor time nor place
> Did then adhere, and yet you would make both:
> They have made themselves, and that their fitness now
> Does unmake you. I have given suck, and know
> How tender 'tis to love the babe that milks me:
> I would, while it was smiling in my face,
> Have pluck'd my nipple from his boneless gums,
> And dash'd the brains out, had I so sworn as you
> Have done to this.

PARTICIPATION AND STUDENT WORK

Virtual Macbeth was opened in 2008, and many non-student visitors as well as groups of learners have experienced the island. Many workshops were held with teachers, followed by work with both postgraduate and undergraduate students as they learned about the potential for teaching in virtual worlds. One obvious benefit of the virtual world workshops was that learners were able to come from all over the globe to participate in the experience. Figure 12.11, for example, shows a group of learners from the United States and Sweden entering the cube of nothingness at the completion of the experience; their bodies beheaded at the end of Macbeth's descent into madness.

VIRTUAL MACBETH | 253

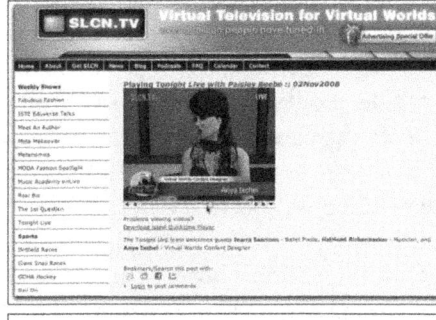
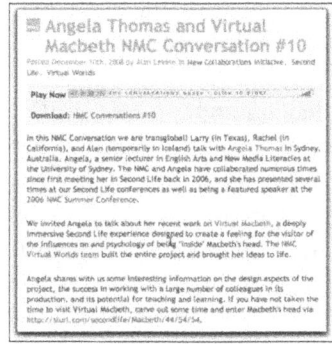

in-world tours,
workshops,
conference talks,
podcasts,
seminars
and tv interviews

Fig 12.11. Virtual Macbeth—students experience decapitation.

Learners who participated in longer workshop sessions created their own content in response to the activities described above. Figure 12.12 shows a sample response to the activity labeled *bloody instructions*. Here students were asked to interpret the relevant speech by searching Google images for relevant illustrations and then using them to create five posters revealing the directions that Lady Macbeth gave to Macbeth.

Fig 12.12. Virtual Macbeth—students create "bloody instructions."

From left to right, the instructions were: (1) invite Duncan to the castle (represented through the image of a Facebook *friend invite*); (2) get him drunk (represented through an advertisement warning about the dangers of alcohol); (3) kill Duncan (represented through an image of a book title about *backstabbing*); (4) blame the guards (represented by an image of three Scottish guards); and (5) *grieve and clamor roar upon his death* (represented through the theatre masks of tragedy and comedy).

The image in Figure 12.13 is a student response to the activity *fair and noble hostess*. This activity asked students to create avatars to reflect both representations of Lady Macbeth: her outward persona of "a fair and noble hostess" and her inward persona filled with ambition that led her to incite Macbeth to murder Duncan. Two students spent time fashioning their avatars (the virtual world character used to represent themselves) and thinking about poses and gestures to reveal the two sides of Lady Macbeth.

Fig 12.13. Virtual Macbeth—students create versions of Lady Macbeth.

The avatar on the right is standing tall, with carefully coiffed dark hair, hands placed behind back, wearing an evening gown and diamond necklace. The avatar was described by students as the epitome of a formal hostess—regal looking, elegant, and polite. The skin is tanned and she has quite dramatic make-up. In contrast, the avatar on the left was designed to show the other side of Lady Macbeth. She is sitting on the ground, wearing more punk-like attire, including a bright red tank top and bright red hair. Her skin is pale, and her face is almost make-up free. She was described by students as being earthy and basic, reflecting Lady Macbeth's base desires. Her red hair and red tank was described as being symbolic of her bloodlust. Positioning her on the ground was also a reference to her gritty determination and desires.

CONCLUSION

The framework above offers a range of learning experiences for exploring the play *Macbeth* within the virtual world of Second Life, and in essence could be adapted to any virtual world. One of the affordances of a virtual world that make it ideal for exploring text is that esoteric or metaphorical qualities of a text can be brought to life in 3D in ways that make them transparent: the internal psyche of Macbeth, for example, can be made physical and explored from within. The ability to transform ones avatar makes it ideal for exploring a narrative from different points of view as those characters. Students are easily able to explore the semiotics of multimodal texts, creating soundscapes, experimenting with lighting effects, making machinima (short films of themselves inside the virtual world), investigating the effect of different camera angles, and discussing the ways in which words, 3D images, sounds, lighting, space, and gesture all work together to construct richly textured layers of meaning. Students can be engaged in intense explorations of a speech, a scene, even a single line of a text, discovering new ways of thinking about meanings of words, or new ways of performing a scene with others. Integrating these kinds of experiences into a wider study of text in classroom contexts offers students multiple ways into a text. Furthermore, such experiences may go some way to widening the gap between home and school literacy practices.

REFERENCES

Ackroyd, J., Neelands, J., Supple, M., & Trowsdale, J. (1998). *Key Shakespeare 2: English and drama activities for teaching Shakespeare to 14–16 year olds*. London: Hodder & Stoughton.

Black, R. W. (2004). Access and affiliation: The new literacy practices of English language learners in an online animé-based fanfiction community. In *Proceedings of the 2004 National Conference of Teachers of English Assembly for Research*. Berkeley, California, USA.

Buckingham, D. (2007). *Beyond technology: Children's learning in the age of digital culture*. Malden, MA: Polity.

Butler, J. (1999). *Gender trouble: Feminism and the subversion of identity*. New York: Routledge.

Chandler-Olcott, K., & Mahar, D. (2003). Adolescents' anime-inspired "fanfictions": An exploration of multiliteracies. *Journal of Adolescent & Adult Literacy, 46*(7), 556–566.

Cope, B., & Kalantzis, M. (2009a). "Multiliteracies": New literacies, new learning. *Pedagogies: An International Journal, 4*(3), 164–195.

Cope, B., & Kalantzis, M. (2009b). A grammar of multimodality. *The International Journal of Learning*, *16*(4), 361–426.
Galarneau, L. (2007). Productive play: Participation and learning in digital game environments. Retrieved from http://lisa.socialstudy games.com/productive_play.pdf
Gee, J. P. (2003). *What video games have to teach us about learning and literacy*. New York: Palgrave Macmillan.
Guzzetti, B. J., & Gamboa, M. (2005). Online journaling: The informal writings of two adolescent girls. *Research in the Teaching of English*, 40, 168–206.
Hinchman, K., Alvermann, D., Boyd, F., Brozo, W., & Vacca, R. (2004). Supporting older student's in and out-of-school literacies. *Journal of Adolescent and Adult Literacy*, *47*(4), 304.
Ito, M. (2003). *A new set of social rules for a newly wireless society*. Retrieved from www.ojr.org/japan/wireless/1043770650.php
Ito, M., Baumer, S., Bittanti, M., Boyd, D., Cody, R., Herr, B., Horst, H. A., Lange, P. G., Mahendran, D., Martinez, K., Pascoe, C. J., Perkel, D., Robinson, L., Sims, C., & Tripp, L. (2009). *Hanging out, messing around, geeking out: Living and learning with new media*. Cambridge, MA: MIT Press.
Jenkins, H. (2006). *Convergence culture*. New York: New York University.
Lankshear, C., & Knobel, M. (2004). "New" literacies: Research and social practice. In *Proceedings of Annual Meeting of the National Reading Conference*. San Antonio, USA.
Lankshear, C., & Knobel, M. (2005). Digital literacies: Policy, pedagogy and research considerations for education. In *Proceedings of the ITU Conference*. Oslo, Norway.
Lankshear, C., & Knobel, M. (2006). *New literacies: Changing knowledge and classroom learning*. London: McGraw-Hill.
Neelands, J. (2000). *Structuring drama work*. Cambridge, UK: Cambridge University Press.
New London Group. (1997). A pedagogy of multiliteracies. *Harvard Educational Review*, *66*, 60–92.
Parks, S., Huot, D., Hamers, J., & H.-Lemonnierr, F. (2003). Crossing boundaries: Multimedia technology and pedagogical innovation in a high school class. *Language Learning and Technology*, *7*(1), 28–45.
Silver, D. (2000). Looking backwards, looking forward: Cyberculture studies. In D. Gauntlett (Ed.), *Web.studies: Rewiring media studies for the digital age* (pp. 19–30). Oxford: Oxford University Press.
Sunderland-Smith, W., Snyder, I., & Angus, L. (2003). The digital divide: Differences in computer use between home and school on low socio-economic households. *L1—Educational Studies in Language and Literature*, *3*, 5–19.
Taylor, T. L. (2009). The assemblage of play. *Games and Culture*, *4*(4), 331–339.
Thomas, A. (2004). Digital literacies of the cybergirl. *E-Learning*, *1*(3), 358–382.
Thomas, A. (2005). Blog fiction and the narrative identities of adolescent girls. In *Proceedings of Blogtalk Downunder*. Sydney, Australia. Retrieved from http://incsub.org/blogtalk/?page_id=109
Thomas, A. (2007). *Youth online: Identity and literacy in the digital age*. New York: Peter Lang.
Thomas, A. (2008). Machinima: Composing 3D multimedia narratives. In L. Unsworth (Ed.), *New literacies and the English curriculum: Multimodal perspectives*. London: Continuum.
Thorne, S. (2003). The Internet as artifact: Immediacy, evolution, and educational contingencies or "The wrong tool for the right job?". In *Proceedings of AERA*. Chicago, Illinois, USA.
Unsworth, L., Thomas, A., Simpson, A., & Asha, J. (2005). *Children's literature and computer-based teaching*. London: Open University Press.
Wenger, E. (1998). *Communities of practice: Learning, meaning and identity*. Cambridge, UK: Cambridge University Press.

FURTHER READING

Lyman, P., Ito, M., Thorne, B., & Carter, M. (2009). *Hanging out, messing around, and geeking out: Kids living and learning with new media.* Cambridge, MA: MIT Press/MacArthur Foundation.

Nicosia, L. (2008). Adolescent literature and Second Life: Teaching young adult texts in the digital world. *New Literacies: A Professional Development Wiki for Educators.* New Jersey: Improving Teacher Quality Project. Retrieved from http://newlits.wikispaces.com/Adolescent+Literature+and+Second+Life

Palfrey, J., & Gasser, U. (2008). *Born digital.* Philadelphia: Basic Books.

WEB RESOURCES

Second Life: http://secondlife.com

Virtual Macbeth wiki: http://virtualmacbeth.wikispaces.com/

Contributors

Tom Apperley, PhD, is an ethnographer who researches digital media technologies. His previous writing has covered broadband policy, digital games, digital literacies and pedagogies, mobile media, and social inclusion. Tom is currently a Senior Lecturer at the University of New South Wales, Australia. He is the editor of the open-access peer-reviewed journal *Digital Culture & Education*, and his open-access print-on-demand book *Gaming Rhythms: Play and Counterplay from the Situated to the Global* was published by The Institute of Network Cultures in 2010. Tom's more recent work has appeared in *Digital Creativity*, *Literacy*, and *Westminster Papers in Culture and Communication*.

Julie Bain is a secondary English teacher and librarian at O'Connor Catholic College in Armidale, NSW. She has a Master of Education from the University of New England and uses digital technologies to build teaching resources, while exploring the ways through which digital technologies can be used to demonstrate student learning and creativity. She has presented at state, national, and international English conferences on the subjects of diversity, transformation, multiplatform story telling and multimodal pedagogy and has been published in *Screen Education* about the affordances of film trailers in English education.

Catherine Beavis is Professor of Education at Griffith University, Australia. She teaches and researches in the areas of English and literacy curriculum, and around digital culture, young people, and new media. Her work has a particular focus on the changing nature of text and literacy, and the implications of young people's experience of the online world for contemporary constructions of English and Literacy curriculum. Recent books include *Digital Games: Literacy in Action* (Wakefield Press, 2012), edited with Joanne O'Mara and Lisa McNeice, and *Literacy in 3D: An Integrated Perspective in Theory and Practice* (ACER Press, Melbourne, 2012), edited with Bill Green.

Paul D. Chandler is a Senior Lecturer in Education at the Australian Catholic University in Melbourne where he teaches education studies, ICT education, multimedia education, and science education. Prior to this appointment, he was Resserch Fellow in Multimodal Pedagogy at the University of New England, working closely with Len Unsworth, Angela Thomas, and Annemaree O'Brien, a position he held concurrently with ICT Pedagogy Officer for the Teaching Teachers for the Future project at the University of Melbourne. Paul's research is focused on the teaching and learning of multimodal authoring.

Winyu Chinthammit is a lecturer and researcher at the Human Interface Technology Laboratory, Australia, School of Computing and Information Systems, University of Tasmania. His areas of research are human computer interaction, advanced human interface technologies, motion sensing systems, and 3D user interface design. One of his PhD publications was awarded "Best Paper Award" at the IEEE Virtual Reality conference and his PhD work was also awarded a U.S. patent. Dr. Chinthammit is a regular contributor to conference committees and a technical reviewer for conferences such as ISMAR, TEI, CHI, and BHCI. He currently resides in Tasmania with wife Pearl, dog Maile, and daughter Allyn.

Kerreen Ely-Harper is a theatre director and filmmaker. Her passion for Shakespeare's texts has led her to direct a number of re-workings: *Making the Green One Red*, a mixed reality instillation work at QUT Creative Precincts, Brisbane; *Foul Whisperings, Strange Matters* (Macbeth in Second Life); *When The Eye Winks at the Hand* (SL machinima); and *Embrace*, a dance film based on *Hamlet*. A graduate of the Victorian College of the Arts, School of Performing Arts (Actor) and School of Film & Television (Director), Kerreen has recently completed a PhD on performing memory and family biography on film.

Ros Lippis is a teacher-librarian who works at Riverside Primary School. She has worked as an ICT support teacher and has a keen interest in all forms of literacy. Several years ago she recognised the need to change some of her teaching practises and has worked to include a multimodal approach to the teaching of literacy. Three years ago she began using *Inanimate Alice* with Grade 6 students.

Annemaree O'Brien is completing her PhD, investigating student use of focalisation in creating 3-D animation narratives, and teaching part-time in postgraduate language and literacy education. She has an extensive background in literacy and media education including Education Programmer at the Australian Centre for the Moving Image and Education Projects Manager for the Australian Children's Television Foundation. Consultancies include children's television curator for the Australian Screen website with the National Film and Sound Archive and English content expert and writer of digital learning objects with Education Services Australia.

Kate Richards has been creating with interactive multimedia for 20 years and exhibits electronic art in Australia and internationally, as well as working as a multimedia producer for cultural and corporate sector clients. Kate joined the University of Western Sydney in 2009 as the coordinator for the Masters of Convergent Media. As a multimedia concept designer, producer, and dramaturge (SparkeMedia), Kate produces both large and boutique scale projects, collaborating with historians, curators, archeologists, and corporate identity to develop, design, and deliver a variety of multimedia formats. She has a particular interest in experience and interactivity design for audiences, including theatre.

Angela Thomas is a Senior Lecturer in English Education at the University of Tasmania, Australia. Her research includes children's literature, multimodal semiotics, feminist theory and the fusion of literature and new media. Her publications include two books: (with Len Unsworth, Alyson Simpson, and Jenny Asha) *Children's Literature and Computer-Based Teaching* (Open University Press, 2005) and *Youth Online* (Peter Lang, 2007), as well as articles and book chapters on topics such as the semiotics of multimodal authoring, fan fiction, fictional blogging, exploring literature in virtual worlds, machinima, and stop motion animation. Angela was a co-creator of the Second Life space Virtual Macbeth, and the augmented reality storytelling application iFiction.

Len Unsworth is Professor in English and Literacies Education at the Australian Catholic University. His book publications include (with Angela Thomas, Alyson Simpson, and Jenny Asha) *Teaching Children's Literature with Information and Communication Technologies* (McGraw-Hill/Open University Press 2005), *e-Literature for Children and Classroom Literacy Learning* (Routledge, 2006), *New Literacies and the English Curriculum* (Continuum, 2008), *Multimodal Semiotics* (Continuum, 2008), and, with Clare Painter and Jim Martin, *Reading Visual Narratives* (Equinox, 2013).

Martin Waller is a primary school teacher and educational researcher based in the United Kingdom. His main teaching and research interests are founded in multiliteracies, critical literacy, digital technologies, and creative learning in relation to the curriculum and educational change. He is also fascinated by children's popular culture and how this can affect learning. Martin currently coordinates e-learning across a large primary school and leads regular professional development events for other teachers. Further information can be found on his website: http://martinwaller.me.

Jenny White is a primary teacher at St. Helens District High School, Tasmania. She had been looking for a more contemporary approach to the teaching of literacy to engage students in an ever-increasing digital society. She had recognised the need to utilise and develop the vast range of digital skills her students already possessed. *Inanimate Alice* provided a platform for developing student creativity and critical thinking within the literacy program, including viewing, writing, and reading.

Index

3DMAP (3D Multimodal Authoring Pedagogy), 79, 92, 93–94, 97
5Haitis (Kerr), 46–47, 50
"Viii, a story" (Colquhoun), 193
21st-century competencies, 63
The 21 Steps (Cumming), 222–223

action
  forms of, 67
  games as, 65–69, 74
Actor, 7
affect, 4, 27
affiliation, 26, 128, 134, 135–137, 138, 142
  See also relationships, interpersonal
Afternoon, a Story (Joyce), 49
Alexander, B., 214, 224
Alice in Wonderland (Carroll), 43
Allen, M., 50
Allen, R., 224
ambience, 26, 29, 34
animation, 106, 107, 125
Anstey, M., 81
Appraisal framework, 8–10

appreciation, 4
  See also engagement, appreciative
AR (Augmented Reality). *See* Augmented Reality (AR)
Asha, J., 48
assessment, of multimodal texts, 98
attitude, 4, 26
Attitude system, 138, 143–146
Augmented Reality (AR)
  characteristics of, 214–215
  components of, 215
  defined, 214
  in education, 218
  locative storytelling, 221–228
  mobile, 217, 219
  practical applications of, 217–218
  walking tours, 221–222
Augmented Reality narrative, 219
Australian Curriculum: English (ACE), 2
  deep studies of literature, 52
  emphasis on meaning-making, 48
  grammatical theme in, 10
  intermodal complementarity in, 37

interpreting and creating multimodal texts in, 11–12
knowledge of grammatical systems in, 7–9
lack of visual grammar of narrative images in, 15
metalanguage in, 12–15, 18–19
multimodal texts in, 23
recognition of multimodal reconceptualization of literacy, 18
requirement for explicit learning of knowledge about language, 6
requirement to address multimodal literacy, 106
systemic functional linguistics in, 19
Australian Research Council, 106
authoring, multimodal
  in blogging project, 159–160
  categories of meaning for, 82–87
  creation of animated movies as, 106
  grammatical design applied to, 82–87
  independent construction of text, 93–97
  influences on teaching approaches, 88–89
  pedagogy of, 87–92, 99
  planning phase, 95–97
  preparation, 99–100
  production sequence in, 93–94
  recommendations, 99
  sample character profile, 101
  sample story outline, 100
  scriptwriting in, 97
  scriptwriting sample, 101
  software for, 99
  storyboarding, 96–97, 102
  undoing work, 96
  and ZooBurst, 220
  See also 3DMAP (3D Multimodal Authoring Pedagogy)
authors, multimodal, 79
Azuma, R., 214, 224

back view, 109–110, 116, 145
Bakhtin, M. M., 52
Bal, M., 127
Barthes, R., 52
Barton, D., 153
Behance LCC, 224
Berry, A., 89
betrayal, 34
biographical locative storytelling projects, 224
Black, D., 223
Blake, Quentin, 27
blog fiction, 51
blogging, 155–157
blogging project
  analysis and findings, 158–168
  comments, 161–163, 170
  and development of competencies, 169–170
  engagement with, 158
  as facilitating a transformative pedagogy, 160
  meaning-making systems in, 160
  safety mechanisms, 157–158
  view of literacy promoted by, 169–170
blogs, 155, 156
bodily orientation of characters, 143–146
Bogost, I., 72
boyd, d., 154
BradField Company, 173, 174
  See also Inanimate Alice
Bradford, C., 71
Brenan, Sarah, 28
Bronte (character), 53, 54–55
Browne, Anthony, 15, 110
Buckingham, D., 153, 157
Buffy (television series), 45
Bull, G., 81
Burn, A., 70, 125

camera work
  and changes in social distance, 140–141
  constructing meaning through, 84–85
  and contact, 142
  and involvement, 145
  and moving image, 126
  and power, 146
  and proximity, 141–142
  and viewer's perception of subject, 138
  and visual meaning-making, 107
Campbell, A., 39
capital, gaming, 69
character, in locative storytelling, 223

character analysis, in *Inanimate Alice*, 179–180t
character movement
    and contact, 142–143
    and involvement, 145
    and power, 146
character sketch, 202–203
Chinthammit, W., 215
Circumstance, 5
circumstances, 3–4, 36
collaboration, in game play, 72
collegiality, pedagogies of, 205
Collerson, J., 80
colour, 26, 27, 58t, 84
    See also ambience
composition, 86
computing, in Augmented Reality, 216
Consalvo, M., 72
contact
    in *The Lost Thing* (movie), 114, 116–117, 118
    and rear view images, 110
Contact system, 108–109, 138, 142–143
contact with viewer, 26
convergence
    in *5Haitis*, 57
    defined, 26
    in *Fox*, 30, 35–36
Cope, B., 48, 88
Cumming, Charles, 222–223
curriculum
    Australian Curriculum: English. *See* Australian Curriculum: English (ACE)
    digital games in, 70–71, 72, 74

Daughters of Freya, 50
Davies, J., 155, 156, 158, 163, 169
deep studies
    of digital fiction, 52, 55–58
    of texts, 27
design, in digital games, 67–68, 74
design elements
    in approach to teaching multimodal authoring, 88–89
    relation with software, 87t
    teaching using VDDDR, 89–92
    See also grammar of design

devices used by writers, 177–178t
digital fiction
    affordances of, 40, 47–51, 173–174
    blended reality fictions, 47
    born digital fiction, 46–47
    and construction of meaning, 59
    deep studies of, 52, 55–58
    digital enhancements to known texts, 42
    digital replications of known texts, 41
    digital reversioning of known texts, 43–46
    digital transformations of known texts, 43
    fan fiction, 43–44
    hypertext, 49
    and interaction with text, 59
    meaning-making resources in, 39
    modes in, 23
    reader control in, 51
    reading and, 51–52
    remixes, 43, 44–46
    spatiality, 49–50
    types of, 40
    See also Inanimate Alice
digital literacy, critical, 46
display, in Augmented Reality, 215
distance education, Augmented Reality in, 218
Distance system, 138, 139–141
divergence, 26, 27, 30
Donnie Darko, 42
Douglas, J. Y., 51
Drac and the Gremlin (Baillie), 10
drawing styles, 112
Dreaming Methods, 46
dugong, 195–196
Dyson, A. H., 167

earthquake. *See 5Haitis* (Kerr)
e-books, 41
Edgar, Margo, 176
editing
    and establishing proximal relationship, 141
    and inferred meaning, 136–137
    and moving image, 126
education, transformative, 200
Electronic Literature as a Model of Creativity and Innovation in Practice (ELMCIP), 46
Electronic Literature Organization, 46

e-literature, 39, 40
    See also digital fiction
Ellison, N., 156, 157
emotions, 26
    See also attitude
empathy, 137
    See also engagement, empathetic
engagement, appreciative, 111–112, 115, 116
engagement, empathetic, 111, 112, 115, 117
English (subject), disengagement with, 192
ergodic processes, 65
e-safety, 157–158
Ettinghausen, Jeremy, 222–223
eye contact, 142–143

fan fiction, 43–44
features, 215–216
Feral Arts, 223
fiction, born-digital, 40, 46–47, 173–174
    See also Inanimate Alice
field, 128
films, modes in, 23
first-person point of view, 135–136
Five Times Dizzy (Wheatley), 10–11
focalisation
    back view images, 109–110
    choice of subject, 137
    choices about, 124–125
    components of, 127
    and development of relationships, 127, 128–129
    metalanguage for talking about, 129
    semiotic resources for, 129–130
    student knowledge of choices for, 147
    student use of resources, 131–134
    use of term, 126–127
focalisation, along-with-character, 134
focalisation, as character, 135–137
focalisation, mediated, 134–137
focalisation, unmediated, 133–134
focalised, 127
focaliser, 127, 132–133
focalising, 127
Focalising systems, 138–146
four resource model, 88
Foursquare, 217

Fox (Wild and Brooks), 27–36
    convergence in, 35–36
    intermodal complementarity in, 29–30
    interpersonal meanings in, 28–29
    visual analysis of, 34–35
    written analysis of, 33–34
Freebody, P., 52

games, digital
    collaboration in, 72
    connection with digital literacy, 64
    contexts of, 71–72
    cooperation between players, 68–69
    in curriculum, 70–71, 72, 74
    and development of out-of-school literacies, 68
    engagement with different knowledges, 72–73
    first-person shooter, 136
    games-as-action, 65–69, 74
    games-as-text, 69–73, 74
    knowledge about, 70–71
    learning through, 72–73
    levels enacted on, 66
    literacy practices in, 64
    "me" as game player, 71
    media panics about, 72
    narrative structures in, 70–71
    player's relation with, 66
    in repertoire of texts, 64
    situations, 68–69
    software's role in, 66
    world around, 71–72
gaming capital, 69
gaming literacy, 64
gaze, 142–143
Gee, J. P., 66, 69
gender, in *Twilight*, 45
Genette, Gerald, 126–127
Genishi, C., 167
Goal, 7
Gorilla (Browne), 110
grammar, functional, 80
    See also systemic functional grammar (SFG)
grammar, use of term, 80–81
grammar, visual. See grammar of design

grammar of design, 13, 80–87, 81, 129, 192, 200, 205, 207–208, 209
　　See also design elements
graphic rendering, in Augmented Reality, 216
Great Expectations, 200–201
Green, B., 48
Guerda (character), 53, 54–55

Haiti, 52–58
Hall, Edward, 139
Halliday, M. A. K., 80, 83–84, 124, 127
Harper, Ian, 173
Haunted London, 224
Hayes, E., 69
Hayles, N. K., 49
Higher School Certificate (HSC), 191
Hinman, R., 224
Hi_ReS1, 42
The Honest Thief (Dostoevsky), 194
HSC (Higher School Certificate), 191
HSC English examination, 191–192
human/computer interaction, 213–214
Hunt, P., 24
hyperlinks, 160–161, 185, 187
hypertext, 49, 50, 51
hypertextuality, of *Inanimate Alice*, 173

ICT (Information and Communication Technologies), 175, 234
　　See also technologies, digital
idea generation, 96
if:book Australia, 46
if:book UK, 46
image, moving, 125, 126, 128–131, 146
images
　　in *5Haitis*, 57t–58t
　　compositional meanings, 14–15
　　construction of viewer/character relationships in, 108–109
　　interactive meanings in, 13–14
　　interrelationship with words, 24–25
　　meaning-making resources of, 12–15, 105, 107, 206
　　understanding of meaning-making in, 106
images, Conceptual, 14
images, contact, 109, 116–117, 118

images, demand, 109
　　See also images, contact
images, narrative, 14, 15
images, observe, 109, 115–116, 117
images, offer, 109
　　See also images, observe
images, rear view, 109–111, 116, 145
Inanimate Alice (BradField Company)
　　as born-digital text, 173–174, 175
　　and ICT competencies, 175
　　integration into literacy program, 176
　　interactivity of, 175
　　pedagogy for teaching, 176–182
　　reasons for teaching, 175
　　reversionings of, 174, 176, 181t, 185–188
　　skills needed for reversionings, 183t, 184t
　　student feedback on, 182–184t, 189
Inanimate Alice Education Portal, 176
Information and Communication Technologies (ICT), 175, 234
Inspiration. *See* software
interactivity, 42, 50–51, 175
interanimation, 24–25, 30
intermodal complementarity, 26, 29–30, 36
intermodality, 15–18, 23, 25
Internet safety, 157–158
Involvement/Detachment, in images, 14
Involvement system, 108, 144–145

Jackson, S., 49
Jenkins, H., 44, 45, 153, 155, 167, 169
Jewitt, C., 200
Joseph, Chris, 173
judgment, 4, 34
Junaio, 226

Kahootz, 82, 85, 93, 106
Kalantzis, M., 48, 88
Kapp, Craig, 219–220
Kerr, Simon, 46–47, 55–58
Knobel, M., 47, 48
Kress, G., 12, 13, 15, 47, 48, 81, 84, 86, 108, 127, 138, 139, 142, 144, 145, 160, 206
Kuleshov, Lev, 137, 141
Kumagai, T., 218

language
  meaning-making resources of, 105
  metafunctions of, 25, 26
  as social resource for making meaning, 25
Lankshear, C., 47, 48
Layar, 217, 221
layout, 14–15
The Leaky Cauldron, 42
Lean, David, 200–201
Learning by Design framework, 88–89
Leaving (Solomon), 194, 195
Lessig, L., 45
Lewis, D., 24, 43–44
lexia, 51, 52
linguistics, Hallidayan, 83–84
  See also systemic functional linguistics (SFL)
literacies, multimodal, 182t
literacies, multiple, 152
  See also Multiliteracies
literacies, new, 74, 151
  competencies of, 153–154, 160, 161, 163–164, 166–168
  using *Inanimate Alice* to teach, 174–184
  See also blogging; Multiliteracies; New Literacy Studies
literacies, out-of-school, 63, 68
literacy
  3D view of, 69
  as communicative practice, 155
  critical view of, 164
  dominant discourses of, 170
  and meaning-making in real world, 167
  nature of, 152
  pedagogisation of, 170
  as social practice, 159, 161–163, 169, 170
  treatment of, 169
  view of, 154
literacy, critical, 70
literacy, critical multimedia, 82
literacy, digital, 64
literacy, gaming, 64
literacy, media, 63
literacy, traditional, 168
literary analysis
  adaptation of software for, 192
literature
  conventions of, 194
  disengagement with, 192
  eras of, 192, 202–205
  teaching of, 192
literature, traditional, 40
The Little Prince (de Saint-Exupéry), 106
locative storytelling, 221–228
The Lost Thing (book), 107
  appreciative engagement in, 111–112, 115, 116
  compared to movie, 110–118
  distancing of reader from characters in, 118
  drawing style in, 112
  front on shots in, 110–111
  narrative in, 118
  observe view in, 115–116
  rear view images in, 110–111
The Lost Thing (movie), 107
  compared to book, 110–118
  contact images in, 116–117, 118
  drawing style in, 112
  empathetic engagement in, 111, 112, 115, 117
  narrative in, 118
  observe images in, 116
  rear view images in, 112–114, 116
Loughran, J., 89
Luke, C., 166, 169

Macbeth (Shakespeare). *See* Virtual Macbeth project
MagicBook, 220–221
Marsh, J., 155, 163
Martin, J. R., 18, 25–26, 37, 128
McGuire, S., 137
McIntosh, Jonathan, 45
McKee, David, 18
meaning
  constructing through camera work, 84–85
  construction of in digital fiction, 59
  construction of through interaction of images and language, 15
  See also intermodality
  function in, 127
  modes of, 17–18
  in phases of narrative in *5Haitis*, 57t–58t

system in, 127
meaning, Hallidayan systems of, 86
meaning, inferred, 136–137
meaning, inscribed, 136
meaning, interpersonal, 84–85
meaning-making
  and grammatical design, 81
  in multimodal modes of communication, 159
  organisational framework for, 80
  in real world, 167
  as socially constructed, 84
meaning-making systems, 17
meanings, compositional / textual, 3, 5, 12, 14–15, 25, 86, 206
meanings, experiential / ideational, / representational, 3–4, 6–7, 12, 14, 25, 35, 206
meanings, interactive / interpersonal, 3, 4, 12, 14, 25, 28–29, 58t, 206
meanings, types of, 3
"me" as game player, 71
media panics, about digital games, 72
Meek, M., 24
Merchant, G., 155, 156, 158, 163, 169, 170
metafunction, interpersonal, 26
metalanguage
  describing meaning-making resources of images, 12–15
  for focalisation, 129
metasemiotic understanding, 1
Michel Rosen's Sad Book (Rosen and Blake), 27
Milgram, P., 214
Millard, E., 160
modality, 7, 86
mode, 128
modernism, literary, 203–204
Mood, 7
Morgan, H., 49, 51
Morgan, W., 49
Morikawa, O., 218
The Mortal Immortal (Shelley), 193
Moulthrop, S., 49
movement, in Augmented Reality, 215–216
movies, animated, 106, 107
moving image, 125, 126
moving image resources, 125, 128–131, 146

Mueck, Ron, 201–202
Mulhall, P., 89
Multiliteracies, 152–153, 154, 160, 161, 163, 164–165, 169, 170
Multiliteracies (New London Group), 152
multiliteracies education, 199
multimodality
  of blogs, 155, 156
  of digital fiction, 47–48
  of *Inanimate Alice*, 173, 174
  and increased confidence in writing, 192
Murphet, J., 136

narrative
  affected by technological affordances, 51–52
  in digital games, 70–71
  in locative storytelling, 222
  mapping of, 195
  shifts in, 27–36
  in ZooBurst platform, 220
narrative, Augmented Reality, 219
narrative, digital, 175, 178t, 200, 209
  See also digital fiction
narrative, distributed, 50
narrative, multimodal, 200
narrative, print, 178t
narrative stages, 7
National Education Technology Plan, 63
New Literacy Studies, 152153, 161, 163, 169, 170
New London Group, 2, 12, 152–153, 156, 164, 199164, 169
New Media Consortium, 235
New Media Writing Prize, 46
New South Wales Syllabus, 193
Not Now, Bernard (McKee), 18

Objectivity, in images, 14
observe, unmediated, 29
observe images
  in *The Lost Thing* (book), 115–116
  in *The Lost Thing* (movie), 115, 116, 117
offer, 29
Omar (character), 53, 54–55
Online Caroline, 50

Painter, C., 17, 18, 25–26, 37, 58t, 109, 112, 128
paratexts, players' use of, 72
Parker, D., 125
participants, relationships between, 127
  See also relationships, interpersonal
Patchwork Girl (Jackson), 49
picture books
  compared with e-books generated by movies, 106
  intermodality in, 23–25
  modes in, 23
  movie versions of, 105–106
    See also *The Lost Thing*
  story lines in, 24
  used to explore intermodal complementarity, 36–37
Piggybook (Browne), 7
PlaceStories (Feral Arts), 223
players
  cooperation of, 68–69
  "me" as, 71
  relation with digital game, 66
  use of paratexts, 72
Pottermore, 42
poverty, words used to create picture of, 55–57
Power, realisation of, 146
PowerPoint. See software
Prestridge, S., 156
procedural rhetoric, 72
Processes, Material, 4, 7
Profumo, S., 224
Project Gutenberg, 41
Proximity, 141–142
Pullinger, Kate, 173
Pumpkin Soup (Cooper), 7

reader, 49, 50–51
reading
  and digital fiction, 51–52
  importance of to writing, 192, 199
  of print *vs.* digital text, 177t
reading, active, 193, 194
Reality-Virtuality continuum, 214
rear view images, 109–111, 112–114, 116, 145
register theory, 127, 128

relationships, interpersonal
  and contact system, 142–143
  design of, 128
  and proximity system, 141–142
  and social distance system, 139–141
remixes, 43, 44–46
Rosen, Michael, 27
Rothery, J., 88
Rowling, J. K., 42
Ruhemann, Andrew, 107

Samson and Delilah (Film), 205, 206, 207–208
scene, defined, 126
scriptwriting, 97, 101
sculptures, Mueck's, 201–202
Second Life, 234, 235, 236
  See also Virtual Macbeth project
SFG (systemic functional grammar), 3–5, 10–11
SFL (systemic functional linguistics), 6, 19, 25, 127
  See also grammar of design
shot, defined, 126
Shrek (book), 8–9, 105–106
Shrek (e-book), 8–9
Shrek (film), 8, 105–106
SimCity series, 66
Simpson, A., 48
situatedness, in digital gaming, 74
smartphones, 217
Snyder, I., 48
social distance
  changes in, 140–141
  and involvement, 144, 145
  in *The Lost Thing* (book), 111–112
  in *The Lost Thing* (movie), 114
  and rear view images, 110
Social Distance system, 109, 139–141
social technologies, 154
  See also technologies, digital; technologies, new
software
  in analysis of trailer, 207
  for digital animation, 106–107
  Kahootz, 82, 85, 93, 106
  for multimodal authoring, 99

relation with design elements, 87t
for reversionings of *Inanimate Alice*, 176
role in digital games, 66
and student engagement with
    English, 209
use of in literary analysis, 192, 198
solidarity, 144–145
The Sound and the Fury (Faulkner),
    203–204
sounds, in *5Haitis*, 57t–58t
spatial continuity, 137
spatial framing, 125
spatiality, 49–50, 58, 174
Steinkuehler, C., 69
Story, Kate, 176
storyboarding, 96–97, 102, 180t
storytelling, Augmented Reality, 219–228
storytelling, locative, 221–228
Strickland, S., 39
Subject, 5
subject, focalised, 137, 138
systemic functional grammar (SFG), 3–5,
    10–11
systemic functional linguistics (SFL), 6, 19,
    25, 127
    See also grammar of design
system network, 127

Taku, F., 218
Tan, Shaun, 43, 107
    See also The Lost Thing
teaching/learning cycle, 88
technologies, digital
    competencies of, 166–167
    developing competencies with, 165–166
    impact of, 169
    in *Inanimate Alice* pedagogy, 180t
    using to communicate literary response,
        192, 195–197
technologies, new
    children's use of, 233
    dangers in ignoring, 153
    and new meaning-making systems, 152
    students' ease with, 174
    and view of literacy, 154
The Tell-Tale Heart (Poe), 194

temporal framing, 125
tenor, 128
texts
    deep studies of, 27
    games as, 69–73, 74
    interaction with, 59
    new types of, 152
    redesigning of, 199–200
texts, born-digital, 173–174
texts, digital
    in ACE, 11–12
    children as producers of, 233
    reading, 177t
texts, multimodal
    in ACE, 23
    assessment of, 98
    camera use in, 84–85
    constructing interpersonal meaning in,
        84–85
    creating the world, 83–84
    defined, 23
    grammatical design, 80–82
    idea generation, 96
    independent construction of, 93–97
    and literacy education, 47
    planning phase, 95–97
    semiotic affordances of, 48
    as series of scenes, 83
texts, print
    in ACE, 11–12
    reading, 177t
texts, visual, 206
Theme, grammatical, 10–11
Theme, Marked, 10
Theme/Rheme system, 5
themes, in *5Haitis*, 52, 55
Theme selection, 10–11
Thomas, A., 48
tone, 26, 27
Tsai, Y.-ta, 224
Twilight (film series), 45

Ulysses (Joyce), 204
Undertow (Tan), 195–196
unmediated observe, 29
Unsworth, L., 37, 48, 145

van Leeuwen, T., 12, 13, 15, 81, 84, 86, 108, 127, 138, 139, 142, 144, 145, 146, 206
VDDDR (View, Deconstruct, Demonstrate, Do, and Reflect), 89–92, 94, 95
verbal meaning-making systems, 17
verb types, differentiating, 6–7
Verstraten, P., 141
video tracking, 215–216
View, Deconstruct, Demonstrate, Do, and Reflect (VDDDR), 89–92, 94, 95
viewer, positioning of, 123–124
    See also focalisation
"Viii, a story" (Colquhoun), 193
Virtual Macbeth project
    background, 234
    design of, 235
    pedagogical framework for, 235–252
    student work, 253–255
    workshops, 252–253
Virtual Reality, 214
virtual worlds
    affordances of, 255
    modes in, 23
    potential for teaching in, 252
    Second Life, 234, 235, 236
    See also Virtual Macbeth project
visual design. See grammar of design
visual meaning-making systems, 17

Walker, J., 48, 51
walking tours, 221–222
Walsh, M., 80, 152
Web 2.0 systems, 155, 156, 157–158, 160–161
The Westwood Experience, 224–226
"The White Dove," 139
Wikitude, 221, 226
words
    in *5Haitis,* 55–57, 57t–58t
    interrelationship with images, 24–25
wreader, 50
writing
    and blogs, 155, 156
    exercises, 202–205
    importance of reading to, 192, 199
    importance placed on, 193
    lack of confidence in, 192, 193, 199
    pedagogical approach to, 199
    student samples, 204–205
    teaching, 199
    See also authoring, multimodal
writing instruction, on fan fiction sites, 44
Wu, Y., 156, 157

Yamashita, J., 218
Yokoyama, K., 218

Zoo (Browne), 10, 15
ZooBurst, 219–220

Colin Lankshear & Michele Knobel
General Editors

New literacies emerge and evolve apace as people from all walks of life engage with new technologies, shifting values and institutional change, and increasingly assume 'postmodern' orientations toward their everyday worlds. Despite many efforts to take account of such changes, educational institutions largely remain out of touch with the range of new ways of making and sharing meanings that increasingly mediate and shape the lives of the young people they teach and the futures they face. This series aims to explore some key dimensions of the changes occurring within social practices of literacy and the educational challenges they present, with a view to informing educational practice in helpful ways. It asks what are new literacies, how do they impact on life in schools, homes, communities, workplaces, sites of leisure, and other key settings of human cultural engagement, and what significance do new literacies have for how people learn and how they understand and construct knowledge. It aims to challenge established and 'official' ways of framing literacy, and to ask what it means for literacies to be powerful, effective, and enabling under current and foreseeable conditions. Collectively, the works in this series will help to reorient literacy debates and literacy education agendas.

For further information about the series and submitting manuscripts, please contact:

>Michele Knobel & Colin Lankshear
>Montclair State University
>Dept. of Education and Human Services
>3173 University Hall
>Montclair, NJ 07043
>michele@coatepec.net

To order other books in this series, please contact our Customer Service Department at:
>(800) 770-LANG (within the U.S.)
>(212) 647-7706 (outside the U.S.)
>(212) 647-7707 FAX

Or browse online by series at:
>www.peterlang.com